Political Jouissance

ALSO AVAILABLE FROM BLOOMSBURY

Žižek Responds!, Dominik Finkelde and Todd McGowan
Surplus-Enjoyment, Slavoj Žižek

Political Jouissance

Edited by
Nicol A. Barria-Asenjo and
Slavoj Žižek

BLOOMSBURY ACADEMIC
LONDON • NEW YORK • OXFORD • NEW DELHI • SYDNEY

BLOOMSBURY ACADEMIC
Bloomsbury Publishing Plc
50 Bedford Square, London, WC1B 3DP, UK
1385 Broadway, New York, NY 10018, USA
29 Earlsfort Terrace, Dublin 2, Ireland

BLOOMSBURY, BLOOMSBURY ACADEMIC and the Diana logo are trademarks of Bloomsbury
Publishing Plc

First published in Great Britain 2024
Reprinted in 2024

A catalogue record for this book is available from the British Library.

Library of Congress Cataloging-in-Publication Data

Names: Barria-Asenjo, Nicol A., editor. | Žižek, Slavoj, editor.
Title: Political jouissance / edited by Nicol A. Barria-Asenjo and Slavoj Žižek.
Description: London ; New York : Bloomsbury Academic, 2024. | Includes bibliographical references
and index. | Summary: "When we oppose or disagree with something important, do we ever really
do it dispassionately? Isn't setting the world to rights or condemning a political opponent always done
with a hint of relish, or at least enthusiasm? This book's challenging essays explore the modes in which
that transgressive pleasure of political 'jouissance' operates. In this collection, the authors seek out
jouissance in the battle against patriarchy, in social revolts, in the age of mechanical surveillance, in the
necrosociety of neoliberalism, or the proliferation of conspiracy theories. Drawing on Lacan's insistence
that jouissance is intrinsically political by its nature, we can understand how readily psychoanalytic ideas
can be put to use across the geopolitical spectrum"–Provided by publisher.
Identifiers: LCCN 2023058359 (print) | LCCN 2023058360 (ebook) | ISBN 9781350352759 (hardback) |
ISBN 9781350352742 (paperback) | ISBN 9781350352773 (epub) | ISBN 9781350352766 (ebook)
Subjects: LCSH: Political psychology. | Emotions–Political aspects. | Political science–Philosophy.
Classification: LCC JA74.5 .P6225 2024 (print) | LCC JA74.5 (ebook) | DDC 320.01/9–dc23/eng/20240214
LC record available at https://lccn.loc.gov/2023058359
LC ebook record available at https://lccn.loc.gov/2023058360

ISBN: HB: 978-1-3503-5275-9
PB: 978-1-3503-5274-2
ePDF: 978-1-3503-5276-6
eBook: 978-1-3503-5277-3

Typeset by Deanta Global Publishing Services, Chennai, India
Printed and bound in Great Britain

To find out more about our authors and books visit www.bloomsbury.com
and sign up for our newsletters.

This book and all my work is for Antonella,
my beautiful daughter and the event of my life.

Contents

Part II Inside and outside the psychoanalytic view of politics 115

Contributors

Slavoj Žižek is Co-Director at the International Center for Humanities, Birkbeck College, University of London. He is a Researcher at the University of Ljubljana, Slovenia. He is also Senior Researcher at the Department of Philosophy, University of Ljubljana and teaches at numerous universities in the US, the UK, France, Switzerland and South Korea. Slavoj Žižek is the author of numerous publications on politics and ideology today. He is a Doctor of Arts (philosophy) at the Department of Philosophy, Faculty of Arts, Ljubljana, and a Doctor of Arts (psychoanalysis) at the Universite Paris-VIII. Currently, he is directing a research project 'Antinomies of the Postmodern Reason' at the Kulturwissenschaftliches Institut, Essen.

Nicol A. Barria-Asenjo has authored columns, essays and academic articles published in national and international media. She is affiliated with Universidad de Los Lagos, Departamento de Ciencias Sociales, Osorno, Chile. She is also the Editor of special issues of scientific and academic journals and is the author of the books *Construcción de una Nueva Normalidad. Notas de un Chile Pandémico* (2021) and *Karl Marx y Antonio Gramsci en el Siglo XXI. Apuntes para re-pensar el porvenir* (2022). She is also Guest Editor of the special issue 'Filosofía y Pandemía' in the journal *Discusiones Filosóficas*, Universidad de Caldas, Colombia.

Darian Leader is a psychoanalyst working in London and a member of the Centre for Freudian Analysis and Research and of The College of Psychoanalysts-UK. He is the author of several books including *Why do women write more letters than they post?*; *Freud's Footnotes*; *Stealing the Mona Lisa: What Art Stops Us From Seeing*; *Why do people get ill?* (with David Corfield); *The New Black: Mourning, Melancholia and Depression*; *What is Madness?*; *Strictly Bipolar*; *Hands*; *Why Can't We Sleep?* (2019) and *Jouissance: Sexuality, Suffering and Satisfaction* (2021). He writes frequently about contemporary art.

Andrea Perunović is a Research Fellow at the Institute for Philosophy and Social Theory, University of Belgrade, Serbia. He studied in the Philosophy, Art and Critical Thought division of the European Graduate School, Saas-Fee,

Switzerland and obtained a doctoral degree in philosophy from the University Paris 8, Saint-Denis, France. His dissertation (directed by François Noudemann) is entitled 'Archéologie de la confiance: prolégomènes d'une pensée défiante' ('Archeology of trust: prolegomena of a distrustful thought'). His theoretical interests gravitate around the fields of ontology, epistemology, psychoanalysis, linguistics and political economy, as well as contemporary francophone philosophy and theory.

Ignacio López-Calvo is Presidential Chair in the Humanities, Director of the Center for the Humanities, and Professor of Literature at the University of California, Merced. He is the author of more than 100 articles and book chapters, as well as nine single-authored books and seventeen essay collections. His latest books are *The Mexican Transpacific: Nikkei Writing, Visual Arts, Performance* (forthcoming); *Saudades of Japan and Brazil: Contested Modernities in Lusophone Nikkei Cultural Production*; *Dragons in the Land of the Condor: Tusán Literature and Knowledge in Peru*; and *The Affinity of the Eye: Writing Nikkei in Peru*.

Pavin Chachavalpongpun is Professor at Kyoto University's Center for Southeast Asian Studies. Earning his PhD from the School of Oriental and African Studies (SOAS), Pavin is the author and editor of several books, including the forthcoming *Rama X: The Thai Monarchy under King Vajiralongkorn* (Yale). He is also the editor of the online journal *Kyoto Review of Southeast Asia* in which all articles are translated from English into Japanese, Thai, Bahasa Indonesia, Filipino, Vietnamese and Burmese. In the aftermath of the Thai coup in 2014, Pavin was summoned by the junta for his criticisms against the monarchy. He rejected the summons. As a result, a warrant was issued for his arrest and his passport was revoked, forcing him to apply for refugee status in Japan.

Jens Schröter, Prof. Dr., has been Chair for Media Studies at the University of Bonn, Germany since 2015. Since October 2018, he has been a speaker of the research project (VW Foundation; together with Prof. Dr. Gabriele Gramelsberger, Dr. Stefan Meretz, Dr. Hanno Pahl and Dr. Manuel Scholz-Wäckerle) 'Society after Money – A Simulation' (four years). He is Director (together with Prof. Dr. Anna Echterhölter PD Dr. Sudmann and Prof. Dr. Alexander Waibel) of the VW-Main Grant 'How is Artificial Intelligence Changing Science?' (Start: 1 August 2022, four years). Winter 2021/22: Fellowship, Center of Advanced Internet Studies. His recent publications include *Medien und Ökonomie, Wiesbaden* (2019) and *Media Futures. Theory and Aesthetics* (2021), co-written alongside Christoph Ernst.

Jesús Ayala-Colqui is Professor of Philosophy at University Scientific of the South. He is co-editor of *Poder y subjetivación en Michel Foucault* (2020) and

Sentido, verdad e historia del ser en Martin Heidegger (2022). He is the editor of two articles, 'Félix Guattari' and 'Technopolitics: Artificial intelligence, algorithms and biotechnology', published in academic journals, and author of several research articles. He is the founder and editor-in-chief of the *Latin American Journal of Humanities and Educational Development*.

Natalia Romé is a Senior Researcher at the Instituto de Investigaciones Gino Germani, Universidad de Buenos Aires, where she coordinates the Program of Critical Studies on Ideology, Technique and Politics. She is also a Chair Professor at the Social Sciences Faculty of the same university and Director of the Master's Program in Communication and Culture. She has published several works, including *La posición materialista*, EDULP, 2015 and *For Theory. Althusser and the politics of time*, Rowman and Littlefield, 2021. romenatalia@yahoo.com

Obed Frausto completed his doctoral studies in philosophy of science with a specialization in social studies of science and technology at the National Autonomous University of Mexico (UNAM). He is currently Assistant Professor of humanities at Ball State University, Indiana, USA. His research interests are political philosophy, social theory, decoloniality and social studies of science and technology. He is co-editor with Jason Powell and Sarah Vitale of the book *The Weariness of Democracy* (Switzerland: Palgrave Macmillan, 2020). He is the author of *Tres tradiciones en la teoría de la legitimidad política* (Barcelona: Terra Ignota, 2021) and *The Power of the Metaphysical Artifact* (Lexington Press, in press).

Tim Themi holds a PhD in philosophy and psychoanalysis from Deakin University and holds honours degrees in philosophy from La Trobe University and in the engineering sciences from the University of Melbourne. His doctoral dissertation was supervised by leading Lacan translator and commentator Russell Grigg and brought together the psychoanalysis of Lacan and the philosophy of Nietzsche on the question of desire and ethics. He is the author of *Lacan's Ethics and Nietzsche's Critique of Platonism* (SUNY 2014), along with numerous refereed articles, and most recently of *Eroticizing Aesthetics: In the Real with Bataille and Lacan* (Rowman 2021). He has taught philosophy and psychoanalysis at the Lacan Circle of Australia, Deakin University, the Melbourne School of Continental Philosophy, the Australian Catholic University, and in screen and media studies at the University of Melbourne.

Daniel Bristow is a practising psychoanalyst and psychoanalytic theorist. He is the author of *Joyce and Lacan: Reading, Writing, and Psychoanalysis* (Routledge: 2016); *2001: A Space Odyssey and Lacanian Psychoanalytic Theory* (Palgrave: 2018); and *Schizostructuralism: Divisions in Structure, Surface, Temporality, Class* (Routledge: 2021).

Alfredo Eidelsztein is a psychoanalyst. He holds a PhD in Psychology from the University of Buenos Aires. He has taught many courses in psychoanalysis at the post-graduate level and directed MA and doctoral dissertations in Argentinean academic institutions and abroad. Eidelsztein is the founder and director of the international scientific society 'Apertura para Otro Lacan' (*Aperture for Another Lacan*). He is the author of *Modelos, esquemas y grafos en la enseñanza de Lacan* (*Models, Schemes, and Graphs in Lacan's Teaching*) (1992, 1995, 2010, 2021) and *El grafo del deseo* (*The Graph of Desire*) (1995). Several of his books have been translated into English, Italian and Portuguese. He has led psychoanalytic seminars in Argentina, Bolivia, Brazil, Chile, Colombia, Costa Rica, Spain, Italy, México and Uruguay.

David Pavón-Cuéllar is a Mexican Marxist philosopher and critical psychologist. He is Professor of Psychology and Philosophy at the Universidad Michoacana de San Nicolás de Hidalgo, Morelia, Mexico. His last books include *Psychoanalysis and Revolution: Critical Psychology for Liberation Movements* (2021), *Marxism and Psychoanalysis: In or Against Psychology?* (2017), *Lacan, Discourse, Event: New Psychoanalytic Approaches to Textual Indeterminacy* (co-written with Ian Parker, 2013) and *From the Conscious Interior to an Exterior Unconscious: Lacan, Discourse Analysis and Social Psychology* (2010).

Graham Harman is Distinguished Professor of Philosophy and Liberal Arts Co-Ordinator Southern California Institute of Architecture (SCI-Arc). He is also a Visiting Professor of Architecture, Yale University, and a Distinguished University Professor at American University in Cairo, Egypt. Harman is Series Editor of the Speculative Realism book series at Edinburgh University Press, co-editor (with Bruno Latour) of the New Metaphysics book series at Open Humanities Press, and Editor in Chief of the journal *Open Philosophy*. Harman is the author of more than twenty books and 300 articles in more than twenty languages. His books include *Architecture and Objects* (2022); *Art and Objects* (2020); and *Speculative Realism: An Introduction* (2018) *Object-Oriented Ontology: A New Theory of Everything* (2018).

Francesca R. Recchia Luciani holds a PhD and is a Professor of Contemporary Philosophies and Gender Studies and History of Human Rights Philosophy at the University of Bari 'Aldo Moro', Italy, where she is responsible for gender policies. Creator and director of the Festival of Women and Gender Studies and of the Course of History and Didactics of the Shoah (UniBA), she has written essays and monographs on Max Weber, Ludwig Wittgenstein, Peter Winch, Simone Weil, Hannah Arendt, Primo Levi, Günther Anders and Jean-Luc Nancy. His research interests encompass the history and critique of human rights theories, the hermeneutics of totalitarianism, and feminist and queer philosophies. She edits 'Post-Filosofie. Journal of philosophical practices and human sciences' and the Melangolo (Genoa) editorial series, 'Xenos. Philosophy, phenomenology and history of otherness'.

Gonzalo Salas is Adjunct Professor at the Universidad Católica del Maule, Chile. He is a psychologist at the University of La Serena; has a PhD in Education from the University of La Salle, Costa Rica; a Postdoctorate in Social Sciences, Arts and Humanities from the National University of Cordoba, Argentina; and was a PhD student in History of Science at the Autonomous University of Barcelona. He was awarded the National Award Colegio de Psicólogos 2018 and recently the Early Scientific Trajectory Contribution Award Maritza Montero, Interamerican Society of Psychology 2021. His main line of research is in the history of psychology. He is a founding member of the Chilean Society for the History of Psychology and IR of the FONDECYT Regular 1211280 Project on Amanda Labarca.

Brian Willems is Associate Professor of literature and film at the Faculty of Humanities and Social Sciences, University of Split, Croatia. He is most recently the author of *Sham Ruins: A User's Guide* (Routledge, 2022), *Speculative Realism and Science Fiction* (Edinburgh University Press, 2017) and *Shooting the Moon* (Zero Books, 2015), and is co-editor of *Reconsidering (Post-)Yugoslav Time: Towards the Temporal Turn in the Critical Study of (Post)-Yugoslav Literatures* (Brill, 2022). He has published essays in collections of Cambridge University Press, Goldsmiths/MIT Press, University of Minnesota Press and others.

Ruben Balotol Jr currently teaches at Visayas State University, Tolosa, Philippines. His research interests are under the theme of postcolonial/colonial studies, psychoanalysis and ideology. He received his Master of Arts in Philosophy from the University of San Jose-Recoletos in Cebu City, Philippines. Aside from doing research and teaching, he is also a co-founder of the Association of Eastern Visayas Studies, Inc. (Philippines).

Mia Neuhaus is a Berlin-based psychologist in training as a psychoanalyst. She studied critical theory, politics and psychoanalysis in Frankfurt/Main, Potsdam and Berlin and holds a Master's degree in philosophy, sociology and psychology. She is working on transgenerational transmission, multidirectional memory and the collective unconscious in Germany's reunification process at Sigmund Freud University Berlin. Currently, she is co-editing a book on solidarity.

Preface
'Political Jouissance'
By Darian Leader

The bad news about 'political jouissance' is that it refers not only to a fault in the Other but also to our own efforts to denounce this. One of the most striking features of psychoanalytically-inspired approaches to social and political problems is not simply the almost total agreement on what's wrong with the world but the collective enthusiasm of our hatreds. Unfortunately, if we want to keep things even vaguely analytical, we might have to question our own investments – yes, our own enjoyment – in our outrage at Trump, Putin, Bolsonaro etc., and the economic systems that are destroying the planet.

We could stop right here and dismiss this as in itself a depoliticizing gesture, but an engagement with this kind of enjoyment does not de facto delegitimatize, and may or may not facilitate different forms of engagement. To take an old example, in the 1960s what was called the 'rape of the planet' was sometimes explained as an unconscious attack on 'mother earth', with the implication that attempts to save the planet would, in turn, be efforts at maternal repair. Today, we are happy to decry the damage to the planet, but we tend to bracket out the implication, even if maternal repair may be as good a reason as any for political activism.

In analysis, questioning political activism is uncommon – unless the analyst does not share the analysand's politics – although the lack of activism is often explored and complained of. Psychoanalysis demonstrated early on that sins of omission can exert as heavy a toll on the subject as acts that are prosecuted. Despite recognizing this, Freud's position was rather conservative here. When Erich Leyens wrote to him of the growing nationalist and anti-Semitic movements in Germany in 1923, Freud replied,

> I should like to advise you against consuming yourself in a hopeless struggle against the 'spiritual' ['Geistes'] currents prevailing in Germany of today. Mass

psychoses are invulnerable to reasoning. The Germans in particular would have had all reason to learn this in this World War. But they do not seem capable of it. Let us leave them alone. (1)

Other analysts of the time took a rather different stance, as is well known, but it is curious to see how, all these years later, personal politics still seem so impermeable to analysis. As Ernest Jones observed, despite serious analytic work, analysands invariably retain their old voting habits, usually a direct replica or the exact opposite of those of a parent (2). The only exceptions to this that I have noticed are the vote swings in those analysts who have become wealthy through the use of ultra-short sessions, who now vote to protect the value of stock market portfolios.

To turn now to the question of political jouissance – or rather, that side of it which involves collective hatreds – we could think of the anti-Trump enjoyment that swept not just the liberal but certainly most of the psychoanalytic world in 2017. It was quite striking to see the very rhetoric deployed by Trump and his supporters now being used against them, and the rapid escalation of 'us' and 'them' vocabulary. The UK had seen a comparable process with the Brexit debate: in the anti-Brexit litany of the left-leaning press, the very nationalism that was supposedly being combatted became a new norm. There were daily references to the wishes and will of 'the British people', to 'we' and 'us' and to 'this country', as if the threat of EU departure had suddenly generated a new nationalism to oppose what was depicted as . . . a new nationalism. And with this, a violence to match.

Interestingly, with Trump-hate, analysts noticed how some of the most vocal anti-Trump voices in the press would, in the privacy of the consulting room, reveal something different. Analysands who were resolute in calling out the American monster and his inhuman policies would weep on the couch as they spoke of their feelings of love and pity for this vulnerable and infantile individual. Yet publicly the love to hate prevailed, together with the sense of righteous indignation that was once seen as a signature of neurosis (and which even God was said to suffer from: see Lactantius, *On the Anger of God*). That is one face of political jouissance: forming oneself through hatred, which is so often the go-to treatment for anxiety, frustration and the experience of powerlessness.

This is also perhaps one of the reasons for the lethargy, in some quarters, regarding environmental action. There is unfortunately no single person who can be blamed, and it turns out that some of our favourite bad guys had actually not been that bad when it came to ecology. Hating corporations or the global financial system is fine, but hatred tends to need an embodied target, a person, a name. Once we have found it, we can love to hate, and bind together in our collective enjoyment of hating. Because we all hate together, we can avoid punishment, and this evasion is surely one of the central variables at play in the different forms of political jouissance.

It is worth observing here how one of the most fundamental dilemmas of human life is the question: When is an act of violence justified? It would indeed be difficult to find a single cultural product today – with obvious exceptions such as the rom-com genre – in which this question is not directly posed at some point: When should the retired hitman or cowboy or soldier take up their guns again, when should the detective act outside the law, when should the mother or father defend their family, when should the ordinary citizen start to fight back, when should the teenager retaliate against the bullies, and when should someone stand up for what's right?

The urgency and the ubiquity of this question might suggest that it is hardly a simple one and that hence a collective sanction can help the subject bear the freight that it carries. We are always on the lookout, perhaps, for opportunities to hate together, as if the collective dimension divests us of the guilt that this might otherwise involve.

If we turn now to the other side of political jouissance – the fault in the Other that we denounce – it is worth going back to the post-Freudian approaches that emphasized not simply an unchecked thanatonic force but also, crucially, the principle of sacrifice that was built into it. Freud's own theory of the death drive ignored this, despite his earlier sensitivity to sacrificial logic in works such as 'Totem and Taboo'. To put it simply, the old are willing to sacrifice the young, a non-reciprocal relation that extends from the story of Oedipus to the Christian narrative to the trenches of the First World War to recent fiction like 'The Cabin in the Woods'. As Elaine Scarry observed, people say 'I'm willing to die for my country' rather than 'I'm willing to kill for my country' (3). And the historical shifts from human to territorial sacrifice have not really been sufficient to keep the gods happy.

When we gloss this with our Lacanian theory of what were once called 'leavings' – the different exudations of the body and their zones – we perhaps miss out on this unthinkable dimension. Let's remember here that our theory of the unthinkable object is actually absolutely thinkable, whereas stuff about sacrificing or pedicating children is not. Including this dimension of sacrifice can illuminate not only the actions of bad men whom we love to hate – they are giving up something to someone, even with their own temples (Trump Plaza etc.) – but also aspects of the global environmental crisis. The planet is not just being pillaged and destroyed but given up to a higher god.

Recognizing these currents, together with the dangers of certain tropes about the environment that can only support fantasies of desecration and defilement, may be helpful in formulating strategies for change and for allowing renewed and increased engagement. At the level of the unconscious, sadly, 'The Planet does not exist', but the mother and the toilet bowl do.

References

Jones, Ernest (1948), 'The Concept of a Normal Mind' (1931), in *Papers on Psychoanalysis*, 5th edn, London: Hogarth, 201–16.

Niederland, William (1956), 'Four Unpublished Letters of Freud', *Psychoanalytic Quarterly* 25: 147–54.

Scarry, Elaine (1985), *The Body in Pain*, Oxford: Oxford University Press, p. 81.

Acknowledgement

Slavoj Žižek and Nicol A. Barria-Asenjo, as editors of the book *Political Jouissance*, are deeply grateful for all the work behind the production of this project. The editors would like to express their gratitude to the entire Bloomsbury editorial and production team. Special thanks to Liza Thompson, Katrina Calsado, Vishnu Prasad, Mohammed Raffi, Giles Herman and Louisa McDonnell.

This book is proof of what commitment, responsibility and solidarity can achieve.

This publication emerges in the midst of confusing times, 2024 has begun and its arrival has left no one indifferent. This project is an important challenge. We sincerely thank all the authors of this project.

Thanks to the authors for their solidarity, friendship and trust. It is a pleasure and an honor to work with intellectuals from the Social Sciences and Humanities of such an academic, theoretical and human level.

Introduction

A Slovene actor said in an interview on 6 February 2022: 'You have to enjoy – even if you don't agree!' Although he referred to playing a role on stage, his remark should be universalized. All of us know the feeling of being haunted by a musical fragment which we find even disgusting – what haunts us certainly brings no pleasure, so the pressure we experience is that of enjoyment. Enjoyment is a superego injunction you have to follow even if you don't agree with it. Victims themselves have to enjoy: the more humans enjoy, the more surplus-enjoyment can be drawn from them – Lacan's parallel between surplus-value and surplus-enjoyment is again confirmed here. Lacan is fully aware that *jouissance* is a political factor: the intrusion into the political can only be made by recognizing that the only discourse there is [. . .] is the discourse of jouissance.'[1] In short, ideology and politics can be explained neither by crude reference to actual class interests nor by discourse-analysis which focuses on the competitive game for discursive hegemony, for which ideology will provide the dominant cognitive mapping of the situation. Even a brief look at racism and sexism suffices to see how, for an ideology to really take hold of us, it has to mobilize the dimension of jouissance. Oppression of women is sustained by the fear that, if not controlled, women will explode in excessive pleasures. Racism envies the Other's enjoyments and perceives this Other as a threat to enjoyments that form our way of life. All such passionate ideological investments are traversed by sadism, masochism and all their perverted combinations like enjoying one's own humiliation. To find our way in the mess we are in today, we thus need to analyse closely the modes of jouissance which sustain the predominant political discourses.

We are thereby raising the old Freudian question: Why do we enjoy oppression itself? That is to say, power asserts its hold over us not simply by oppression (and repression) which are sustained by a fear of punishment but by bribing us for our obedience and enforced renunciations – what we get in exchange for our obedience and renunciations is a perverted pleasure in renunciation itself, a gain in loss itself. Lacan called this perverted pleasure surplus-enjoyment: there is no 'basic enjoyment' to which one adds the surplus-enjoyment; enjoyment is always a surplus, in excess. It is the reference to Marx, especially to Marx's notion of surplus-value *Mehrwert*, that enabled Lacan to deploy his 'mature' notion of *objet a*, the object-cause of desire, as surplus-enjoyment (*plus-de-jouir*, *Mehrlust*). Freud made the first step in this direction when he talks about *Lustgewinn*, a 'gain of pleasure', which does not designate a simple stepping up of pleasure but the additional pleasure provided by the very formal detours in the subject's effort to attain pleasure. Exemplary is here the reversal that characterizes hysteria: renunciation to pleasure reverts into pleasure of/in renunciation, repression of desire reverts into desire of repression and so on. Such a reversal lies in the very heart of capitalist logic: as Lacan pointed out, modern capitalism began with *counting* the pleasure (of gaining profit), and this counting of pleasure immediately reverts into the *pleasure of counting* (profit).

In the following pages, the authors invited to this volume, who bring together mainly psychoanalysis and politics, will approach from different theoretical perspectives what we have identified as the 'modalities of political jouissance'. To go into the specifics, the reader will discover that our book has been divided into two parts, in which we approach from different disciplines the phenomenon that links the psychoanalytical conjectures related to 'jouissance' and its implications in the current challenges that the political conjuncture shows us.

Therefore, to introduce the specifics and the topics addressed in the book, we present in this Introduction a form of 'abstract' to each work. Part I, entitled 'Jouissance: The political crisis in neoliberalism', begins with Chapter 1, 'On the material existence of ideology' by **Slavoj Žižek**, where we find the following statement:

> In such a moment, we should make a step back and, instead of just analyzing the content of today's ideologies, we should focus on their more formal features. What do we mean when we say that we believe or not in an ideology? (Of course, such a statement is impossible: an ideology never calls itself that, it is always another who is caught in ideology.) Today, more than ever, we should bear in mind that there are beliefs which function socially, even if no-one really believes.

In Chapter 2, 'Neoliberalism, liber-fascism and cyber-liberalism: Modalities of enjoying symptoms in current capitalism' by **Jesús Ayala-Colqui** and **Nicol A. Barria-Asenjo**, concepts such as neoliberalism, ideology and hegemony, in light of the diverse ramifications that each concept has, leaving in an abstract void the implications with the dilemmas of the time, are approached.

Chapter 3 'Mistrust and political jouissance: From a "tickle" to the "blaze of petrol"', by **Andrea Perunović**, configures different approaches to the notion of 'mistrust' with the aim of answering the following question: What exactly do we mean when we use the word 'mistrust' today? Chapter 4, entitled 'Neoliberalism's political jouissance and the environmental crisis in Latin America', is authored by **Ignacio López-Calvo**. In this chapter, the author moves the

> concept of jouissance or libidinal enjoyment to the political domain – and therefore to the level of the symbolic and the social – to explore its connection with the unchecked excesses and transgressions of extractivist neoliberalism. This sadistic, ecocidal mode of jouissance at the heart of today's neoliberal ideology touches upon another side of the Lacanian concept, described as 'illicit, incurred in acts that apparently transgress laws or socially prescribed limits'.

In short, the chapter addresses the question of political jouissance in light of the ecological crisis and the unbridled race of capital accumulation, which has increasingly brought the planet to a point of no return.

In Chapter 5, a particular reality is approached under the title 'Hyper-royalism: A Thai modality of political jouissance' by **Pavin Chachavalpongpun**, an author who historically and philosophically analyses the implications of political enjoyment in the political crisis, affirming by generating a map of the material, psychological and spiritual conditions of the population of his country because 'After all, Thailand is known as the "Land of Smiles", supposedly because people are happy. And the monarchy is one reason for the Thai jouissance [. . .] I define hyper-royalism as a modality of political jouissance – a fantasy that has been created around the royal institution in Thailand'.

As we progress through the book, we next come to Chapter 6 by **Jens Schröter**, 'The joy circuit', where he writes that 'these artworks critically reflect on the circuit and its social and historical grounding and show moreover reflexively that mapping the structure of technology into the visible realm does not grant us access'. The author, using art as a tool for analysis, proposes a way out insofar as 'we embed ourselves into the technological pulse, into the abstract machine and use this energy to disrupt our stabilized subjectivity'.

In Chapter 7, 'Uncanny politics', **Natalia Romé** writes the following at the beginning,

> The current conditions of our social life have proved to be particularly harmful to our mental health [. . .] In the sixties Louis Althusser developed his theory of ideology in order to theorize the complex mediations that connect the social historical with the unconscious psychic. The concept of ideology was, nevertheless, discarded in the following decades by various theoretical traditions that preferred to work with the categories of discourse, performativity, identity, among others.

Throughout her contribution, the Argentine-born intellectual introduces us to concepts such as 'ideology' in relation to Althusser's ideas and puts them in dialogue with contemporary voices.

Chapter 8 is entitled 'Necro-society and jouissance: The acrobat, Lilith, and the Romantic machine' by **Obed Frausto**. Using the conceptual machinery of Freud, Lacan and Foucault, he proposes to 'understand the connections within organic and biological forces that are located in the instincts, and comprehend how capitalism extrapolates these forces to allow capital accumulation to continue, while maintaining social order and motivation among individuals'.

Finally, to conclude Part I in Chapter 9, 'Jean-Luc Nancy: A philosophy for a transformative existence', Italian philosopher **Francesca R. Recchia Luciani** writes that 'Thanks to entertainment and social networks, the overexposure of bodies is disproportionately expanding in the media and communication society' and then tries to answer the question: 'What is the role of sex in the contemporary hypersexualized and objectified system?'

For this purpose, she resorts to Nancy's ideology, to analyse the dilemmas of our time.

Part II 'Inside and outside the psychoanalytic view of politics', begins with Chapter 10, 'Daydream and emancipation: Against surplus-enjoyment, repression and their parallax of lack and excess', co-authored by **Nicol A. Barria-Asenjo**, **Slavoj Žižek**, **Brian Willems**, **Andrea Perunović**, **Ruben Balotol Jr.** and **Gonzalo Salas**. The authors state:

> In this research, we will start by exposing the paradox of 'surplus-enjoyment' (the Lacanian plus-de-jouir), showing that its parallax structure of lack and excess is also applicable to the phenomenon of (surplus) repression. Linking his concept with the Hegelian Aufhebung, understood as a 'failed negation of negation' or a 'negation of negation' as failure, we will focus in detail on the central example illustrating our theoretical positions, which is Iciar Bollain's film Tambien la Lluvia (Even the Rain). In analyzing its narrative structures that address the neocolonial reality, we will tend to approach indirectly, by reading the medium of cinematic narration, the 'neocolonial question'.

Chapter 11, 'Perverted erotics in the political unconscious: Lacan and Bataille', written by **Tim Themi**, concludes 'that the ethico-political perversions of greed, violence, corruption, are not symptomatic of a lack of repression, but of proper outlets for the drives as expressible in Bataille's philo-erotic renewal of aesthetics, augmented here by Lacan's clarifications on perversion in response to Freud'.

Chapter 12, 'In the absence of politics: A matter of life and death drive', takes a clinical-historical turn. Author **Daniel Bristow** asks the reader to take as our central theme the retreat from politics of the great psychoanalyst Wilhelm Reich (1897-1957). At one time one of the most remarkable practitioners within the Vienna Psychoanalytic Society, Reich started out as a committed Marxist and Communist, but became increasingly drawn to far more esoteric domains over his extraordinary life and career after outrightly rejecting Sigmund Freud's concept of the death drive. In exploring here the political ramifications of jouissance – the idea of its modality as 'the only discourse there is' politically, as Jacques Lacan implies – in its combinations with the death drive, this essay will revolve around the core question: what would be a psychoanalysis without the death drive?

Chapter 13, 'Synchronic interactions among discourse, knowledge (saber) and jouissance. Politibiology and/or biopolitics', by Argentine psychoanalyst **Alfredo Eidelzstein**, contains the following opening remarks upon which the author develops his research:

> Even outside psychoanalysis, it is commonplace to consider that jouissance and the drives [pulsiones] are prior to and more primitive than discourse and knowledge (saber; Fr. savoir). It is then concluded that the former are a generating factor or source of ideologies and political views. In the philosophical tradition this is asserted as the claim that res extensa has priority over res cogitans. In more colloquial terms it is claimed that the biological body comes before thought and speech. And in the medical field the conviction, allegedly supported by scientific evidence, is that genes, neurons, and hormones precede everything that is subjective in nature.

In Chapter 14, 'The jouissance of capital: Notes for a Lacanian critique of political economy' by **David Pavón-Cuéllar**, the author states that

> Marx shows that the true subject of capitalism is 'us' and not capital. However, to prove it, he must first show how the capitalist system usurps our place as subjects and objectively constitutes itself, through the objective fantasy, as a self-generated totality in which there is no place for us. This must be shown because it is not obvious to the common sense of individuals who imagine themselves to be free and masters of their actions in a capitalist society.

Following this conjecture, the author develops a Marxist-Lacanian reading focused on the notion of jouissance and its economic-social implications.

In Chapter 15, 'Aggression and the future', German-born thinker **Mia Neuhaus** writes that 'Perhaps the unspoken content of the catchphrases that emerge at the moment a rupture becomes visible, and find such a resonance that they become winged and capable of guiding action, can allow some conclusions to be drawn about the unconscious passions of our time that are negotiated in them' drawing on concepts and ideas from various social science thinkers, bringing us closer to the spectres of violence that are perceptible in the light of global struggles.

In the final two chapters of Part II, the philosophical-psychoanalytical look is approached in implication with political conjuncture – in Chapter 16, 'AOC and her boyfriend's leg' by **Slavoj Žižek,** and in Chapter 17, 'Jouissance the Levinas way' by **Graham Harman**.

Note

1   Jacques Lacan, *The Other Side of Psychoanalysis. The Seminar of Jacques Lacan, Book XVII* (New York: Norton 2007), 78.

References

Lacan, Jacques (2007), *The Other Side of Psychoanalysis. The Seminar of Jacques Lacan, Book XVII*, New York: Norton, 78.

Jouissance
The political crisis in neoliberalism

Chapter 1

On the material existence of ideology

Slavoj Žižek

Today we live in a strange era. Religious and national fundamentalisms are rising at the same time that cynical disbelief is rising. In such a moment, we should take a step back and, instead of just analysing the content of today's ideologies, we should focus on their more formal features. What do we mean when we say that we believe or not in an ideology? (Of course, such a statement is impossible: an ideology never calls itself that, it is always another who is caught in ideology.) Today, more than ever, we should bear in mind that there are beliefs which function socially, even if no one really believes. I remember, from my youth, in socialist Yugoslavia, the official ideology was not taken seriously even by the state apparatchiks – and in this way, it functioned perfectly. The apparatchiks got in a panic when someone took the official ideology too seriously – this was for them the first step towards becoming a dissident. But this didn't mean that individuals simply didn't believe – they acted as if they believed, and this was what mattered. They believed in and through their activity.

Niels Bohr, who gave the right answer to Einstein's 'God doesn't play dice' ('Don't tell God what to do!'), also provided the perfect example of how a fetishist disavowal of belief works in ideology: seeing a horse-shoe on his door, the surprised visitor said that he doesn't believe in the superstition that it brings luck, to what Bohr snapped back: 'I also do not believe in it; I have it there because I was told that it works also if one does not believe in it!'

This perspicuous example compels us to complicate a little bit Pascal's 'Kneel down and you will believe!', adding an additional twist to it. In the 'normal' cynical functioning of ideology, belief is displaced onto another, onto a 'subject supposed to believe', so that the true logic is: 'Kneel down and you will thereby *make someone else believe*!' One has to take this literally and even risk a kind of inversion of Pascal's formula: 'You believe too much, too directly? You find your belief too oppressing in its raw immediacy? Then kneel down, act as if you believe, and *you will get rid of your belief* – you will no longer have to believe yourself, your belief will already ex-sist objectified in your act of praying!'

That is to say, what if one kneels down and prays not so much to regain one's own belief but, the opposite, to get rid of one's belief, of its over-proximity, to acquire a breathing space of a minimal distance towards it? To believe – to believe 'directly', without the externalizing mediation of a ritual – is a heavy, oppressing, traumatic burden, which, through exerting a ritual, one has a chance of transferring it onto an Other. . . . If there is a Freudian ethical injunction, it is that one should have *the courage of one's own convictions*: one should dare to fully assume one's identifications. And exactly the same goes for marriage: the implicit presupposition (or, rather, injunction) of the standard ideology of marriage is that, precisely, there should be no love in it. The Pascalean formula of marriage is therefore not 'You don't love your partner? Then marry him or her, go through the ritual of shared life, and love will emerge by itself!', but, on the contrary: 'Are you too much in love with somebody? Then get married, ritualize your love relationship, in order to cure yourself of the excessive passionate attachment, to replace it with the boring daily custom – and if you cannot resist the passion's temptation, there are extra-marital affairs.'

The next feature of ideology is what I take the risk to call the *ideological unconscious*: an ideological edifice implies and relies on a set of claims which are necessary for its functioning but which should not be stated publicly. In the autumn of 2006, Sheik Taj Din al-Hilali, Australia's most senior Muslim cleric, caused a scandal when, after a group of Muslim men had been jailed for gang rape, he said: 'If you take uncovered meat and place it outside on the street [. . .] and the cats come and eat it . . . whose fault is it – the cats' or the uncovered meat? The uncovered meat is the problem.' The explosively scandalous nature of this comparison between a woman who is not veiled, and raw uncovered meat distracted attention from another, much more surprising premise underlying al-Hilali's argument: if women are held responsible for the sexual conduct of men, does this not imply that men are totally helpless when faced with what they perceive as a sexual provocation, that they are simply unable to resist it, that they are totally enslaved to their sexual hunger, precisely like a cat when it sees raw meat? In contrast to this presumption of the complete lack of male responsibility for their own sexual conduct, the emphasis on public female eroticism in the West relies on the premise that men *are* capable of sexual restraint, and that they are not blind slaves of their sexual drives.

The final feature I want to emphasize is the material existence of ideology, and here things get complicated. In his classic text, *Ideology and Ideological State Apparatuses*, Althusser makes the point about the material support of ideology: military, legal and ideological apparatuses, institutional and educational 'machines' and so on, claiming that this material support of ideology is ignored by Marxists from Marx onwards. For traditional Marxists, materialism means that ideology (still conceived in an idealist way, as a form of 'social consciousness' as a domain of ideas, as an inverted ideal mirror of reality) is grounded in the extra-ideological material process of social (re)production ('being determines consciousness'); what they ignore is the proper material existence of ideology in ISAs (ideological state apparatuses), in a complex institutional network of practices and rituals. However, Lacan goes here one step further from Althusser: there is *a specific materiality of ideas themselves*, immanent to the 'ideal' symbolic order, insofar as this order cannot be reduced to (an expression of) meaning but functions as a 'meaningless' machine, the machine that is the big Other beyond any concrete materialization in institutions or material practices. Let me elaborate this crucial point. According to Althusser, what distinguishes the state from other social apparatuses is that

everything that operates in it and in its name, whether the political apparatus or the ideological apparatuses, *is silently buttressed by the existence and presence of /the/ public, armed physical force*. That it is not fully visible or actively employed, that it very often intervenes only intermittently, or remains hidden and invisible – all this is simply one further form of its existence and action. [. . .] one had to make a show of one's force so as not to have to make use of it; [. . .] it suffices to deploy one's (military) force to achieve, by intimidation, results that would normally have been achieved by sending it into action. We may go further, and say that *one can also not make a show of one's force so as not to have to make use of it*. When threats of brute force, or the force of law, subject the actors in a given situation to obvious pressure, there is no longer any need to make a show of this force; there may be more to be gained from hiding it. The army tanks that were stationed under the trees of Rambouillet Forest in May 1968 are an example. They played, by virtue of their absence, a decisive role in quelling the 1968 riots in Paris.

So first, one makes a show of one's force so as not to have to make use of it; then, one does not make a show of one's force so as not to have to make use of it. We are effectively dealing here with a kind of negation of negation: first, we 'negate' the direct use of force by replacing it with a mere show of force (say, in a tense situation in which authorities expect forceful popular demonstrations, they decide to parade columns of tanks through the popular quarters of the city, expecting that this show of readiness to defend public order at any price will dissuade the protesters); then, this 'negation' is itself 'negated', there is no show of force, with the authorities expecting that this absence will have an even more forceful deterring effect than the open display of force – since the protesters know there is a police (or military) force ready to confront them, its very absence (invisibility) makes it all the more ominous and omnipotent. (Is Israel not doing this for years? It gives hints that it has nuclear weapons, but it never admits this publicly. Nuclear weapons are an exemplary case of violence that works as a potential threat – their actual use would have meant a total destruction of all parties.) The first 'negation' operates at the level of the Imaginary: the real brutal use of force is substituted by a fascinating spectacle destined to deter protesters. The second 'negation' operates at the level of the Symbolic: it is only within the symbolic order of differentiality that 'the presence-absence (a presence rendered effective by its very absence)' functions, that is, that absence can count as a positive feature, a feature even more powerful than presence. (Another example: when we do something wrong and expect our figure of authority to explode in fury and shout at us, if this figure does not explode but remains cold and calm, the effect can be even more threatening, since there is always something of the release of tension in the open explosion of fury – OK, this is it, now we've seen it . . .). And it is this properly symbolic dimension that Althusser ignores, as it is clear from a footnote attached to the quoted passage, in which Althusser draws attention to how Perry Anderson likened 'the presence-absence (a presence rendered effective by its very absence) of the state's armed forces to the monetary gold reserves of the Central Banks': the 'little piece of the real' (the armed force, gold reserve) which can remain in the background since it can perform its function even without being used, can perform its function *even if it doesn't exist at all* – it is enough that people believe that there are armed forces hidden in the background (or gold reserves in an inaccessible bank vault). The real in the background which serves as the ultimate guarantee and support of the public power is a spectral entity – it not only doesn't need to exist in reality, but if it appears and directly intervenes in reality, it risks losing its power, since, as Lacan made it clear, omnipotence (*toute-puissance*) necessarily reverts into 'all-in-potency' (*tout en puissance*): a father who is perceived as 'omnipotent' can only sustain this position if his potency/power remains forever 'potential', a threat which is never actualized. The full use of force, painful as it can be, makes it part of reality and as such by definition limited. This – and not only the shame at what they were doing – was the reason the Chinese authorities made their crackdown at Tiananmen Square, with (at least) hundreds of dead, a non-event: it was a direct exercise of raw force, but it took place at night, invisible, a nightmarish-spectral event of rumours; peace and order were immediately restored, all traces of conflict erased, the appearance of life going on as normal was immediately restored. If a regime gets involved in open warfare against its own population, it risks losing not only the minimum of its legitimacy but the very strength of its power. (And the same goes for gold reserves: imagine they all get poisoned by strong radiation and thus of no physical use – scenario of GOLDFINGER: if people continue to accept them as a point of reference, nothing would have changed.)

There is another feature of ideology and its prohibitions – I want to illustrate it by *The Laws of Manu*, the ancient Indian text which is one of the most exemplary texts of ideology in the entire history of humanity. While its ideology encompasses the entire universe, inclusive of its mythic origins, it focuses on *everyday practices as the immediate materiality of ideology*: how (what, where, with whom, when . . .) we eat, defecate, have sex, walk, enter a building, work, make war and so on. Here, the text uses a complex panoply of tricks, displacements and compromises whose basic formula is that of universality with exceptions: in principle yes, but . . . *The Laws of Manu* demonstrates breathtaking ingenuity in accomplishing this task, with examples often coming dangerously close to the ridiculous. For example, priests should study the Veda, not trade; in extremity, however, a priest can engage in trade, but he is not allowed to trade in certain things like sesame seed; if he does it, he can only do it in certain circumstances; finally, if he does it in the wrong circumstances, he will be reborn as a worm in dogshit. Is the structure here not exactly the same as that of the famous Jewish joke on the marriage mediator who reinterprets every deficiency of the bride-to-be as a positive asset: 'She is poor . . .' '. . . so she will know how to handle the family money, making most of it!' 'She is ugly . . .' 'So the husband will not have to worry that she will cheat on him!' 'She stutters . . .' 'So she will keep quiet and not annoy the husband with incessant prattle!', and so on till the final 'She really stinks!' 'So what do you want her, to be perfect, without any failure?' The general formula of this procedure is to state one general rule, to which the whole of the subsequent treatise constitutes nothing but a series of increasingly specific exceptions. A specific injunction is stronger than a general one. In other words, the great lesson of *The Laws of Manu* is that the true regulating power of the law does not reside in its direct prohibitions, in the division of our acts into permitted and prohibited, but in *regulating the very violations of prohibitions*: the law silently accepts that the basic prohibitions are violated (or even discreetly solicits us to violate them), and then, once we find ourselves in this position of guilt, it tells us how to reconcile the violation with the law by way of violating the prohibition in a regulated way. In the finale of Mozart's *Clemenza di Tito*, we get a ridiculously sublime explosion of mercies. Just before the final pardon, Tito himself is exasperated at the proliferation of treasons which oblige him to proliferate acts of clemency:

> The very moment that I absolve one criminal, I discover another. [. . .] I believe the stars conspire to oblige me, in spite of myself, to become cruel. No: they shall not have this satisfaction. My virtue has already pledged itself to continue the contest. Let us see, which is more constant, the treachery of others or my mercy. [. . .] Let it be known to Rome that I am the same and that I know all, absolve everyone, and forget everything.

One can almost hear Tito complaining: 'Uno per volta, per carita!' – 'Please, not so fast, one after the other, in the line for mercy!' Living up to his task, Tito forgets everyone, but those whom he pardons are condemned to remember it forever:

> 'SEXTUS: It is true, you pardon me, Emperor; but my heart will not absolve me; it will lament the error until it no longer has memory.
>
> TITUS: The true repentance of which you are capable, is worth more than constant fidelity.'

This couplet from the finale blurts out the obscene secret of *Clemenza*: the pardon does not really abolish the debt, it rather makes it infinite – we are forever indebted to the person who pardoned us. No wonder Tito prefers repentance to fidelity: in fidelity to the Master, I follow him out of respect, while in repentance, what attached me to the Master is the infinite indelible guilt. In this, Tito is a thoroughly Christian master. One usually opposes the Jewish rigorous Justice and the Christian Mercy, the inexplicable gesture of undeserved pardon: we, humans, were born in sin, we cannot ever repay our debts and redeem ourselves through our own acts – our only salvation lies in God's Mercy, in His supreme sacrifice. In this very gesture of breaking the chain of Justice through the inexplicable act of Mercy, of paying our debts, Christianity imposes on us an even stronger debt: we are forever indebted to Christ, and we cannot ever repay him for what he did to us. The Freudian name for such excessive pressure which we cannot ever remunerate is, of course, the *superego*. (One should not forget that the notion of Mercy is strictly correlative to that of Sovereignty: only the bearer of sovereign power can dispense mercy.) Accordingly, it is Judaism which is conceived as the religion of the superego (of man's subordination to the jealous, mighty and severe God), in contrast to the Christian God of Mercy and Love. However, it is precisely through *not* demanding from us the price for our sins, through paying this price for us Himself, that the Christian God of Mercy establishes itself as the supreme superego agency: 'I paid the highest price for your sins, and you are thus indebted to me *forever*.'

But is this eternalized superego the ultimate truth of Christianity? There is an alternate option which defines what I call Christian atheism/materialism: What if we imagine Christ's death on the Cross not as an act of deliberate sacrifice but as an act of endorsing one's death and impotence? Christ's death sets us free because it deprives us of any transcendent support because it exposes us to a weak impotent God who can only offer sympathy to our suffering.

Today, however, ideology no longer functions like that – a rupture is thus taking place in what philosophers call the 'ethical substance' of our life. This rupture is getting too strong for 'normal' democracy, and it is gradually drifting towards a kind of civil cold war. Trump's perverted 'greatness' is that he effectively acts – he is not afraid to break the unwritten (and written) rules to impose his decisions. Our public life is regulated by a thick web of unwritten customs and rules which teach us how to practice the explicit (written) rules. While Trump (more or less) sticks to explicit legal regulations, he tends to ignore the unwritten silent pacts which determine how we should practice these rules. Instead of just blaming Trump, the Left should learn from him and do the same. When a situation demands it, we should shamelessly do the impossible and break the unwritten rules. Unfortunately, today's Left is in advance terrified of any radical acts – even when it is in power, it worries all the time: 'If we do this, how will the world react? Will our act cause panic?' Ultimately, this fear means: 'Will our enemies be mad and react?' In order to act in politics, one has to overcome this fear and assume the risk, taking a step into the unknown.

Politicians are making desperate appeals for a return to civility, but this is not enough: it doesn't take into account the fact that the rise of 'brutal' populism filled in the lack opened up by the failure of the liberal consensus. Violent protests are the return of the repressed of our liberal societies: a symptom which enacts what cannot be formulated in the vocabulary of liberal multiculturalism. Usually, we accuse people that they just speak instead of doing something – the ongoing protests are the exact opposite, people act violently because they don't have the right words to express their grievance.

But there is another aspect of unwritten rules. Every order of culture implies its obscene underground: what one is not allowed to talk about publicly. This space of the obscene operates at multiple levels, from rumours about the dark side of the private life of political leaders and the use of dirty language and indecent insinuations, to cases which are much more 'innocent' and as such even more crucial – here is an extreme case of the prohibition of publicly stating the obvious. In the last years of his life, Deng Hsiao-Ping officially retired, but everybody knew that he continued to pull the strings of power. When one of the high Chinese party apparatchiks referred to Deng as the de facto leader of China in an interview with a foreign journalist, he was nonetheless accused of publicly disclosing a state secret and severely punished. So a state secret is not necessarily what only a few are allowed to know – it can also be something that everybody knows – everybody except what Lacan calls the big Other, the order of public appearance. . . .

One should not lose sight of what is so surprising about this rise of shameless obscenity of the alt-right so well noted and analysed by Angela Nagle in her *Kill All Normies*. Traditionally (or in our retroactive view of tradition, at least), shameless obscenity worked as subversive, as an undermining of traditional domination, as depriving the Master of his false dignity. I remember from my own youth how, in the 1960s, protesting students liked to use obscene words or make obscene gestures to embarrass figures of power and, so they claimed, denounce their hypocrisy. However, what we are getting today, with the exploding public obscenity, is not the disappearance of authority, of Master figures, but its forceful reappearance – we are getting something unimaginable decades ago, obscene Masters.

Should we link this rise of public obscenity to the alleged abandonment of truth? Big media are telling us again and again that we live in a post-truth era, and that this abandonment of truth in public discourse is the greatest threat to our democracy. In the debates about the explosion of fake news in (not only) our media, liberal critics like to point out three events which, combined, continuously bring about what some call the 'death of truth'. First, it is the rise of religious and ethnic fundamentalisms (and its obverse, stiff Political Correctness) which disavow rational argumentation and ruthlessly manipulate data to get their message through: Christian fundamentalists lie for Jesus, Politically Correct Leftists obfuscate news which shows their preferred victims in a bad sight (or denounce the bearers of such news as 'Islamophobic racists'), and so on. Then, there are the new digital media which enable people to form communities defined by specific ideological interests, communities where they can exchange news and opinions outside a unified public space and where conspiracies and similar theories can flourish without constraints (just look at the thriving neo-Nazi and anti-Semitic websites). Finally, there is the legacy of postmodern 'deconstructionism' and historicist relativism which claim that there is no objective truth valid for all, that every truth relies on a specific horizon and is rooted in a subjective standpoint that depends on power relations, and that the greatest ideology is precisely the claim that we can step out of our historical limitation and look at things objectively. Critics of the 'death of truth' oppose in historicist relativism the idea that facts are out there, accessible to an objective disinterested approach, and that we should distinguish between freedom of opinions and freedom of facts. Liberals can thus comfortably occupy the privileged ground of truthfulness and dismiss both sides, alt-right and radical Left.

Problems begin with the last distinction: in some sense, there ARE 'alternate facts' – not, of course, in the sense that the Holocaust did or did not happen. (Incidentally, all Holocaust revisionists that I know, from David Irving on, argue in a strict empirical way of verifying data – none of them evokes postmodern relativism!) 'Data' are a vast and impenetrable domain, and we always approach them from (what hermeneutics calls) a certain horizon of understanding, privileging some data and omitting others. All our histories are precisely that – stories, a combination of (selected) data into consistent narratives, not photographic reproductions of reality.

Lacan wrote that, even if what a jealous husband claims about his wife (that she sleeps around with other men) is all true, his jealousy is still pathological: the pathological element is the husband's need for jealousy as the only way to retain his dignity, identity even. Along the same lines, one could say that even if most of the Nazi claims about the Jews were true (they exploit Germans, they seduce

German girls . . .) – which they are not, of course – their anti-Semitism would still be (and was) a pathological phenomenon because it repressed the true reason why the Nazis needed anti-Semitism in order to sustain their ideological position. In the Nazi vision, their society is an organic whole of harmonious collaboration, so an external intruder is needed to account for divisions and antagonisms.

The same holds for how, today, the anti-immigrant populists deal with the 'problem' of refugees: they approach it in the atmosphere of fear, of the incoming struggle against the Islamization of Europe, and they get caught in a series of obvious absurdities. For them, refugees who flee terror are equalized with the terrorists they are escaping from, oblivious to the obvious fact that, while there are among the refugees also terrorists, rapists, criminals and so on., the large majority are desperate people looking for a better life. The cause of problems which are immanent in today's global capitalism is projected onto an external intruder. We find here 'fake news' which cannot be reduced to a simple inexactitude – if they (partially, at least) correctly render (some of) the facts, they are all the more dangerously a 'fake'. Anti-immigrant racism and sexism are not dangerous because they lie; they are at their most dangerous when the Lie is presented in the form of a (partial) factual truth.

For example, an anti-Semitic historian could easily write an overview of the role of the Jews in the social life of Germany in the 1920s, pointing out how entire professions (lawyers, journalists, art) were numerically dominated by Jews – all (probably more or less) true, but clearly in the service of a lie. The most efficient lies are lies with truth, lies which reproduce only factual data. Or take the history of a country: one can tell it from the political standpoint (focusing on the vagaries of political power), on economic development, on ideological struggles, on popular misery and protest . . . each of the approaches could be factually accurate, but they are not 'true' in the same emphatic sense. There is nothing 'relativist' in the fact that human history is always told from a certain standpoint, sustained by certain ideological interests. The difficult thing is to show how some of these interested standpoints are not ultimately all equally true – some are more 'truthful' than others. For example, if one tells the story of Nazi Germany from the standpoint of the suffering of those oppressed by it, that is, if we are led in our telling by an interest in universal human emancipation, this is not just a matter of different subjective standpoint: such a retelling of history is also immanently 'more true' since it describes more adequately the dynamics of the social totality which gave birth to Nazism. All 'subjective interests' are not the same – not only because some are ethically preferable to others but because 'subjective interests' do not stand outside social totality; they are themselves moments of social totality, formed by active (or passive) participants in social processes. The title of Habermas's early masterpiece *Knowledge and Human Interest* is perhaps today more current than ever.

There is an even greater problem with the underlying premise of those who proclaim the 'death of truth': they talk as if once before (say, until the 1980s), in spite of all manipulations and distortions, truth did somehow prevail, and that the 'death of truth' is a relatively recent phenomenon. Already a quick overview tells us that this was not the case: how many violations of human rights and humanitarian catastrophes remained invisible, from the Vietnam War to the invasion of Iraq. Just remember the times of Reagan, Nixon, Bush. . . . The difference was not that the past was more 'truthful' but that the ideological hegemony was much stronger, so that, instead of today's greater melee of local 'truths', one 'truth' (or, rather, one big Lie) basically prevailed. In the West, this was the liberal-democratic Truth (with a Leftist or Rightist twist). What is happening today is that, with the populist wave which unsettled the political establishment, the Truth/Lie which served as the ideological foundation of this establishment is also falling apart. And the ultimate reason for this disintegration is not the rise of postmodern relativism but the failure of the ruling establishment which is no longer able to maintain its ideological hegemony.

We can now see what those who bemoan the 'death of truth' really deplore: the disintegration of one big Story more or less accepted by the majority which brought ideological stability to a society. The secret of those who curse 'historicist relativism' is that they miss the safe situation in which one big Truth (even if it was a big Lie) provided the basic 'cognitive mapping' to all. In short, it is those who deplore the 'death of truth' that are the true and most radical agents of this death: their motto is the one attributed to Goethe, '*besser Unrecht als Unordnung*', better injustice than disorder, better one big Lie than the reality of a mixture of lies and truths.

Does this mean that the only honest position is postmodern relativism, which claims that we should accept the mixture of lies and (small) truths as our reality and that every big Truth is a lie? Definitely not. What it means is only that there is no return to the old ideological hegemony – the only way to return to Truth is to reconstruct it from a position engaged in universal emancipation. The paradox to be accepted is that universal truth and partiality do not exclude each other: in our social life, universal truth is accessible only to those who are engaged in the struggle for emancipation, not to those who try to maintain 'objective' indifference. To return to our example: anti-Semitism (but also every other form of racism) is wrong absolutely, even if it is supported by partial 'truths' (exact data). There are not only true and false data, but there are also true and false subjective standpoints since these standpoints themselves are part of 'data', of social reality.

The obscene public space that is emerging today thus changes the way the opposition between appearance and rumour works. It is not that appearances no longer matter since obscenity reigns directly; it is rather that spreading obscene rumours or acting obscenely paradoxically sustains the appearance of power.

A political leader can act in undignified ways, make obscene gestures and so on, but all this only strengthens his position as a master. Trump surprised us again and again with how far he is willing to go with his vulgar obscenities. As a climax of Trump's attacks on the ex-FBI lawyer Lisa Page, at a Minneapolis rally in October 2019, he performed a mock re-enactment of her texts with Mr Strzok, her ex-lover, as though the couple were in the middle of a sexual act, imitating her orgasmic throes. Lisa Page understandably exploded with rage – but the same story seems to repeat itself: Trump survives yet again what his enemies consider to be the final straw that should destroy him.

When we are shocked by what some politicians like Trump or Modi say, we explode in critical rage: 'How is this possible? It is unacceptable and outrageous!' However, by way of reacting in this way, we miss the point: the big Other (the moral authority we are addressing and relying on) is no longer here, our complaint is pointless, and there is no one listening to it. When there was a war in Bosnia almost three decades ago, I remember the reports on the suicides of the raped women: they survived the rape, and what kept them alive was the conviction that they must live to tell their story to their community. But it often happened that there was nobody in their community ready to listen to them – they were viewed with suspicion, treated as participating in and co-responsible for their humiliation, and this experience drove them to suicide. Something similar awaits those who explode in rage about today's political obscenities.

Ideology is thus not just an explicitly formulated edifice of ideas and ideals – ideology includes how this edifice functions in our daily lives and institutions. Look at how ideology is at work in our dealing with the Covid pandemic. The predominant form of thinking about the pandemic was a combination of predictable motifs: in a pandemic not only did our social and economic tensions explode, but the pandemic also reminded us that we are part of nature, not its centre, so we have to change our way of life – limit our individualism, develop new solidarity and accept our modest place in the life on our earth. Or, as Judith Butler put it,

> an inhabitable world for humans depends on a flourishing earth that does not have humans at its center. We oppose environmental toxins not only so that we humans can live and breathe without fear of being poisoned, but also because the water and the air must have lives that are not centered on our own. As we dismantle the rigid forms of individuality in these interconnected times, we can imagine the smaller part that human worlds must play on this earth whose regeneration we depend upon – and which, in turn, depends upon our smaller and more mindful role.

But is it not too simple to insist that 'the water and the air must have lives that are not centred on our own', that is, that we have to adopt a more modest role on the earth? Is it not that global warming and other ecological threats demand of us collective interventions into our environment which will be incredibly powerful, direct interventions into the fragile balance of forms of life? When we say that the rise of average temperature has to be kept below 2 degrees Celsius, we talk (and try to act) as general managers of life on earth, not as a modest species. The regeneration of the earth obviously does not depend upon 'our smaller and more mindful role' – it depends upon our gigantic role which is the truth beneath all the talk about our finitude and mortality. What we get here is the extreme form of the gap at work already in modern science and subjectivity: modern science and subjectivity which aim at mastering nature are strictly co-dependent with the vision of humanity as just another species on the earth. If we have to care also about the life of water and air, it means precisely that we are what Marx called 'universal beings', as we would be able to step outside ourselves, stand on our own shoulders and perceive ourselves as a minor moment of the natural totality. In premodern times when humanity perceived itself as the crown of creation, this paradoxically implied a much more modest stance. This is the paradox we have to sustain in these crazy days: to accept that we are one among the species on earth, and simultaneously to think and act as universal beings. To escape into the comfortable modesty of our finitude and mortality is not an option, it is a path to catastrophe.

So, to conclude, I would like to deal with an event which is going on now. From time to time, the Slovene government does something that makes me deeply ashamed of being a citizen of Slovenia. Now is one of such moments: as an act of solidarity with Israel, the Slovene government (together with those of Austria and the Czech Republic) decided to add the Israeli flag to the Slovene and European flags flown in front of official buildings. The official explanation was that Israel is under rocket attack from Gaza and has to defend itself – no usual calls for mutual restraint, just a clear assignation of guilt.

But the ongoing crisis did not begin with rockets from Gaza, it began in East Jerusalem where Israel is again trying to evict Palestinian families. The frustration of the Palestinians is easily understandable: for over fifty years (since the 1967 war), they are stuck on the West Bank in a kind of limbo, with no identity, refugees in their own land. This protraction is in Israel's interest: they want the West Bank, but they don't want to directly annex it because in this case, they would have to make the West Bank Palestinians Israeli citizens. So the situation just drags on and is from time to time interrupted by negotiations which were perfectly described by a Palestinian participant: both sides sit at opposite sides of a table with a pizza in the middle, and while they negotiate about how to divide the pizza, one side constantly eats its parts. . . . The Palestinian predicament found its most desperate expression in a series of individual suicidal attacks on Jews in Jerusalem a couple of years ago – there was no collective movement or mind behind them, just the horror of having no prospect of a way out. When, as a sign of solidarity with protesting Palestinians in the West Bank, Hamas began to launch rockets against Israel, this act (which should be condemned) served Netanyahu perfectly: a genuine desperate West Bank protest against the Israeli ethnic cleansing became yet another Hamas-Israel conflict with Israel just responding to rocket attacks – although now Netanyahu himself had to admit that the civil unrest in Israel was a greater threat than the rockets from Gaza. One of the focal points of the protests is the Israeli city of Lod with a strong Palestinian presence: Lod's mayor has described events as a 'civil war'. Gangs from both sides are terrorizing individuals, families and stores, up to direct lynchings. Far-right Jewish Israelis, often armed with pistols and operating in full view of police, moved into mixed areas. The most dangerous aspect of the situation is that the Israeli police are dropping even the pretence of acting as a neutral agent of the law and public safety – sometimes they even applaud the Jewish mob that terrorizes Palestinians. In short, the rule of law is disintegrating in Israel, at least for its Palestinian citizens – they are left to themselves, alone, and they cannot appeal to any higher agency that would intervene when they are attacked. This scandalous situation is just a consequence of something that has gone on in Israel in the last few years: the openly racist extreme Right (which wants to assert what they obscenely call Israel's 'full sovereignty' over the West Bank and treats Palestinians who live there as unwelcome intruders) is more and more recognized as legitimate and becoming part of the public political discourse. This racist stance was, of course, always the unspoken de facto foundation of Israeli politics, but it was never publicly acknowledged, it was just the secret (although known to everyone) motivation of Israeli politics whose public official position was always (till recently) the double-state position and respect of international laws and obligations. Now that this appearance of respect for the law is dissolving, it is not enough to say that we get the reality that was always the truth behind the appearance: appearances are essential, they oblige us to act in a certain way, so that without the appearance the way we act changes also. The distance between appearance and the dark reality behind it enabled Israel to present itself as a modern state of law in contrast to the Arab religious fundamentalism, but with this public acceptance of the religious fundamentalist racism, Palestinians are now a force of secular neutrality while the Israelis act like religious fundamentalists.

The big goal of Jewish fundamentalists is to reoccupy the Mount, destroy the al-Aksa mosque, and replace it with a new temple which stood there before the Romans (not the Arabs) destroyed it. Does this not remind us of India, where the Hindu nationalists want to destroy mosques and build there a Hindu temple? No wonder India now has good relations with Israel: Narendra Modi is pursuing a similar ethnic homogenization of India against the Muslim minority. The wider context of this escalation of events in Israel makes the entire picture even darker: first in France, then in the US, a considerable group of military officers and generals published a letter warning against the threat to the national identity and the way of life of their country. In France, the letter attacks the tolerance of the state against Islamization, and in the United States, they warn about the 'socialist' and 'Marxist' politics of the Biden administration. The myth of the depoliticized character of the armed forces is dispelled: a considerable part of the army supports the nationalist agenda. In short, what happens now in Israel is part of a global trend.

But what does this mean for the Jewish identity? As one of the Holocaust survivors said: in the past, an anti-Semite was a person who disliked Jews; now, an anti-Semite is a person whom Jews dislike – which Jews? The title of a recent dialogue on anti-Semitism and BDS in *Der Spiegel* was: 'Wer Antisemit ist, bestimmt der Jude und nicht der potenzielle Antisemit' ('Who is an anti-Semite determines the Jew and not the potential anti-Semite'). OK, sounds logical, the victim should decide their victim status, so in the same sense that this holds for a woman who claims she was raped, it should hold also for Jews – but there are two problems here: (1) Should then not the same also hold for Palestinians on the West Bank who should determine who is stealing their land and depriving them of elementary rights? (2) Who is 'the Jew' who determines who is anti-Semite? What about quite numerous Jews who support BDS or who, at least, have doubts about the politics of the State of Israel on the West Bank? Is not the implication of the quoted stance that, although empirically Jews, they are in some 'deeper' sense not Jews, they betrayed their Jewish identity? (I was once ferociously attacked as anti-Semitic for just using the term 'the Jews' . . .).

Carlo Ginzburg proposed the notion that shame for one's country, not love of it, may be the true mark of belonging to it. A supreme example of such shame occurred back in 2014 when hundreds of Holocaust survivors and descendants of survivors bought an ad in Saturday's *New York Times* condemning what they referred to as 'the massacre of Palestinians in Gaza and the ongoing occupation and colonization of historic Palestine': 'We are alarmed by the extreme, racist dehumanization of Palestinians in Israeli society, which has reached a fever-pitch', said the statement. Maybe, today, some Israelis will gather the courage to feel shame apropos of what the Israelis are doing on the West Bank and in Israel itself – not, of course, in the sense of shame of being Jewish but, on the contrary, of feeling shame for what the Israeli politics in the West Bank is doing to the most precious legacy of Judaism itself. I certainly am for what the Slovene government is doing.

Chapter 2

Neoliberalism, liber-fascism and cyber-liberalism

Modalities of enjoying symptoms in current capitalism

Jesús Ayala-Colqui and
Nicol A. Barria-Asenjo

It is commonplace to affirm that the dominant political discourse of current capitalism is neoliberalism. But what exactly is neoliberalism? The usual narrative consists of pointing out that after the crisis of the welfare state and the Fordist model of capitalist production at the end of the 1970s, the United States and supranational organizations such as the World Bank and International Monetary Fund assumed government policies that would affect an emptying of social rights, deregulation of the economy, a generalized privatization of goods and services and finally a financialization of the economy in order to 'restore class dominance'.[1] This narrative is often Eurocentric, as it places the governments of Thatcher in the United Kingdom and Reagan in the United States as paradigms, ignoring the fact that Latin America was one of the main experimental laboratories of neoliberalism.[2] Indeed, already in 1973, the military dictatorship of Pinochet imposed neoliberal ideas in Latin America with blood and fire at the hands of the Chicago Boys, a group of Chilean economists indoctrinated by Friedman.[3] Nevertheless, neoliberalism is not the exclusive work of this economist. Previously there is the theoretical work of Hayek who emigrated to the United States where he was a colleague of Hayek at the University of Chicago. And before this is von Mises, his teacher. It is important to remember that even neoliberalism has differences and nuances: 'Three neoliberal currents can be distinguished: the ordoliberal German school (Eucken, Röpke and Rüstow), the Austrian school (von Mises and Hayek) and the Chicago school (Simons, Friedman, Buchanan and Becker).'[4] All these authors first came together in the Lippmann Place in Paris in 1938 and later in the Mont Pelerin Society in 1947, a think tank created expressly to disseminate their ideas around the globe.[5] What would be in essence the difference between neoliberalism and liberalism? In his seminal 1979 course 'Naissance de la biopolitique', Foucault established three distinguishing features: first, while liberalism places the market under state supervision, neoliberalism places the state under market control; second, while liberal governmentality assumes that subjects are atomic units that are related through exchange, neoliberal governmentality posits that these individualities are linked through competition; third, while the governmental reason of the eighteenth century postulated that the subject is a partner in the exchange and still a worker, that of the twentieth century stipulated that the subject ceases to be a worker who produces value to become a human capital and an entrepreneur of himself.[6] It is based on an excessive business vision of human beings that it is natural to consider that all activities should be private and managed according to the logic of the market. Likewise, if the subject is reduced to being a mere capital, its objective should not be the negation of that network of social relations that extract its surplus value, but simply entrepreneurship and investment. And since companies compete with each other, individuals would have no other alternative than to launch into a brutal confrontation where the defeat of others (poverty, precariousness, inequality and indigence) is justified in advance by the same rules of the market. In this way, the power that the bourgeoisie exercises over the proletarian layer is not only a government over them but above all a self-government of the workers over themselves. Dardot and Laval point out in this regard:

> competition and the entrepreneurial model constitute a general mode of government, far exceeding the 'economic sphere' in the habitual sense of the term. And that is precisely what we see everywhere. The requirement of 'competitiveness' has become a general political principle, which governs reforms in all areas, even those furthest removed from commercial confrontations in the world market. It is the clearest manifestation that we are dealing not with a 'creeping commodification', but with an extension of market rationality to existence in its entirety through the generalization of the enterprise-form. It is this 'rationalization of existence' which, ultimately, can have the effect (as Mrs Thatcher stressed) of 'changing the heart and soul'.[7]

In neoliberalism, the idea of business entrepreneurship is regulated by capital valorization flows and, more precisely, by specific economic frameworks that place the emphasis on fictitious capital, that is, on financial assets. In order to speed up competition, industrial and commercial companies have undertaken, under the neoliberal auspices of market deregulation, a radical financialization of their activities. This same financial logic applies to people:

> banks have turned toward individual and household income as a source of profit, often combining trading in open markets with lending to households, or collecting household savings [. . .]. individuals and households have come increasingly to rely on the formal financial system to facilitate access to vital goods and services, including housing education, health, and transport. The savings of households and individuals have also been increasingly mobilized by the formal financial system.[8]

Also, under neoliberal conditions, each subject assumes his life as a financial bet: a certain amount or certain time is invested in this or that activity in order to produce a certain profitability, and, above all, one indebts oneself through to be able to finance oneself as long as capital In fact, what greater form of fictitious capital than to impose the fiction that we are all entrepreneurs? Now, neoliberalism does not cause successful entrepreneurs, but rather indebted and depressed subjects. Lazzarato has shown that in reality, this entrepreneur is a 'debtor', which can be both employment and unemployment, both working and non-working.[9] Berardi, in his turn, places as a counterpart to the rhetoric of competition the reality of depression: 'When economic competition is the dominant psychological imperative of the social consortium, we can be positive that the conditions for mass depression will be produced.'[10]

What in Foucault and his successors – for example, in Lazzarato, Dardot and Laval – is about a mode of subjectivation and, more broadly, about a veridiction (véridiction) or a game of truth (jeu de vérité) that modifies subjectivity of the subjects,[11] in Althusser and in his successors – for example, in Žižek (beyond the criticism that the Slovenian may make of the French Marxist) – it is an ideological framework that shapes the actions of the subjects.

Althusser wrote, in effect, that ideology is far from being a mere set of representations or ideas: it is, above all, an apparatus (appareil) that has a subjection-effect, that is, ideology has a material existence that functions in apparatuses (school, family, the media, etc.) and that is manifested in the practices and acts of the subjects: 'ideology existing in a material ideological apparatus, prescribing material practices regulated by a material ritual, which practices exist in the material acts of a subject acting in all good conscience in accordance with his belief'.[12] Thus, ideology performs an interpellation (l'interpellation) so that individuals become subjects, which literally means that they become subjected (soumis). Such subjection is based on the use of a guarantee 'that everything really is so' and that the subjects 'will receive their reward'.[13]

What Althusser says about ideology we can apply to neoliberalism. In this case, neoliberalism challenges individuals to be entrepreneurs of the self because only by being entrepreneurs does this offer a guarantee: the reward of personal success, economic stability, well-being and enjoyment. It is the subjection of competition that represents an imaginary relationship of the individual with the conditions of his existence, since with this the reality of debt and the devastation of capitalist exploitation are eluded. Thus, neoliberalism is ideological not so much in the sense that it is a true or false political-economic doctrine, but in the sense that it is an interpellation that, through specific institutions, mobilizes the practices of the subjects.

Žižek complements Althusser's approach by introducing, from psychoanalysis, an unconscious order that transcends specific apparatuses and institutions. In fact, he distinguishes three senses of ideology:

> What thereby comes into sight is a third continent of ideological phenomena: neither ideology qua explicit doctrine, articulated convictions on the nature of man, society and the universe, nor ideology in its material existence (institutions, rituals and practices that give body to it), but the elusive network of implicit, quasi-'spontaneous' presuppositions and attitudes that form an irreducible moment of the reproduction of 'non-ideological' (economic, legal, political, sexual . . .) practices.[14]

In other words, ideology is not only reduced to a doctrinal component or an institutional functioning but also involves a set of presuppositions that spontaneously and implicitly determine our actions. Starting with Sohn-Rethel, Žižek takes up the notion of real abstraction to explain how this last sense of ideology originates. In capitalist society, the commodity appears abstractly in a double sense: the sphere of production is abstracted so that it appears as something exclusive to exchange between free agents and its use value is abstracted so that the commodity appears as something that has only one exchange value. It is this commodity form that is found as a presupposition in every social relationship since everything starts from abstract work.[15] Thus, every time we relate to others we establish relationships 'as if' we were atomistically free and even every time we act cognitively we start from intellectual categories that assume quantitative abstractions as real. Sohn-Rethel writes:

> the abstractness of that action cannot be noted when it happens because the consciousness of its agents is taken up with their business and with the empirical appearance of things which pertain to their use. One could say that the abstractness of their action is beyond realization by the actors because

their very consciousness stands in the way. Were the abstractness to catch their minds their action would cease to be exchange and the abstraction would not arise.[16]

To the extent that it is not cognitively apprehended as such in the acts of society, Žižek can say that it is unconscious: 'the "real abstraction" is the unconscious'.[17]

In order to scrutinize the unconscious character of this third sense of ideology, Žižek resorts to the psychoanalytic notion of 'fantasy' (le fantasme). For psychoanalysis, this is not a mere arbitrary whim that we add to reality but an area that is both symbolic and imaginary[18] that structures reality itself. In this sense, 'The fundamental level of ideology, however, is not that of an illusion masking the real state of things but that of an (unconscious) fantasy structuring our social reality itself'.[19]

But if fantasy produces reality, that means that what it offers us is not the real itself. Indeed, the real for psychoanalysis is nothing but a traumatic core that is unassimilable for the subject.[20] In order to avoid a confrontation with reality, psychoanalysis explains that it is precisely unconsciously repressed through the production of fantasies. What is the reality of capitalist society beyond all the illusions that can be naively or self-interestedly invented about it? What is real is exploitation, domination, oppression, in a word: the antagonism of the class struggle. For this reason, in capitalism, the ideological fantasy would do no more than cover up this materiality already contained in the commodity form.

However, psychoanalysis also points out that there is a 'return of the repressed'. This happens through the 'symptom' (le symptôme). Already Freud pointed out that the subject tends to a repetition (Wiederholung) of his acts and inhibitions from what is repressed: 'he repeats everything that has already made its way from the sources of the repressed into his manifest personality [. . .]. He also repeats all his symptoms'.[21] Originating from the repressed, precisely because it cannot be expressed as such given its traumatic character, the symptom is always a metaphor[22] that replaces the real itself. The symptom causes, however, a paradoxical unpleasant pleasure, that is, an enjoyment (jouissance) that explains the pregnancy of its repetitions: 'the subject can "enjoy his symptom" only in so far as its logic escapes him'.[23]

Brief, for Žižek, capitalist ideology in an unconscious sense produces both fantasies and symptoms that not only secretly determine each action of the subjects but also tritely organize their ways of enjoying and desiring.

What status can we give, then, to neoliberal discourse? If neoliberalism can be considered an ideology, it should be noted that it is not (only) in the sense of a set of ideas, representations, economic-political doctrines, nor in the sense of a practice that materializes in government institutions and policies, but in the sense that it is an ideological fantasy that operates spontaneously in each act of the subjects before any conscious and deliberate reflection, generating repetitive symptoms that reduce the subject to a predetermined circuit of unpleasant pleasure. We affirm then that the fundamental fantasy of capitalism is none other than the market as a necessary, effective and free instance where atomistic individualities concur. Now, what neoliberalism adds is a specific configuration of this ideological discourse based on three dimensions. First, the fantasy of the anteriority and ontological priority of the market over the state and above all possible social bonds. The market appears as the deus ex machina that explains society. It would be, contradictorily, a reality that is, at the same time, a contract between individuals as well as an original factum. But it is also the result and the end: a proper and properly organized society can only be mercantile. Outside of it, there would be nothing but inefficiency, despotism, irrationality and violence. All activity must be organized according to the logic of the superior and eternal of the free market. Second, neoliberalism brings the fantasy of competition. Mercantile reality is nothing more than a conglomeration of competitions: between producers, owners, rentiers, investors, individuals, companies, countries, animals against non-animals and so on. In this way, social Darwinism is renewed: only some adapt in the fight for scarce resources and the rest perish. There is, therefore, no inequality, injustice or poverty: they are just the counterpart of an uninterrupted and natural process of bids and contests. A result among others is revealed as necessary in order for there to be a winner of the competition. Third, the fantasy of the entrepreneurial self. In this unstable terrain, the subjects cannot be workers, they are contenders whose objective is to value their human capital. It is not that there are exploited and exploiters but only a homogeneous horizon where we are all entrepreneurs and compete to obtain the highest possible income. For this, every gesture, every detail, every event is an investment. If we fail, it is a simple stock market issue: we invested wrongly and we did not know how to value our existential company. In short, it is these three fantasies that constitute the neoliberal unconscious that spontaneously structures our actions without perhaps having read a book or having come into contact with an institution that replicates the ideas of von Mises, Hayek, Friedman or Becker.

But these three figures are also three modalities where the symptom of capitalist exploitation that organizes the enjoyment of the subject is repeated. Indeed, in the ferocious deregulation of the market, the brutality of competition and the becoming-company of subjectivity, the subject is condemned to a suffering that is considered acceptable and inevitable: it is a necessary sacrifice to obtain success. This constant martyrdom, certainly unpleasant, is constantly repeated only because the promised pleasure of capital is promised. Furthermore, ways to externalize this enjoyment are developed through self-help, motivational coaching and success stories. As Dean notes: 'In sacrificing everything to the system, the player, the investment, banker or entrepreneur, acts as if such a sacrifice is necessary for success, thereby subverting the fantasy that we are all winners.'[24]

The first thesis that we want to present in this paper, based on our previous inquiries,[25] is the following: the real abstraction of the commodity form of capital acquires, in the three senses of ideology (doctrine, institution and social unconscious), multiple historical configurations, which are not mutually exclusive, but rather overlap, reinforce, intensify and eventually replace each other definitively.

It is not entirely correct to point out that we live in neoliberalism. Neoliberalism is dead, but it is an unwelcome corpse. Does this have any relation to the proliferation of products and merchandise of popular culture that take as a topic the zombies that, after being clinically dead, continue to literally fuck us? There is another discursivity of capital that has certainly not replaced neoliberalism, but has been attached, has been superimposed and, in some circumstances, has made it irrelevant. We are referring to what we have called, with regard to Bolsonaro in Latin America and the new far-right parties, 'liber-fascism'.[26]

Many current theorists have resorted to two kinds of approaches to explain the emergence of new extreme right or alt-right groups. On the one hand, some have pointed out that these are violent resurgences and prolongations of neoliberalism: thus, they have spoken of a 'fascist moment of neoliberalism'[27] or an 'authoritarian liberalism'.[28] That is, it is not a new phenomenon but a modification of something already existing. On the other hand, others have indicated that it is a reissue and recovery of fascism: thus we have concepts such as 'neo-fascism'[29] and 'late fascism'[30] where, beyond the differences, the analogies with traditional fascism are clearly emphasized. It is here a variable return of the same. But are Bolsonaro and the new far-right parties really simply a modification of neoliberalism or a new version of fascism?

First of all, fascism is not an abstract universal but a concrete historical phenomenon. Therefore, a comprehensive political analysis must not fall into excessive generalizations or imprecise anachronisms. Poulantzas, when carrying out his study on fascism, wrote that it belongs to a very limited historical period, namely, a crisis of capitalism that required the constitution of exceptional regimes.[31] Are the parties of the extreme right the same answer to the debacle of the industrial model? Although the proposals by Fassin, Chamayou or Toscano are totally meritorious, the truth is that we belong to another era with quite specific problems, for example, the exhaustion of the neoliberal model, the spread of fake news on social networks, xenophobic violence, the formation of urban militias, the resonance of conspiracy theories and a profoundly reactionary gesture that is expressed in an explicit apology for the free market. What would happen if, instead of reissues or extensions of something already existing, that was the emergence of a new discourse, a new type of government and a new form of subjectivity?

Undoubtedly there are neo-fascist conformations, that is, groups that, for example, nostalgically claim the figures of Nazism displaying nationalist and authoritarian practices. However, Bolsonaro in Brazil, Aliaga in Peru, Kast in Chile, Hernández in Colombia and Milei in Argentina are not just followers of Hitler or Goebbels. They are characterized because their conspiracy conservatism is a way of carrying out the fiction of the free market. In them, there is not simply a 'fascist', 'violent' or 'authoritarian' version of the entrepreneur of himself of neoliberalism, but a new subjectivity, namely, the defender of himself.[32] Indeed, while in neoliberalism the subject is taken as a business individuality that must sacrifice and invest in itself to value itself in a competition of all against all, in libertarian fascism it is assumed as an individuality that is threatened by two fundamental enemies: on the one hand, the state and the corrupt political caste and, on the other hand, 'communism' or 'cultural Marxism' that would undermine the ontological consistency of the self.[33] This is the core from which an apology for the free market unfolds, since only in this market is the individual free from all state and cultural coercion, from any offensive that wants to undermine the pristine and essential axiological condition of people. Likewise, if liber-fascism is xenophobic, nationalist and, ultimately, forms urban militias, it is only because the imperatives of the defender of himself are present in them: it is the other-non-liberal-fascist who endangers the integrity of the former, hence it must be eliminated.[34] In summary,

> while at the level of the production of subjectivity and modes of governmentality, neoliberalism is characterized by the assumption of competition and the entrepreneur of himself, in addition to hedonism, entrepreneurship and cynicism; and while neo-fascism is definished by the adoption of nationalism, populism and authoritarianism; liber-fascism is defined by the postulation of mercantilism and the defender of himself, in addition to segregationism, conservatism and conspiracy.[35]

If we now return to Žižek's notion of ideology, then it is appropriate to carry out an inquiry into the liberal-fascist ideological fantasy. As we have pointed out, the commodity form is not only the fundamental fantasy of capitalism but it is realized in different historical configurations. Thus, libertarian fascism articulates this fantasy of the free market through three elements. First, the fantasy of an individuality endangered both by supra-individual, collective and state authorities as well as by ideas and practices that question economic, political and social conservatism.

It is not necessary that liber-fascism be transmitted in public speeches or on social networks (as a doctrine), but spontaneously more and more people feel threatened by immigrants (thus constituting a social unconscious). The reverse of this fantasy is, of course, violence: verbal, physical, and psychological aggression against anyone who dares to endanger the fragile ontological and axiological stability of the self. This is what produces subjectivities put on the defensive: what we have called 'the defender of himself'. The corollary, and in no way the foundation or essence of liber-fascism, is thus exacerbated nationalism, generalized xenophobia, imperative segregation and visceral hatred towards the non-liberal-fascist who is called 'communist', 'feminist', 'environmentalist' or 'terrorist'. Thus, to extrapolate a statement by Žižek, in this new way of fantasizing: the slogan is 'enough of enjoyment, enough of debauchery: a victim is necessary'.[36] Therefore, it is not necessary to invest in oneself but to defend oneself from others. Thus neoliberal competition is replaced by liberal-fascist aggression. Secondly, liberal-fascism brings with it the fantasy that the market is the highest level of self-defence, in such a way that it can be agreed with absolutely conservative positions: 'economically liberal, socially conservative'. One is therefore no longer a capital but a human 'property' that must be placed in a safe place against corrupt governments and the global threat of communism. The market is no longer an area of exchange, if not a protection zone for threatened integrity. Third, liberal-fascism brings the fantasy of the lack of fantasies where evidence and argumentation do not matter, but only the subjective certainty of what puts us in danger: thus, every rumour becomes a truth to be followed and defended. The consequence of this is the ad nauseam proliferation of fake news and conspiracy theories that spread massively on social networks, creating a kind of alternative reality where all connection with reality is already forgotten. These are, then, the fantasies that repress the reality of capitalism: the class struggle and exploitation. However, it should not be thought that the liberal-fascist unconscious annuls the neoliberal: on the contrary, these discursivities overlap, reinforce, mix, repel and feed each other as 'ideologies' of the government of capital. Thus, the subjects live in a multiplicity of fantasies that, beyond their phenomenal diversity, express the essence of capital: the secret of merchandise as a constitutive abstract on of society.

Now, we want to indicate that there is currently a third discursivity of capitalism that is not reduced to neoliberalism and liber-fascism: we call it cyber-liberalism.[37]

Probably a bunch of renegade liber-fascists protesting in the streets, storming parliaments and calling their opponents to death gets a lot of attention. However, there is another discursiveness of capital that has silently imposed itself. It is one that, under the cloak of objectivity, scientificity and inexorable progress, has taken life by storm without criticism or express deliberation. We are referring to that set of regimes of knowledge that propose a technical solution to every social problem, that favours the computerization of every human relationship, the algorithmization of reality and that, finally, speaks to us in terms of optimization and technological advance: cyber-liberalism. What is cyber-liberalism? As we have argued, we define this 'new' political figure as a government strategy that through information technologies seeks to implement strategies of control over the subjects in order to modulate every detail of capitalist production and consumption.[38]

We must banish the misconception that the discourses where the free market and technology converge are simply (neo)liberal. Practices that support technology initiatives like Alphabet (Google), Meta (Facebook), Apple, Microsoft, Amazon, Tesla and so on do not simply propose the ideology of competition and the entrepreneur himself. Superimposed on this political configuration is another register that, on the one hand, prolongs its notions and, on the other hand, exceeds them, transmuting them into another substance. What is the novelty of this form of government and this discursive proposal?

Some theorists have already tried to characterize the range of statements that unilaterally consider the benefits of technology for the benefit of the abstract individuality of the capitalist market. They have used the term 'technoliberalism' in this regard. Malaby, addressing the video game Second Life, defines this term as a 'combination of distrust of vertical authority, faith in technology, and faith in the legitimacy of emerging effects', which adds to neoliberalism the emphasis on technological manipulation.[39] Fish, for his part, sees in technoliberalism a contradictory 'digital discourse' that updates the aporias of liberalism: 'Technoliberalism designates a specific type of digital discourse, namely, how the Democratic elite dialogue on technology in attempts to mitigate the tensions of liberalism, the simultaneous attractions of capitalism, individualism, populism, and progressivism.'[40] Sadin, in turn, sees in technoliberalism a 'world view' that seeks to institute an automated organization of society and, thereby, disqualify all human action, in such a way that the enlightened deliberative principles would lose political effectiveness.[41]

We distance ourselves from the point of view of these three authors for the following reasons. Firstly, we do not see in this new political configuration a simple addition or a simple update of either liberalism or neoliberalism. Secondly, we start from a class approach that places the accent on the class struggle. This prevents us from an abstract outlook that views technical advancements as autonomous. Our approach suggests that this discourse is a novel political strategy for management of the economy, in view of the fact that it serves to oversee the exploitation of classes in order to value capital.[42] In this sense, it would be an 'ideology': it is not only a doctrine prophesied by the Silicon Valley gurus or a partial inspiration of some governments; it is, above all, a social unconscious that installs its particular fantasies in the subjects, causing them to act spontaneously according to the technologized designs of capital. We call it cyber-liberalism because we are interested in emphasizing the prefix 'cyber' that refers to control through technology and information that conveys such an ideology. When Norbert Wiener proposed the term 'cybernetics' he pointed out:

We have decided to call the entire field of control and communication theory, whether in the machine or in the animal, by the name Cybernetics, which we form from the Greek χυβερνήτης or steersman. In choosing this term, we wish to recognize that the first significant paper on feedback mechanisms is an article on governors.[43]

Where does cyber-liberalism originate and what characteristics does it possess? Barbrook and Cameron were already aware of the birth of a new type of discursive regime in California in the 1990s, which mixed technological determinism with the affirmation of capitalist individuality, although they limited themselves to calling it 'dotcom neoliberalism'.[44] Now, the history of cyber-liberalism is much more complex. In fact, it combines utopian and especially rebellious elements that create a kind of technological counterculture[45] and, at the same time, seek social alternatives where technology solves political problems and, especially, allows the individuality of the most beyond state coercion and collective impositions.[46] Thus, unlike neoliberalism which proposes a surveillance of the state by the market, cyber-liberalism 'drinks' from anarcho-capitalism and proposes to suppress all political mediation beyond the immediate abstraction of the individual:

> this approach falls short of the concept of liberty, since the only liberty that matters here, is that of the capitalist market, which is itself the outcome of the free agency of totally individuals motivated by their purely private interest in the accumulation of capital and consumerism [47]

What cyber-liberalism adds is a conception of the market that can be optimized by means of cybernetic, digital and algorithmic technologies. They replace the invisible hand of liberal exchange and the cynical reality of competition with the 'automated hand' of individual in-mediation. It is no longer about individuals subjected to exchange or competition but about individuals who realize themselves abstractly and, even more, are ontologically optimized by means of a market algorithm.[48] Consequently, they propose technologized automatism of the market where there is not so much exchange or competition but technical modulation of individualities. Likewise, this means that at the level of the formation of subjectivity, an absolutely unique formation is obtained: we call it, in contrast to the entrepreneur of himself and the defender of the self, the enhancer of himself. In effect, it is assumed that only through technology, be it through a computer, a cryptocurrency, an algorithm, an application, a virtual reality or a modification by bioengineering, can that individual be fully realized without state, natural, physical, biological or collective coercion. And, by extension, all reality is improved thanks to technological developments. It is what Morozov has called 'the folly of technological solutionism'.[49] This culminates the myth of progress spurred by an aura of neutral scientificity that conceals specific class interests, given that technology does not benefit humanity but rather the valorization of companies and results in the exploitation of people in a regime of 'platform capitalism'.[50]

But cyber-liberalism is not only the product of engineers, technophiles, anarcho-capitalists, innovators, entrepreneurs and visionaries of cheap science fiction but also of theorists of capitalism. For example, Bell, the same author who pointed out in 1960 the 'end of ideology', proposed in 1973 the advent of a 'post-industrial society' where the valorization of value would be possible 'without exploitation' thanks to the development of technology.[51] Therefore, cyber-liberalism is an ideology, in the Marxist-psychoanalytic sense, that spreads assuming itself as non-ideology, as a discourse connatural to the advances in technology and the progress of society.

If we adopt the ideological approach of materialist psychoanalysis, then cyber-liberalism must work at the level of unconscious drives and through fantasies. What are the myths of cyber-liberalism? First, the fantasy that reconciling the market and technology will contribute to resolving all of society's dilemmas. This fantasy has several levels. It starts from the idea that technological progress is necessary and inevitable, then assumes that technology is consistent with the abstract individuality of capitalism and, finally, considers that the virtuous synthesis of technological determinism and ontological libertarianism provides the solution to all ills of humanity. Under the premise of this fantasy, we have the biggest slogans of the technology companies in Silicon Valley. Thus, Facebook promises a more connected world, Google proposes free access to information and Apple postulates unlimited comfort and a complementary nature of human activities through customized apps. Second, the fantasy that 'there is only technique, individuals and nothing else'. Indeed, cyber-liberalism takes up the libertarian spirit of Ayn Rand: it is the technological geniuses and visionaries, whether in act or potential, who rebel against tyrannical governments and other instances of intermediation that go beyond the immediacy of individuality. Cryptocurrencies, metaverses, genetic modifications, all of these will help to banish those damn intermediaries that weaken the individual power of the subject and condemn him to a world of collective impositions. It is in this digital space that she proposes that everything will be possible for the individual: 'Yes, in cyberspace, "everything is possible," but for the price of assuming a fundamental impossibility: you cannot circumvent the mediation of the interface, its "by-pass," which separates you (as the subject of enunciation) forever from your symbolic stand-in.'[52]

Third, cyber-liberalism spurs the fantasy of the enhancer of himself. Unlike neoliberalism and liber-fascism, the individual is not a subject that simply must compete or defend himself but must improve himself. Therefore, the enhancer of the self radicalizes the imperative of the 'entrepreneur of himself': we are not only an existential start-up that must innovate,[53] but we are a technical-monetary instance that must biologically modify itself in order to value itself in the midst of a frenetic succession of innovations. For this, we start with external ergonomic accessories (telephones, computers, etc.) that gradually become internal until finally becoming a transhumanist modification of the self. Thus one falls into the imperative of becoming a bio-hacker and a geek at the risk of worsening not only economically but also ontologically. One of the most outstanding exponents of current cyber-liberalism is, without a doubt, Raymond Kurzweil, director of engineering at Google, who brings together these three fantasies under the heading of the 'singularity': a future moment where technology surpasses all human capacity and we entered an unsuspected dimension that would culminate, deterministically, in the insurmountable evolution of humanity.[54] It is, therefore, the last step in the improvement not only of the capitalist individual through technology but also of the market and nature understood as an agent of improvement as valuable capital. In all these fantasies, which prolong the real abstraction of the commodity form, the real class struggle and exploitation are repressed by a technological paradise of 'continuous improvement'.

In this sense, we arrive at a second thesis that we have already suggested in previous works:[55] there are currently three ideological configurations that, with their respective singularities and levels (doctrinal, institutional and unconscious), carry out the real abstraction of merchandise in contemporary society: neoliberalism, liber-fascism and cyber-liberalism.

Finally, we would like to propose a third thesis on the specifically unconscious level of what, for convenience, we call 'ideology': each discursive configuration of capital corresponds not only to a set of particular fantasies but also to a conglomeration of distinctive symptoms.

Indeed, in our opinion, in the case of neoliberalism, the characteristic symptom is nothing but stress. There is an imperative here to enjoy the fact of being entrepreneurs subjected to extreme competition. Such constant confrontational activity, where debt is the rhythm of our existence, leads to unavoidable stress and, should we fail, leads to depression. If once it was a melancholy in the face of the technological developments of modernity, now the imposition of performance and competitiveness condemn us to the alternation and continuum of stress-depression.[56] In the case of liber-fascism, the repetitive symptoms are fear and anger. The liberal-fascist is not subject to competition but to defence. This originates because, in the most intimate of his being, he feels threatened by those who question his capitalist and conservative status: the communists or the cultural Marxists (feminists, environmentalists, anti-racists, etc.). As a result of this fear, on the one hand, we find the dissemination of fake news and conspiracy theories in order to make intelligible the traumatic core of their confrontation with the other non-liberal-fascists. On the other hand, fear leads to violence. That the liberal-fascists assault parliaments, call for the death of a political enemy or simply display their firearms in the streets indicates the weakness of their fears in the face of an invented threat that serves as an addictive calm: it is the enjoyment, then, of fear-anger that allows the libertarian-fascist to be libertarian-fascist. Finally, in the case of cyber-liberalism, the symptoms are attention-deficit, hyperactivity disorder and burnout. The cyber-liberal technology companies seek that the subjects are using their products uninterruptedly in order to extract the greatest amount of information from them. But this does not result in an improvement in attention span, but on the contrary in a loss in the ability to concentrate given the breadth of information that circulates at high speeds.[57] Here we see the pathological nature of the use of technology in cyber-liberalism: the subject enjoys what makes him suffer, he enjoys his addiction to technological platforms even though they give him an attention deficit and an inability to concentrate on a single activity that forces one to perform multiple tasks at once. Unlike neoliberalism, cyber-liberalism is a joyous continuum of attention deficit-hyperactivity-depression that is crowned with a feeling of individual exhaustion. As a consequence of this permanent online activity, the subject suffers from burnout:[58] he feels that he cannot take it anymore and, nevertheless, he continues working and connected. It is this individual exhaustion that reinforces the fantasy that it is necessary to 'improve' oneself through technology.

It goes without saying that these symptoms are not mutually exclusive but rather, given that the three fundamental fantasies of capital coexist, they overlap, they reinforce each other and they complement each other. For all these reasons, neoliberalism, liber-fascism and cyber-liberalism are not mere discursivities that are reduced to a linguistic, representational or public policy existence. They are, above all, ways of organizing our existence and instances of production of subjectivities that start from the commodity form as a real abstraction. And, even more, these are the three fundamental modalities that, through their particular fantasies, organize the ways of enjoying our symptoms in today's society.

If in this chapter we have explained neoliberalism, liber-fascism and cyber-liberalism from Lacanian psychoanalysis (this being one grid of interpretation among others), what political strategy can be drawn against these three ways of organizing social practices? The answer is linked to the 'end of the cure'. For psychoanalysis, this is achieved through a process that consists of going through fantasy and an identification with the symptoms.[59] What does this mean? It simply consists of the subject going beyond the fantasy and seeing that behind it there is nothing but simply the symptom as a support for the subject: the very thing that constitutes us is nothing but the decentring of our being. Well then, the political strategy against the three fundamental fantasies of capital consists, therefore, of grasping the reality of the class struggle from our symptomatology. If Silvia Lippi has pointed out that the proletarian can only become aware of himself from his symptoms,[60] then only the stressed, scared, angry, inattentive and burnt-out proletarian can become a communist and revolutionary if such symptoms are taken no longer as the immediate enjoyment of our capitalist fantasies but as the material prolegomenon of all political activity. In other words, it is about politicizing our symptoms and our mental discomforts in order to traverse the fantasies that limit us to a predetermined and narrow circle of enjoyment. This is why Marx was, after al , 'the inventor of the symptom'.

Notes

1 David Harvey, 'Neoliberalism as Creative Destruct on', *Annals of the American Academy of Political and Social Science* 610, no. 1 (March 2007): 22.

2 Nicol A. Barria-Asenjo, '¿Liberación de las ataduras capitalistas-neoliberales? Una exploración en los estallidos sociales de Chile', *Teoría y Crítica de la Psicología* 15 (2021): 21.

3 Juan Valdes, *Pinochet's Economists. The Chicago School of Economics in Chile* (Cambridge: Cambridge University Press, 1995).

4 Jesús Ayala-Colqui, 'El nacimiento del "liberfascismo" y los distintos modos de gestión de la pandemia en América Latina', *Prometeica-Revista de Filosofía y Ciencias* 24 (February 2022): 184.

5 Dieter Plehwe, 'Introduction', in *The Road from Mont Pelerin. The Making of the Neoliberal Thought Collective*, ed. Philip Mirowski and Dieter Plehwe (Cambridge, MA: Harvard University Press, 2009), 2.

6 Michel Foucault, *The Birth of Biopolitics. Lectures at the College de France, 1978–1979* (London: Palgrave Macmillan, 2008), 116, 118, 226.

7 Pierre Dardot and Christian Laval, *The New Way of the World: On Neoliberal Society* (London: Verso, 2014): 16.

8 Costas Lapavitsas, *Profiting without Producing. How Finance Exploits Us All* (London: Verso, 2013): 161.

9 Maurizio Lazzarato, *The Making of the Indebted Man: An Essay on the Neoliberal Condition* (Cambridge: Semiotext(e), 2012), 162.

10 Franco 'Bifo' Berardi, *The Soul at Work. From Alienation to Autonomy* (Los Angeles: Semiotext(e), 2009), 100.

11 Jesús Ayala-Colqui, 'Los conceptos de veridicción y subjetivación en el "último" Foucault. Acerca del advenimiento de una est-ética-política y su orientación crítica', in *Poder y subjetivación en Michel Foucault*, ed. Jesús Ayala-Colqui, Mauricio Lugo Vasquez and Luis Daniel Soto Núñez (Lima: Universidad Nacional Mayor de San Marcos, 2020), 379.

12 Louis Althusser, *On the Reproduction of Capitalism. Ideology and Ideological State Apparatuses* (London: Verso, 2014), 187

13 Ibid., 197.

14 Slavoj Žižek, 'The Spectre of Ideology', in *Mapping Ideology*, ed. Slavoj Žižek (London: Verso, 1994), 15.

15 Jesús Ayala-Colqui, 'Subjetividad y subjetivación en Marx: una lectura confrontativa a partir de Heidegger y Foucault', *Tópicos (México)* 61 (December 2021): 127.

16 Alfred Sohn-Rethel, *Intellectual and Manual Labour. A Critique of Epistemology* (London: The Macmillan Press, 1978), 27.

17 Slavoj Žižek, *The Sublime Object of Ideology* (London: Verso, 2009), 11.

18   Jacques Lacan, *Formations of the Unconscious. The Seminar of Jacques Lacan. Book V* (London: Polity Press, 2017), 398.

19   Žižek, *The Sublime Object of Ideology*, 30.

20   Jacques Lacan, *The Seminar of Jacques Lacan Book XI: The Four Fundamental Concepts of Psychoanalysis* (New York: Penguin, 1994): 55.

21   Sigmund Freud, *The Standard Edition of The Complete Psychological Works of Sigmund Freud. Volume XII* (Toronto, The Hogarth Press, 1981): 151.

22   Jacques Lacan, *Écrits* (New York: W. W. Norton & Company, 2005): 439.

23   Žižek, *The Sublime Object of Ideology*, 16.

24   Jodi Dean, 'Enjoying Neoliberalism', *Cultural Politics an International Journal* 4 (2008): 70.

25   Jesús Ayala-Colqui, 'Viropolitics and Capitalistic Governmentality: On the Management of the Early 21st Century Pandemic', *Desde el Sur* 12, no. 2 (June 2020): 380.

26   Jesús Ayala-Colqui, 'El nacimiento del "liberfascismo" y los distintos modos de gestión de la pandemia en América Latina', 186.

27   Éric Fassin, 'Le moment néofasciste du néolibéralisme', *Mediapart*, June 2018.

28   Grégoire Chamayou, *La société ingouvernable. Une généalogie du libéralisme autoritaire* (Paris: La Fabrique, 2018).

29   Andrea Mammone, '*The Eternal Return?* Faux Populism and Contemporarization of Neo-Fascism across Britain, France and Italy', *Journal of Contemporary European Studies* 17, no. 2 (2009): 171–92.

30   Alberto Toscano, 'Capitalism without Capitalism. Fascism According to Žižek', *Res Pública. Revista de Historia de las Ideas Políticas* 23, no. 3 (2020): 367–73.

31   Nicos Poulantzas, *Fascism and Dictatorship* (London: Verso, 1997), 310.

32   Jesús Ayala-Colqui, 'El nacimiento del "liberfascismo" y los distintos modos de gestión de la pandemia en América Latina', 186.

33   Ibid.

34   Ibid., 187.

35   Ibid., 186.

36   Slavoj Žižek, 'Everything Provokes Fascism (interview with Andrew Herscher)', *Assemblage* 33 (1997): 63.

37   Jesús Ayala-Colqui, 'La apuesta política de Silicon Valley: ¿Tecnoliberalismo o ciber-liberalismo?', *Revista Latinoamericana de Humanidades y Desarrollo Educativo* 1, no. 1 (June 2022): 2.

38   Jesús Ayala-Colqui, 'El nacimiento del "ciberalismo". Una genealogía crítica de la gubernamentalidad de Silicon Valley', *Bajo Palabra* 32, (2023), 221-254.

39   Thomas Malaby, *Making Virtual Worlds: Linden Lab and Second Life* (Ithaca: Cornell University Press, 2009), 16.

40   Adam Fish, *Technoliberalism and the End of Participatory Culture in the United States* (London: Palgrave Macmillan, 2010), 108.

41   Éric Sadin, *La silicolonisation du monde. L'irrésistible expansion du libéralisme numérique* (Paris: L'Échapée, 2016).

42 Jesús Ayala-Colqui, 'La apuesta política de Silicon Valley: ¿Tecnoliberalismo o ciber-liberalismo?', 8.

43 Norbert Wiener, *Cybernetics. Or Control and Communication in the Animal and the Machine. Reissue of the 1961 second edition* (Cambridge: The MIT Press, 2019): 18.

44 Richard Barbrook and Andy Cameron, 'The Californian Ideology', *Science as Culture* 6, no. 1 (1996): 44–72.

45 Fred Turner, *From Counterculture to Cyberculture Stewart Brand, the Whole Earth Network, and the Rise of Digital Utopianism* (Chicago: The University of Chicago Press, 2006).

46 Finn Brunton, *Digital Cash. The Unknown History of the Anarchists, Utopians, and Technologists Who Created Cryptocurrency* (Princeton: Princeton University Press, 2020).

47 Ippolita, *In the Facebook Aquarium. The resistible rise of anarcho-capitalism* (Amsterdam: Institute of Network Cultures, 2015), 48.

48 Jesús Ayala-Colqui, 'La apuesta política de Silicon Valley: ¿Tecnoliberalismo o ciber-liberalismo?', 7.

49 Evgeny Morozov, *To Save Everything, Click Here: The Folly of Technological Solutionism* (New York: Public Affairs, 2013).

50 Nick Srnicek, *Platform Capitalism* (London: Polity Press, 2016).

51 Daniel Bell, *The Coming of Post-Industrial Society* (New York: Basic Books, 1999), 8.

52 Slavoj Žižek, *Sex and the Failed Absolute* (London: Bloomsbury Academic, 2019), 173.

53 Massimiliano Nicoli and Luca Paltrinieri. El tránsito del empresario de sí mismo a la start-up existencial en el marco de las transformaciones de la racionalidad neliberal', *Recerca* 24, no. 1 (2019): 49.

54 Ray Kurzweil, *The Singularity Is Near: When Humans Transcend Biology* (New York: Viking Press, 2005).

55 Jesús Ayala-Colqui, 'Viropolitics and Capitalistic Governmentality', 380.

56 Joke J. Hermsen, *La melancolía en tiempos de incertidumbre* (Barcelona: Siruela, 2019).

57 Zaheer Hussain and Mark D. Griffiths, 'The Associations between Problematic Social Networking Site Use and Sleep Quality, Attention-Deficit Hyperactivity Disorder, Depression, Anxiety and Stress', *International Journal of Mental Health and Addiction* 19 (2021): 686.

58 Arie Shirom, 'Job-related Burnout: A Review', in *Handbook of Occupational Health Psychology*, ed. James Campbell Quick and Lois E. Tetrick (Washington, DC: American Psychological Association, 2003), 246.

59 Žižek, *The Sublime Object of Ideology*, 59, 80, 143.

60 Silvia Lippi, 'Proletarian/Laborer/Worker', in *The Marx Through Lacan Vocabulary. A Compass for Libidinal and Political Economies*, ed. Christina Soto van der Plas, Edgar Miguel Juárez-Salazar, Carlos Gómez Camarena, and David Pavón-Cuéllar (London: Routledge, 2022), 183.

References

Althusser, Louis (2014), *On the Reproduction of Capitalism. Ideology and Ideological State Apparatuses*, London: Verso.

Ayala-Colqui, Jesús (2020), 'Los conceptos de veridicción y subjetivación en el «último» Foucault. Acerca del advenimiento de una est-ética-política y su orientación crítica', in Jesús Ayala-Colqui, Mauricio Lugo Vasquez, and Luis Daniel Soto Núñez (eds), *Poder y subjetivación en Michel Foucault*, Lima: Universidad Nacional Mayor de San Marcos.

Ayala-Colqui, Jesús (2020), 'Viropolitics and capitalistic governmentality: On the management of the early 21st century pandemic', *Desde el Sur* 12(2): 377–95.

Ayala-Colqui, Jesús (2021), 'Subjetividad y subjetivación en Marx: Una lectura confrontativa a partir de Heidegger y Foucault', *Tópicos (México)* 61: 109–44.

Ayala-Colqui, Jesús (2022), 'El nacimiento del "liberfascismo" y los distintos modos de gestión de la pandemia en América Latina', *Prometeica-Revista de Filosofía y Ciencias* 24: 182–99.

Ayala-Colqui, Jesús (2022), 'La apuesta política de Silicon Valley: ¿Tecnoliberalismo o ciber-liberalismo?', *Revista Latinoamericana de Humanidades y Desarrollo Educativo* 1(1): 1–10.

Ayala-Colqui, Jesús (2023), 'El nacimiento del "ciberalismo". Una genealogía crítica de la gubernamentalidad de Silicon Valley', *Bajo Palabra* 32: 221–54.

Barbrook, Richard and Andy Cameron (1996), 'The Californian Ideology', *Science as Culture* 6(1): 44–72.

Barria-Asenjo, Nicol A. (2021), '¿Liberación de las ataduras capitalistas-neoliberales? Una exploración en los estallidos sociales de Chile', *Teoría y Crítica de la Psicología* 15: 19–37.

Bell, Daniel (1999), *The Coming of Post-Industrial Society*, New York: Basic Books.

Berardi, Franco (2009), 'Bifo', in *Precarious Rhapsody: Semocapitalism & the Pathologies of Post-Alpha Generation*, New York: Minor Compositions.

Brunton, Finn (2020), 'Digital Cash', in *The Unknown History of the Anarchists, Utopians, and Technologists Who Created Cryptocurrency*. Princeton: Princeton University Press.

Chamayou, Grégoire (2018), *La société ingouvernable. Une généalogie du libéralisme autoritaire*, Paris: La Fabrique.

Dardot, Pierre and Christian Laval (2014), *The New Way of the World: On Neoliberal Society*, London: Verso.

Dean, Jodi (2008), 'Enjoying Neoliberalism', *Cultural Politics an International Journal* 4: 47–72.

Fassin, Éric (2018), 'Le moment néofasciste du néolibéralisme', *Mediapart*, June.

Fish, Adam (2010), *Technoliberalism and the End of Participatory Culture in the United States*, London: Palgrave Macmillan.

Foucault, Michel (2008), *The Birth of Biopolitics. Lectures at the College de France, 1978–1979*, London: Palgrave Macmillan.

Freud, S. (1981), *The Standard Edition of The Complete Psychological Works of Sigmund Freud. Volume XII*, Toronto: The Hogarth Press.

Harvey, David (2007), 'Neoliberalism as Creative Destruction', *Annals of the American Academy of Political and Social Science* 610(1): 22–44. https://doi.org/10.1177/0002716206296780.

Hermsen, Joke J. (2019), *La melancolía en tiempos de incertidumbre*, Barcelona: Siruela.

Hussain, Zaheer and Mark D. Griffiths (2021), 'The Associations between Problematic Social Networking Site Use and Sleep Quality, Attention-Deficit Hyperactivity Disorder, Depression, Anxiety and Stress', *International Journal of Mental Health and Addiction* 19: 686–700. https://doi.org/10.1007/s11469-019-00175-1.

Ippolita (2015), *In the Facebook Aquarium. The resistible rise of anarcho-capitalism*, Amsterdam: Institute of Network Cultures.

Kurzweil, Ray (2005), *The Singularity Is Near: When Humans Transcend Biology*, New York: Viking Press.

Lacan, Jacques (1994), *The Seminar of Jacques Lacan Book XI: The Four Fundamental Concepts of Psychoanalysis*, New York: Penguin.

Lacan, Jacques (2005), *Écrits*, New York: W. W. Norton & Company.

Lacan, Jacques (2017), *Formations of the Unconscious. The Seminar of Jacques Lacan. Book V*, London: Polity Press.

Lapavitsas, Costas (2013), *Profiting without Producing. How Finance Exploits Us All*, London: Verso.

Lazzarato, Maurizio (2012), *The Making of the Indebted Man: An Essay on the Neoliberal Condition*, Cambridge: Semiotext(e).

Lippi, Silvia (2022), 'Proletarian/Laborer/Worker', in Christina Soto van der Plas, Edgar Miguel Juárez-Salazar, Carlos Gómez Camarena, and David Pavón-Cuéllar (eds), *The Marx Through Lacan Vocabulary. A Compass for Libidinal and Political Economies*, London: Routledge.

Malaby, Thomas (2009), *Making Virtual Worlds: Linden Lab and Second Life*, Ithaca: Cornell University Press.

Mammone, Andrea (2009), 'The Eternal Return? Faux Populism and Contemporarization of Neo-Fascism across Britain, France and Italy', *Journal of Contemporary European Studies* 17(2): 171–92.

Morozov, Evgeny (2013), *To Save Everything, Click Here: The Folly of Technological Solutionism*, New York: Public Affairs.

Nicoli, Massimiliano and Luca Paltrinieri (2019), 'El tránsito del empresario de sí mismo a la start-up existencial en el marco de las transformaciones de la racionalidad neliberal', *Recerca* 24(1): 37–60.

Plehwe, Dieter (2009), 'Introduction', in Philip Mirowski and Dieter Plehwe (eds), *The Road from Mont Pelerin. The Making of the Neoliberal Thought Collective.* Cambridge, MA: Harvard University Press, 1–42.

Sadin, Éric (2016), *La silicolonisation du monde. L'irrésistible expansion du libéralisme numérique*, Paris: L'Échapée.

Shirom, Arie (2003), 'Job-related Burnout: A Review', in James Campbell Quick and Lois E. Tetrick (eds), *Handbook of occupational health psychology*, Washington, DC: American Psychological Association, 245–64.

Sohn-Rethel, Alfred (1978), *Intellectual and Manual Labour. A Critique of Epistemology*, London: The Macmillan Press.

Srnicek, Nick (2016), *Platform Capitalism*. London: Polity Press.

Toscano, Alberto (2020), 'Capitalism without Capitalism. Fascism According to Žižek', *Res Pública. Revista de Historia de las Ideas Políticas* 23(3): 367–73.

Turner, Fred (2006), *From Counterculture to Cyberculture. Stewart Brand, the Whole Earth Network, and the Rise of Digital Utopianism*, Chicago: The University of Chicago Press.

Valdes, Juan (1995), *Pinochet's Economists. The Chicago School of Economics in Chile*, Cambridge: Cambridge University Press.

Wiener, Norbert (2019), *Cybernetics. Or Control and Communication in the Animal and the Machine. Reissue of the 1961 second edition*, Cambridge: The MIT Press.

Žižek, Slavoj (1994), 'The Spectre of Ideology', in Slavoj Žižek (ed.), *Mapping Ideology*, London: Verso, 1–33.

Žižek, Slavoj (1997), 'Everything Provokes Fascism (interview with Andrew Herscher)', *Assemblage* 33: 58–75.

Žižek, Slavoj (2009), *The Sublime Object of Ideology*, London: Verso.

Žižek, Slavoj (2019), *Sex and the Failed Absolute*, London: Bloomsbury Academic.

Chapter 3

Mistrust and political *jouissance*

From a 'tickle' to the 'blaze of petrol'

Andrea Perunović

An introductory rant

Seemingly, mistrust has become the predominant trait of our contemporary political cultures. Mistrust in democracy, mistrust in institutions, mistrust in media or mistrust in science, are just some of the forms that the presupposed general mistrust takes in the dominant public discourses. But what exactly do we mean when we use the word 'mistrust' today? For example: we rarely designate the rationally founded, Cartesian doubt, that develops complex metaphysical arguments before unfortunately falling again into the warm hug of certitude. Even less, and to our greater damage one could claim, we relate mistrust to Montaigne who was free to give himself up 'to doubt and uncertainty' (Montaigne 1993: 131), and who, by echoing Dante, claimed to be equally pleased with doubt as with knowledge. Rather, what we observe in today's discursive productions are two dominant interpretations of mistrust, which seem to be disposed like the two faces of Janus: turned back-to-back and looking in opposite directions. Hence, on the one side, mistrust is presented as a rational reaction to the political crises of neoliberal democracy. Such mistrust is engendered in the *subjective lack* of popular trust and is seen as a rationally explainable consequence of the weakening of institutions, growing authoritarianism, populism and so on. On the other side, mistrust is understood equally as a manifestation of irrational forces, as an *objective surplus*[1] that drives certain political judgements and actions that seem profoundly incompatible with the existing dominant values – think just of the dominant readings of conspiracy theories or extreme right narratives.

Being rather insufficient than erroneous, both 'faces of mistrust' express first and foremost a monotone neoliberal cry for the renewal of solid trust in consensual politics, a desperate effort to make things 'go back to normal', by presupposing a common cause of mistrust – namely, the *post-truth*. Repeatedly, we seem to hear the same refrains: 'We are living in the *post-truth era*', '*Truth* isn't what it used to be', '*Truth* and *lie* became undistinguishable!' therefore, 'We can't *trust* in anything or anyone anymore!' But what if nothing went wrong with truth as such? For example, with Lacan we have learned that 'the truth is not whole' and that it is accessible only through 'half-saying', 'because about the other half there is nothing to be said' (Lacan 2006: 51). What if the appearance of the signifier 'post-truth' was nothing else but a *symptom* of the repressed Hegelian *bad infinite*[2] of the dialectical relation between *trust* and *mistrust* – that has obviously escalated in the past two decades or so? In this sense, while the rational mistrust as subjective lack seems to tell us more about trust than about mistrust, the interpretation of mistrust as the irrational objective surplus, appears as a more prospective starting point for an analysis of the stratified and ambiguous relation between mistrust and political *jouissance*.

Thus, the task of this text will consist in laying out different aspects of mistrust in regard to political *jouissance*. The central theoretical argument that will be exposed in the following lines consists of the presumption that mistrust offers enjoyment to its subjects – and that acts of mistrusting, or mistrustful behaviours, are inherently enjoyable. More precisely, different types of mistrust seem to allow the experience of different types of enjoyment. From there will arise the question of the political relevance of mistrust-enjoyment nexus which, we will claim, has become a predominant factor in our contemporary political lives. So, in the first place, we will expose the trust/mistrust dialectical relation and mistrust's ontological becoming as the determinate negation of trust. Furthermore, the psychic manifestations of trust/mistrust dialectics will be seen through the lens of psychoanalytic concepts such as denial and disavowal, thus sketching the first possible links between mistrust and *jouissance*. Finally, the Freudian notions of *Misstrauen* and *Unglauben* will serve as two paradigms of mistrust, that will be related to different Lacanian articulations of *jouissance*: (1) *Misstrauen* will be linked with *jouissance* of the Other and surplus *jouissance* as sneaking around the Thing and the formation of *objet petit a*; (2) *Unglauben* with the transgressive *jouissance* engaged on a death-driven pathway to the Thing. Throughout these developments, we will expose a gradation of libidinal intensities that spans across the different modalities of mistrust, in view of offering the reader a certain critical standpoint, from which the vicissitudes of mistrust could be seen at the core of the global contemporary political (and/or conceptual) crises. The following theoretical inquiry will be illustrated by a choice of examples from conspiracy theories and far-right ideological discourses.

Trust vs mistrust: Negation, denial, disavowal

Our departing (and somewhat hyperbolic) hypothesis presupposes *trust*[3] as the ontological foundation of both subjects and societies. Thus, human animals can be characterized as *homo fidei* and societies as sets of relations, or rather ties, that are established by – and engendered in – trust. Yet, according to common-sensical discursive productions concerning the ontogenesis of mistrust, it seems that mistrust emerges in front of trust as its *abstract negation* – remember the rationally explainable interpretations of mistrust, where mistrust is simply taken as the annihilation of trust. But could this be logically possible? Can this process of the ontogenesis of *mistrust* – which obviously implies mediation – result in *nothingness* that is always supposed to be *immediate*? While for Hegel this scenario is formally possible, he claims that it would enact the cessation of all scientific progress (that would leave us without any potential knowledge about trust and mistrust whatsoever). Luckily, his definition of *determinate negation* shows up to be way more useful for grasping mistrust beyond the bad infinity that draws a decisive limit between trust and mistrust as finite, and finally, empty oppositions:

> The one thing needed to *achieve scientific progress* [. . .] is the recognition of the logical principle that negation is equally positive, or that what is self-contradictory does not resolve itself into a nullity, into abstract nothingness, but essentially only into the negation of its *particular* content; or that such a negation is not just negation, but is *the negation of the determined fact* which is resolved, and is therefore determinate negation; that in the result there is therefore contained in essence that from which the result derives – a tautology indeed, since the result would otherwise be something immediate and not a result. Because the result, the negation, is a *determinate* negation, it has a *content*. It is a new concept but one higher and richer than the preceding – richer because it negates or opposes the preceding and therefore contains it, and it contains even more than that, for it is the unity of itself and its opposite. (Hegel 2010: 33)

Once we start to consider mistrust as the determinate, and not the abstract negation of trust, we clearly see that mistrust first appears in recognizing trust as *position* and *positivity*, from which it will come into being as its *reflection*. In that sense, mistrust always structurally contains trust. Moreover, if we continue following Hegel's argument, mistrust should be understood also as a 'higher and richer' concept than trust. Hence, when we mistrust *something*, we do not cease to believe. On the contrary, in mistrust, our beliefs become even stronger – because they represent the unity of themselves and their opposites, the unity of negation and affirmation of the object of (mis)belief. In consequence, negative beliefs are charged with a significantly 'higher' quantity of libidinal investment (and put to work different mechanisms of the libidinal economy), than our positive ones. Moreover, what exactly makes mistrust a 'richer' concept than trust? The qualities that are prescribed by the prefix *mis-* (deriving from the Latin *minus*) show up to be decisive ontological features of mistrust. Besides negating the notion which it precedes, the prefix *mis-* has a pejorative dimension that defines the term to which it is joined as 'bad' or 'wrong'. So, we could say in a rather banal Manichean fashion: *trust* is always 'good' trust, while mistrust is always 'bad' or 'wrong' *trust*. Therefore, mistrust seems to appear as an inherently *transgressive* category. But is it all that simple? Mistrust defies the Law imposed by trust, while simultaneously interiorizing it and finding its backing in it. Seen from a psychoanalytic point of view, trust and mistrust could correlate then to two counterpart mechanisms of libidinal economy, namely, to *pleasure principle* and *jouissance*. The Law of trust can be thus understood as the Law of the pleasure principle (*homeostasis*) that 'follows from the principle of constancy' (Freud 1920: 9), while its transgression necessary for accessing *jouissance* (Lacan 1997: 177) corresponds to the transgressive character of mistrust. Yet, sheer transgression seems to be present only in the more extreme forms of mistrust and a whole gradation of mistrustful behaviours still causes *jouissance*. Enjoyment doesn't reside only beyond the red line drawn by the pleasure principle, where we meet the Thing itself, but is rather inherently present all along the transgressive path, from pleasure (principle) to enjoyment; or, to drive things back to the precise context of our inquiry – *jouissance* takes place in the entire process of dialectical reflection between trust and mistrust, and not only when mistrust appears in its accomplished, extreme form of existence. As Lacan puts it in order to depict this *crescendo* of libidinal intensities covered by *jouissance*: '*It begins with a tickle and ends up in a blaze of petrol*' (Lacan 2006: 72, my italics).

So, the first psychoanalytic term that we will consider in order to grasp the psychic manifestations of trust/mistrust dialectics as a passage from pleasure principle to *jouissance*, is *Verneinung* (translated to English as *negation* or *denial*). Denial marks the ambiguous passing from trust to mistrust, the moment of ontological uncertainty and hesitation when mistrust appears in the very form of belief. In a famous Freudian example, the analysand says: 'You ask who this person in the dream can be. It's not my mother', and the analyst emends 'So it is his mother' (Freud 1925: 233). Here we can see that when stepping into denial, the analysand is expressing something he *believes* to be perfectly *incredible*. With the appearance of the incredible, a part of the formerly repressed unconscious material (which was repressed by the neurotic structure of trust in the first place) resurfaces in the consciousness in the form of a denied fact, as the *incredible object of belief*. This object represents a new knowledge for the subject, which is obtained solely by what Jean Hyppolite calls *misrecognition* (Lacan 2005: 753). If we reformulate this idea, we can say that 'The *incredible* is known only by being *mistrusted*'.

In the process of denial, the repression (which is the main psychic mechanism of trust) is negated and preserved, sublated (*aufgehoben*) in mistrust. When we deny something, the ego basically lifts the repression from a certain unconscious material, but just redirects it from *Id* to external reality. *Verneinung* is a sign of a certain metamorphosis and transposition of repression, in which repression (*Verdrängung*) of affects and ideas becomes rejection (*Verwerfung*) of representations. In that manner, when there is denial, we also see the psychotic structures of mistrust trying to overtake the neurotic ones, on which the 'good' trust was initially based. In denial, *jouissance* is challenging the pleasure principle, but without fully confronting it. Thus, the 'tickle' of *jouissance* introduces itself alongside mistrustful behaviour that is denial, in the form of the new possibility for the subject of no longer fully obeying the boring balance between the pleasure and reality principles. Denial could be thus understood as the doorway of enjoyments that some other, more extreme mistrustful attitudes, promise to offer.

Let's give an example to make our point. When we hear the phrase that begins with: 'I'm not a racist, but . . .', we can rightfully expect that what follows will be utterly racist. This initial denial of racism isn't simply cynicism. It is a declaration of solid belief in something that *is not* – namely in one's own *non*-racist[4] stance. The narrative that follows this will likewise become more trustworthy than an openly racist one, making the subject able to freely *enjoy* his racist speech, without being judged by others or having to deal with self-reproaches! Žižek explains something correlative in the following manner: 'an ideological identification exerts a true hold on us precisely when we maintain an awareness that we are not fully identical to it, that there is a rich human person beneath it: "not all is ideology, beneath the ideological mask, I am also a human person", is the very form of ideology, of its "practical efficiency"' (Žižek 1998: 8). We read: in order for trust to obtain its full fiduciary potential, it must become mistrust! The mechanism of denial thus reveals what Alenka Zupančič calls an 'internal interval', a certain crack in the dialectics of trust and mistrust that undermines 'their complementariness and symmetry' (Zupančič 2012). The same crack shows up to be revealed by the act of denial in the dialectics of some basic psychoanalytic categorical couples – and most importantly for us – in the pleasure principle/*jouissance* dialectics.

The second psychoanalytic notion that animates the liminal space between trust and mistrust is disavowal (*Verleugung*). In the example of a boy who dismisses the fact that women do not have a penis, Freud sees fetishistic disavowal as a peculiar technique for confronting the castration complex, by simultaneously accepting the fact that the penis is absent while sticking to the belief that it is still there by creating a symbolic substitute for it, a fetish.[5] In disavowal, on the contrary to the denial, everything is affirmed by a very energetic action, that maintains the coexistence of contradictory tendencies in the psyche. The basic formula of disavowal: '*Je sais bien, mais quand même*', 'I know very well, but still', is crucial for making possible the simultaneous coexistence of trust and mistrust. Moreover, as Alenka Zupančič nicely shows, this formula has progressed today, so: 'it is not "I know very well, but I nevertheless continue to believe the opposite", but it is rather, "I know very well, and this is why I can go on ignoring it"' (Perunović 2021: 762). The French right-wing politician Nadine Morano gave us a decade ago a scholarly example of disavowal by saying: 'You are trying to tell that I am racist, whence I have friends who indeed are Arab, and amongst them my best friend who is Chadian, *so even darker than the Arabs*'. In simple terms, what Morano unconsciously says here is: 'I am a racist and I know it very well. Why the hell are you bothering me with something nobody cares about? Let's just ignore it and keep on being racist without naming it.'

In this sense, we see that, when mistrust overtakes trust through disavowal, *jouissance* starts to appear as something more than a tickle, it clearly overruns the pleasure-reality (principles) nexus, as the subject steps into the waters of enjoyment in an affirmation of meanings that tendentiously ignore reality. The initial mistrustful negation that appeared with denial, is turned within disavowal into an affirmation, showing how the dialectical progression between trust and mistrust brings, with every stage of its development, new amounts of enjoyment and new shifts in the general mechanism of our libidinal economy. Mistrust turns likewise into an affirmative force that negates reality by the very act of affirmation, bringing thus to its subject of enunciation the enjoyment that is only to be found in creating affirmative, excessive, surplus significations.

In this vein, perfect examples of fetishist disavowal are conspiracy theories, in which, according to Zupančič again, 'you have this kind of clear coincidence of absolute mistrust, or paranoid mistrust towards all kinds of things, particularly in official versions of events, authorities, and so on; but at the same time, also this incredible trust or belief in whatever'(Perunović 2021: 763). So, in *chemtrail* conspiracy theories, we could say that one can believe that we are sprinkled with chemicals from the sky, only by knowing well that the white trails we see in the sky are simply the vapour that aircraft leave behind them (the so-called 'contrails'). It is by believing in this simple fact in the first place, that one can disavow it afterwards, in order to be able to enjoy the belief in its substitute form (the hazardous chemicals taking the place of vapour). This positive belief in chemtrails materializes and directs the mistrust towards the big Other, which is embodied in official authorities. It also creates surplus signifiers – which bring surplus-enjoyment – by presupposing the existence of a mysterious agency that could be understood as the *Other of the Other*, that secretly enacts 'mind (or weather) control' by means of chemtrails. Yet in the end, this quasi-subversive mistrust found in conspiracy theories, shows up, dialectically enough, to be nothing else but 'the metaguarantee of the consistency of the big Other' (Žižek 1998: 16). So, in fetishistic disavowal, the disavowed knowledge (in which one trusts despite everything) gives ground to the fetish that makes the paradox of the mistrustful belief possible. Within disavowal, the dialectical movement between trust and mistrust closes a full circle, making mistrust the very condition of trust. In the fetish, the opposition between trust and mistrust reaches the stage of a resolved contradiction. That testifies precisely how *jouissance* can be experienced in mistrustful behaviours by only seemingly transgressing the Law of trust, just to finally reinforce it.

From Misstrauen *to* Unglauben, from 'sneaking around' to 'sheer transgression'

In the following paragraphs, we will be finally able to approach the two concrete types of mistrust that are in direct correlation with political *jouissance* and demonstrate the gradation of libidinal intersities inherent to mistrustful enjoyments. The first type of mistrust that we will evoke is the Freudian *Misstrauen*. As we will see below, *Misstrauen* relates both to the *jouissance* of the Other and to the surplus-enjoyment (*plus-de-jouir*) as 'sneaking around the thing' (*das Ding*). *Misstrauen* could be considered as representing a structural paradigm of a more 'moderate' and the most common kind of mistrustful enjoyment. Let's take an example that will show us its conceptual, psychological and political significance. In the essay 'On the Sexual Theories of Children', we read that a child, shaken by the birth of their younger sibling, decides to ask his parents where babies come from. Most often on this occasion, according to Freud, 'The child receives either evasive answers or a rebuke for his curiosity, or he is dismissed with the mythologically significant piece of information which, in German countries, runs: "The stork brings the babies; it fetches them out of the water"' (Freud 1908: 213). Freud then enumerates a few examples to depict the infantile mistrust that is awakened by such an *incredible* mythological answer (which operates as symbolic castration), and one seems to be particularly interesting for our inquiry. When given the 'stork brings the babies' explanation, one boy allowed 'his disbelief[6] to find expression in a hesitant remark that he knew better, that it was not a stork that brought babies but a heron' (ibid., 215). This 'hesitant remark' is still quite something – an expression of mistrust (*Misstrauen*) directed against the big Other. The child stood up against the beliefs of his parents – and subsequently against the whole tradition – that qualifies him as inapt to hear the truth about sexuality. He even created a surplus signifier to counter the piece of narrative imposed on him by the big Other. Politically speaking, this could be considered a genuine little uprising! Although, a miserably failed one, as we will see.

When the child proclaims that 'he knows better', and that it is 'not a stork that brought babies but a heron', this phrase can be seen in a twofold manner, or as having two simultaneous sequences. Firstly, it can be seen as a negative repetition of the mythological discourse – of the knowledge of the big Other. Through it, the very lack of the big Other is (mis)recognized. Thus, the 'not a *stork*' part of the phrase is an expression of the recognized Kantian *negative quantity*, or negative magnitude, of the big Other. By identifying this negative quality, the child doesn't only recognize that the signifier 'stork' is referring to nothing at all (as all signifiers do), and thus denies its relevance, but that the infinite battery of signifiers that constitute the Other serves to cover 'the horrible, obscene Thing' (Žižek 2008: 105). Due to this discovery, the child finds itself in front of a *forced choice*[7] of becoming a (divided) subject, by repeating the logic of the signifier. And this process doesn't go without enjoyment. What is enjoyable in this forced choice of negative repetition, and what bears the political significance, is that the child experiences *jouissance* as the *possession* and *usage* of the knowledge of the Other (*il jouit du savoir de l'Autre*). When mistrusting the knowledge of the big Other, by repeating it in the form of negation, the boy adopts what Lacan calls the master's discourse, thus becoming from a *slave* that he was, the *master* who 'brings about this operation of the displacing, of the conveyancing of slave's knowledge' and who as such 'doesn't desire to know anything at all – he desires that things work' (Lacan 2006: 24).

However, this dialectical shift simultaneously brings a surplus with it: a surplus signifier and a surplus *jouissance*. It is not a stork, *it is the heron*, he says! By creating a metonymy of the *stork* (the *heron*), the child experiences an 'irruption, a falling into the field, of something not unlike *jouissance* – a surplus' (ibid., 20). His mistrust *is* his fall in the social field. The signifier (*heron*), that he created by metonymy with the big Other's signifier (*stork*), is nothing but the *objet petit a*, a reflection of his own constitutive lack. This is where it seems that things already stop working for the ephemeral mistrustful master, where the initial *jouissance* of the Other found in the negative repetition is brought about as its own squandering. With this surplus *jouissance*, 'something is produced as a defect, as a failure' (ibid., 46). So, the appearance of the surplus signifier in the act of affirmation ('it *is* a heron') provokes the surplus *jouissance* residing in the *objet petit a* of the newly formed divided subject that the child has become. Now, the child's constitutive lack is at stake, and not anymore, the one of the big Other. This shift happens precisely because the lack that is reflected in the *objet petit a* is what 'remains of the Thing after it has undergone the process of symbolization' (Žižek 2008: 105).

The symbolization of the Thing, followed by its residue which takes form of *objet petit a* for its subject, shows up to be the main feature of *Misstrauen*'s quasi-transgressive strategy. In the form of mistrust that is the Freudian *Misstrauen*, 'we don't ever transgress. Sneaking around is not transgressing. Seeing a door half-open is not the same as going through it' (Lacan 2006: 19), yet the surplus-enjoyment is certainly present in the formation of *objet petit a*. Further on, this enjoyment can be experienced only in secrecy and without ever truly confronting the Thing. It is rather an intimate creation of a signifier, that will produce a personal surplus signification marking the gap in the subject (of mistrust) in front of the Law (of trust) – the Law to which it always finally obeys. What Freud is reporting seems to justify our hypothesis: 'from the time of this first deception and rebuff . . . [the child] nourish a distrust of adults and have a suspicion of there being something forbidden which is being withheld from them by the "grown-ups", and that they consequently hide their further researches under a cloak of secrecy'(Freud 1908: 215).

This entire process of the appearance of *Misstrauen*, from the repetition of the *jouissance* of the Other to surplus-enjoyment, confirms clearly our departing hypothesis, according to which *jouissance* follows the whole dialectical process leading from trust to mistrust (and back to trust). *Misstrauen*'s model of mistrustful enjoyment seems to apply to many conspiracy theories, such as the *Qanon* for example, that cause *jouissance* in the repetition and the denial of the contents of the mainstream media, while also generating surplus-enjoyment in the creation of the phantasmatic (surplus) significations – of what they presume to be *another Truth*.[8] Similar goes for the climate change deniers, who repeat and negate the scientific discourse on climate change, while at the same time producing and proliferating quasi-scientific arguments about its causes and consequences. What Freud's narrative teaches us clearly is that *Misstrauen* is always initially triggered from the outside and top-down, with a final outcome which is the preservation of the *status quo* that guarantees the eventual return to 'good' trust. We can think simply of the mentioned climate change deniers' mistrust, that ends up reinforcing the trust in the capitalist mode of production. Or, we can think about the anti-vax discourses, that direct the mistrust towards vaccines, all while expressing a blind trust in the pharmaceutical industry by accepting and propagating drugs like hydroxychloroquine and ivermectin as alternative treatments, reinforcing thus its hyper-capitalist market logic, exactly by paradoxically creating narratives on Big Pharma as the *Other of the Other*. Those examples could multiply almost infinitely here because in all conspiracy theories, we find elements of *Misstrauen* and peculiar modalities of political *jouissance* it brings.

Yet, the becoming of mistrust isn't limited only to *jouissance* as sneaking around the Thing and proliferating *objets petit a* as remains of its symbolization. It can as well imply the transgression of the Law of trust, that runs straight to the

Thing. We speak then about the more extreme forms of mistrust, with a highly pronounced destructive drive component, that causes *jouissance* such as it is most commonly defined: as *pleasure-in-pain*. Another Freudian term, namely the *Unglauben*, causes this *jouissance* of *sheer transgression*, that runs over the Law straight to the 'the absolute void, the lethal abyss which swallows the subject' (Žižek 2008: 105). With it, we reach the tip of the *crescendo* of enjoyments that are to be found in mistrustful behaviours. And while there are different types of *Unglauben*,[9] for our needs we shall stick here to the paranoiac disbelief, in which *jouissance* appears truly as a 'blaze of petrol'. The contemporary examples of paranoiac *Unglauben* range from Anders Breivik to alt-right movements, from Mohammed Merah to the Islamic State. Most recently, Putin's military actions and discursive productions concerning the invasion of Ukraine can be seen as a symptom of the paranoid mistrust causing the characteristic transgressive *jouissance* of *Unglauben*. So, how precisely does the structure of *Unglauben* look?

Unglauben is a fundamentally unconscious process, which presupposes the *primordial rejection of belief*. It is tightly intertwined with paranoia since the latter is a condition which has *Unglauben* as its primary symptom. This primary symptom is crucial in the libidinal structure of paranoia because it 'permits the avoidance of self-reproach' (Freud 1986a: 167). Thus, in paranoia, *mortification* is the main pathological aberration of 'the normal affective psychic state' (ibid., 162) and its 'defense is manifested in disbelief' (Freud 1986b: 188). In that sense, the *Unglauben* manifests itself in the extreme forms of denial and disavowal. One should deny and disavow the reality as a whole and reject the symbolic order in a very specific way, in order to access the *jouissance* which *Unglauben* has to offer. What does this very specific way of rejection of the symbolic order consist of? What does the quest of transgressive *jouissance* tell us about the structure of *Unglauben*? Lacan mentions something that could provide an answer to our questions: 'At the basis of paranoia itself, which nevertheless seems to us to be animated by belief, there reigns the phenomenon of the *Unglauben*. This is not the not believing in it, but the absence of one of the terms of belief, of the term in which is designated the division of the subject'(Lacan 1998: 238). The absent term of belief in *Unglauben* is the founding speech, also named by Lacan *fides*, which 'makes possible the deepest level of the relationship of man to reality, namely, that which is articulated as faith' (Lacan 1997: 54). The founding speech guarantees the subject-to-subject relation of 'good trust' in the 'speech that gives itself' (Lacan 1993: 37). In the founding speech, the *divided subject* is posited on the one side, and the *subject supposed to know* on the other. Yet, in *Unglauben*, the sole term of belief that is left is the 'lying speech'. When the lying speech is no longer in a dialectical relation with the foundational speech, the subject supposed to know takes over the position of the divided subject, thus *forclosing* the big Other. It is in this act of foreclosure of the Other, that *jouissance* is experienced by the subject of *Unglauben*, as transgression of the Law and immediate access to the Thing. What was seen initially in our reading of denial and disavowal as a 'crack' in trust/mistrust dialectics, through which the subject could only have a glimpse of the negative magnitude of the Thing, now becomes a lethal abyss which irresistibly attracts the subject into its void, promising the ultimate and incomparable form of *jouissance*.

Unglauben thus represents the death-driven 'moving force of paranoia [which] is essentially the rejection of a certain support in the symbolic order, of that specific support around which the division between the two sides of the relationship to *das Ding* operates' (Lacan 1997: 54). Without the mentioned support in the symbolic order, the barriers on the path to the Thing (The Good, the Shame and the Beauty) fall, which opens the way to sheer transgressive *jouissance* that can now flow freely through the mistrustful subject, which has taken the form of the 'Jar of Danaides'. The *jouissance* that *Unglauben* brings 'might be described as the testing of a faceless fate or as a risk that, once it has been survived by the subject, somehow guarantees him of his power' (ibid., 195). This enjoyable 'acceptance of death' (ibid., 189) indicates that our primary intuition that mistrust is in its final form a transgressive category, finds its justification in the structure of paranoiac disbelief. Yet, this final *Aufhebung* of trust/mistrust dialectics that is reached in *Unglauben*, should be understood as a total failure, since with its upcoming, mistrust appears simply as *blind faith*.

Notes

1 The notions of 'subjective lack' and 'objective surplus', understood as 'two faces of discursive production', are a reference to Samo Tomšič's book *The Capitalist Unconscious* (Tomšič 2015: 52).

2 '[The] bad infinite is in itself the same as the perpetual *ought*; it is indeed the negation of the finite, but in truth it is unable to free itself from it; the finite constantly resurfaces in it as its other, since this infinite only is with reference to the finite, which is its other. The progress to infinity is therefore only repetitious monotony, the one and the same tedious alternation of this finite and infinite' (Hegel 2010: 113).

3 The word 'trust' will be used here as a coverall term, regrouping different notions such as faith, confidence, belief, credit and so on; but also, maybe more importantly, the repressed meanings deriving from their Indo-European linguistic heritage, such as obedience, persuasion, consolation, solidity, etc (Benveniste 1969: 115).

4 Lacan explains the negative particles of discourse, such as the 'non', in the following way: 'the *Verneinung*, far from being the pure and simple paradox of that which presents itself in the form of a "no," isn't just any old "no." There is a whole world of no-saying (*non-dit*), of interdiction (*interdit*), since it is in that very form that the *Verdrängt* which is the unconscious, essentially presents itself. But the *Verneinung* is the most solid beachhead of that which I would call the "intersaid" (*entre dit*)' (Lacan 1997: 64–5).

5 'Yes, in his mind the woman *has* got a penis, in spite of everything; but this penis is no longer the same as it was before' (Freud 1927: 154).

6 The word that Freud uses here is *Misstrauen*.

7 Dominik Finkelde nicely summarizes the Lacan's concept of forced choice as 'the unconscious submission that an individual has to endure in the genealogy of its ego-function' (Finkelde 2021: 145).

8 Alenka Zupančič is rightly pointing that 'The paradigmatic idea of conspiracy theories is not that "there are many truths", but that *there exists another Truth*' (Zupančič 2022: 235).

9 Alongside the paranoiac *Unglauben*, in Freud we encounter also 'obsessional neurotic's disbelief' and 'dialectical disbelief'. For a comprehensive archaeology on *Unglauben*, see Guérin, Lenormand, and Rassial 2014.

References

Benveniste, Émile (1969), *Le vocabulaire des institutions indo-européennes, tome 1: Economie, parenté, société*, Paris: Les Éditions de Minuit.

Finkelde, Dominik (2021), 'Abjection Accomplished: On Jouissance as an Ontological Factor', *Continental Theory & Thought: A Journal of Intellectual Freedom* 3(2): 143–66, | ISSN: 2463-333X.

Freud, Sigmund (1986a), 'Draft K', in Jeffrey Masson(ed.),*The Complete Letter of Sigmund Freud to Wilhelm Fleiss 1887–1904*, Cambridge, MA and London: The Belknap Press of Harvard University Press, 162–9.

Freud, Sigmund (1986b), 'May 30, 1896', in Jeffrey Masson (ed.), *The Complete Letter of Sigmund Freud to Wilhelm Fleiss 1887–1904*, Cambridge, MA and London: The Belknap Press of Harvard University Press, 187–90.

Freud, Sigmund (1908), 'On the Sexual Theories in Children', in James Starchey (ed.), *The Standard Edition, Edition of Complete Psychological Works of Sigmund Freud*, Vol. IX, London: The Hogarth and the Institute of Psychoanalysis, 205–26.

Freud, Sigmund (1920), *Beyond the Pleasure Principle*, in (ed. James Starchey) *SE*, Vol. XVIII, London: The Hogarth Press.

Freud, Sigmund (1925), *Negation*, in (ed. James Starchey) *SE*, Vol. XIX, London: The Hogarth and the Institute of Psychoanalysis, 233-240.

Freud, Sigmund (1927), *Fetishism*, in (ed. James Starchey) *SE*, Vol. XXI, London: The Hogarth and the Institute of Psychoanalysis, 147-158.

Guérin, Nicolas, Marie Lenormand, and Jean-Jacques Rassial (2014), 'Freudian Modalities of Disbelief', *International Journal of Psychoanalysis*, doi:10.1111/1745-8315.12181.

Hegel, Georg Wilhelm Friedrich (2010), *The Science of Logic*, Cambridge: Cambridge University Press.

Lacan, Jacques (1993), *The Seminar of Jacques Lacan, Book III, The Psychoses 1955–1956*, New York and London: W.W. Norton & Company.

Lacan, Jacques (1997), *The Seminar of Jacques Lacan, Book VII, The Ethics of Psychoanalysis*, New York and London: W.W. Norton & Company.

Lacan, Jacques (1998), *The Seminar of Jacques Lacan, Book XI, The Four Fundamental Concepts of Psychoanalysis*, New York and London: W.W. Norton & Company.

Lacan, Jacques (2005), *Écrits*, New York and London: W.W. Norton & Company.

Lacan, Jacques (2006), *The Seminar of Jacques Lacan, Book XVII, The Other Side of Psychoanalysis*, New York and London: W.W. Norton & Company.

(de) Montaigne, Michel (1993), *Essays*, London: Penguin Books.

Perunović, Andrea (2021), 'Subject and (Post)Truth between Philosophy and Psychoanalysis: An Interview with Alenka Župančič', *Filozofija i društvo / Philosophy and Society*, 32(4): 757–69.

Tomšič, Samo (2015), *The Capitalist Unconscious: Marx and Lacan*, London and New York: Verso.

Žižek, Slavoj (1998), 'The Inherent Transgression', *Cultural Values* 2(1): 1–17. doi:10.1080/14797589809359285.

Žižek, Slavoj (2008), *The Plague of Fantasies*, London and New York: Verso.

Zupančič, Alenka (2012), 'Not-Mother: On Freud's *Verneinung*', *e-flux Journal* #33, https://www.e-flux.com/journal/33/68292/not-mother-on-freud-s-verneinung/.

Zupančič, Alenka (2022), 'A Short Essay on Conspiracy Theories', in Adrian Johnston, Boštjan Nedoh, and Alenka Zupančič (eds), *Objective Fictions: Philosophy, Psychoanalysis, Marxism*, Edinburgh: Edinburgh University Press, 222–49.

Chapter 4

Neoliberalism's political jouissance and the environmental crisis in Latin America

Ignacio López-Calvo

The Lacanian term *jouissance* is usually associated, in psychoanalytical discourse, with enjoyment, desire, 'negative pleasure' and the impossibility of a sexual relationship because of the prohibition of the father. Yet the ambiguity with which Lacan defines it or, rather, his refusal to define it enables the term for use in other realms. As Paul Verhaeghe explains,

> *Enjoyment* is a very ambiguous term, particularly as it always evokes the idea of pleasure. Lacan will never define this concept very clearly, providing us with only vague indications. We learn that 'it begins with a tickle and ends in a blaze of petrol!' (83). In fact, jouissance is the opposite of pleasure: *Unlust*, *déplaisir* (89). This imprecision is deliberate: for Lacan, enjoyment is by definition undefinable; it is that which escapes symbolization. (205)

In this chapter, I transfer the concept of jouissance or libidinal enjoyment to the political domain – and therefore to the level of the symbolic and the social – to explore its connection with the unchecked excesses and transgressions of extractivist neoliberalism. This sadistic, ecocidal mode of jouissance at the heart of today's neoliberal ideology touches upon another side of the Lacanian concept, described as 'illicit, incurred in acts that apparently transgress laws or socially prescribed limits' (Hook 605).

Indeed, according to Derek Hook, who discusses resorting to the concept of jouissance for the understanding of racist attitudes, 'this is the whole point of jouissance as a kind of erotics of the negative: Overstepping a boundary, the fact that something illicit is involved, a contravention, increases both the subject's enjoyment of such behaviors and the bonding potential of such behaviors enormously. Jouissance then exceeds both the boundaries of pleasure and the norms of moral or social orthodoxy' (609). In this sense, in today's neoliberal world, the endless thirst for power, capital and raw materials has become a form of perverse libidinal gratification, a painful jouissance. This transgressive and excessive kind of pleasure is the unreachable 'Thing' (to use Lacan's term), the pursuit of the desired object in the service of the pleasure principle.[1] Many governments and predatory corporations seem to believe – wrongly, needless to say – the fantasy of nature as an endless resource that must be possessed and taken advantage of (President Jair Bolsonaro's attitude towards rampant deforestation in the Brazilian Amazon basin, for example, is a case in point). The traditional enjoyment of nature as a refuge from the stress of contemporary life, which provides us with comfort and well-being, has ultimately become political jouissance, that is, the incessant and unfortunately often legal exploitation of natural resources in search of power and capital accumulation, producing an increasingly self-destructing pain that must soon be stopped for human survival's sake. Unless some collective restraint is soon exercised, the day will come when the neoliberal pleasure (its political jouissance) associated with endless capital accumulation and exploitation of more-than-human (as well as human) resources will backfire, as climate change may reach (or may have already reached) a point of no return.

The political jouissance – in the secondary, legal meaning of the French term as 'having the right to use' or 'enjoyment of usufruct rights and property' – directed towards natural resources, as in over-extraction and the 'legal' contamination of water and air, is currently backfiring through the acceleration of climate change and other natural disasters. In Lacanian terms, the pleasure principle that leads predatory corporations to indiscriminately look for libidinal pleasure in the pursuit of the desired object (capital accumulation in this case) through the exploitation of natural resources to the point of committing ecocides, reaches the point of what Lacan described in *Seminar VII* as 'the acceptance of death' (189). Put differently, neoliberal, predatory extractivism, as a dangerous, malignant jouissance, is driving us into extinction; tellingly, in these pandemic times, instead of rebuilding our economies away from contaminating fossil fuels and towards clean, reusable energy as we should, some governments continue to spend public funds on fossil fuel subsidies.

Lacan equates the transgression of the pleasure principle with pain since the subject can only manage a certain amount of pleasure: pleasure then becomes suffering, the excess of jouissance (surplus-enjoyment). Read through an ecocritical lens, one can conclude that the desire (unconscious or not, it can never be satisfied) of accumulation of capital, raw materials, and power in the pursuit of enjoyment and at the expense of the natural world develops into a dangerous, evil jouissance (painful principle, malevolent enjoyment) beyond the pleasure principle. This excessive kind of pleasure compels subjects to transgress prohibitions (e.g., the destruction of our natural habitat), thus bringing human beings each day closer to extinction. One must therefore wonder whether there is a (conscious or unconscious) death drive in this type of self-destructive, neoliberal, extractivist capitalism. According to Slavoj Žižek, 'Desire's *raison d'être* is not to realize its goal, to find full satisfaction, but to reproduce itself as desire' (*The Plague of Fantasies*, 39). In other words, unconscious desire can never be satisfied, just like the desire for capital accumulation and raw material extraction in neoliberal capitalism cannot be satisfied either. Repetition occurs in the endless desire for additional raw materials, which brings us to Lacan's idea that '*Jouissance* necessitates repetition'. As Slovenian philosopher Alenka Zupančič points out, 'it is precisely on account of this that jouissance goes against life, beyond the pleasure principle, and takes the form of what Freud called the death drive' (158). Considering that our planet's natural resources are finite, there is no doubt that the economic philosophy (neoliberalism, market fundamentalism) and the economic system (laissez-faire, free-market capitalism) must change.

Going back to the Lacanian concept of jouissance, people's right to the enjoyment of nature has become entangled with the excessive 'enjoyment' of nature extractive corporations, who take all the natural resources, including water, for themselves, leaving the public with a lack (castration, in Lacanian terms), feeling that they have been robbed from that enjoyment by that blameworthy Other. Citizens, younger generations, in particular, are increasingly becoming hopeless. In this manner, extractivist corporations' ecocidal, libidinal enjoyment transgresses the Law, in the sense of the universal, fundamental principles that underlie social relations and make social exchanges and existence possible. The thrill of their transgressive acts of environmental injustice leaves behind a 'stain' (a term used by Lacan) that is as much symbolic as it is tragically material, as real as the 2010 Deepwater Horizon oil spill in the Gulf of Mexico, the largest marine oil spill in history. Stated otherwise, the libidinal thrill of aggressively transgressing socially prescribed limits in the form of ecocidal acts of environmental injustice goes hand in hand with a death drive that, in this case, is not individual but collective: a shortcut to human extinction.

Academic activism and environmental injustice in Latin America

After this brief psychoanalytical exploration of neoliberal extractivism, a deliberation on what to do about it seems to be in order. First, it should be clear that the responsibility to change this dynamic should not be conceived as individual; it is, instead, collective, structural. Thus, Elizabeth R. DeSombre points out, in her chapter 'Refuge and environmental responsibility', that we should avoid the temptation of personalizing our responsibility for preventing climate change through our individual behaviour:

> What is needed, then, is systemic action – a change to the overarching systems and structures within which we act in ways that have environmental implications. . . . We need environmental policy to require industry to pay the costs of the environmental externalities it creates (which then incentivizes reducing those harms). When industry has to pay for the environmental harms it creates – either through a tax on emissions or a rule that restricts emissions – it will figure out the most effective way to reduce those emissions. (221)

She adds that we must change the systems and structures within which critical decisions about environmental problems take place.

For this goal, scientists and economists are not entirely well equipped. I argue that the environmental humanities are a privileged site from which new concepts and conceptual frameworks can be generated as critical tools aimed at changing not only legislation but also our collective consciousness, thus saving the natural environment and ourselves along the way. Indeed, the environmental humanities represent a potential tool to stop the anthropogenic climate crisis. From the perspective of Latin American studies, critical concepts and ideas coming from socio-environmental approaches such as ecocriticism, the hydrohumanities[2] and the environmental humanities can help change the collective frame of mind and the dominant political discourse to positively influence policymaking towards greener, more sustainable futures. In this way, the environmental humanities may bring Western worldviews that oppose the domain of culture (the Symbolic, in Lacanian terms) to the order of nature (the Imaginary) closer to Indigenous understandings of our place, as humans, in the natural world.

Activist research aimed at achieving environmental justice may expose which critical political decisions are made in the interest of capital rather than in that of citizens. One example of this type of activist, environmental humanities research that may influence policymaking is the 2019 article 'Toxic Bodies: Water and Women in Yucatan', in which Ángel Polanco Rodríguez and Kata Beilin first expose environmental injustice related to the contamination of groundwater by carcinogenic, agricultural pesticides in the Yucatán Peninsula and how it is affecting the health of local women, and then suggest potential solutions:

the passage of toxins between bodies of water, soil, and human flesh, and the resulting illnesses and struggle for health are deeply significant processes in which culture becomes transformed by an economy in which gain is more important than health and well-being. . . . On June 5, 2018, while everybody's attention was taken by the World Cup, the Mexican government signed ten decrees that eliminated protection of three hundred water basins containing 55 percent of the available water in the country. From now on, there will be no legal obstacles for concessions to corporations needing water for their industrial ventures such as fracking, mining, soft drink and beer production, and others. (185)

This type of research may also explain, for a general audience – better than scientific or economic discourses – why a desire to protect the natural environment or a desire for self-preservation must prevail over the rule of capital and the market. This desire can prevent what Lacan calls 'going beyond a limit in jouissance' (*Écrits* 825) and, quite apropos of climate change, 'the burning hearth' (*Seminar XIII*). To this extent, the environmental humanities offer a cognitive mapping of the Anthropocene's severe climate change and related environmental disasters, including mass extinction, loss of animal habitat, expanding drought, fire seasons, retreating glaciers and rising sea levels as symptoms of our potential demise. Mobilizing society to passionately engage with environmental issues, including through political means and activism against environmental injustice, is a struggle worth fighting. This type of intersubjective concern acknowledges the ethical need to allow future generations the right to enjoy nature and to inherit a healthy planet from us.

Within the environmental humanities field, Karl Kusserow, in his *Picture Ecology: Art and Ecocriticism in Planetary Perspective* (2021), points at the Judeo-Christian tradition and capitalism as two of the main ideological justifications for environmental degradation. Indeed, the Judeo-Christian tradition, starting with the biblical book of Genesis, has encouraged a self-centred, anthropocentric worldview that positions human beings (or, rather, certain humans) at the centre of the universe and conceives of the more-than-human world (animals, plants, minerals) as resources to be utilized and exploited by us – other species are meant to be at our service. Added to this dangerous worldview, capitalist ideology's extractivist logic, together with its goal of market-driven, competitive, perpetual growth and profit, fails to acknowledge the limited nature of our planet's natural resources. As such, capitalism has often prioritized economic growth over environmental justice.

In fact, green Marxists tend to view environmental injustice as the defining feature of capitalism, which has primarily depended on colonial and neocolonial extractivism. Jason W. Moore, for example, argues, in his 2015 *Capitalism in the Web of Life. Ecology and the Accumulation of Capital*, that the way in which neoliberal capitalism – a 'world-ecology' with an endless thirst for power, capital and raw materials – has organized nature is the primary source of today's climate crisis. The economy, he maintains, is not separate from the environment, as there has been an undeniable nexus between environmental history and the history of capitalism since the sixteenth century. Capitalism (modernity, industrial civilization) extracted wealth from nature, degrading it along the way, but soon nature will take its revenge. Along these lines, Eduardo Gudynas has coined a new term for this type of abusive activity, which is different from extractivism: 'extrahección', which he defines as 'the appropriation of natural resources imposed with violence and breaking the framework of human and Nature's rights',[3] including the criminalization of citizens' protest (16).

These ideologies and religious beliefs have opened the door to the mass extinction of animals and plants due to climate change and the loss of their habitats. It has also brought about unethical factory farming (intensive animal farming or industrial livestock production), which excels at cutting costs while maximizing production at the expense of animal suffering. These practices are becoming increasingly unsustainable for our planet and our well-being. Besides the concern with the welfare of livestock such as poultry, cattle, pigs and fish, which often end up being unethically abused, this type of intensive agribusiness creates significant health risks and environmental degradation, including pollution of soil, air and groundwater, greenhouse gas emissions, climate change, biodiversity loss, the harming of wildlife and deforestation for animal feed production. Therefore, in contrast with the assumed interconnectedness between humans and the natural world more typical of Indigenous epistemologies in Latin America, which have often been ignored or erased by epistemic violence, Western imaginings of human beings at the centre of creation have resulted in animal abuse, environmental destruction, mass extinction and, as stated, may one day lead to our own extinction.

The anthropogenic environmental crisis has made us reconsider, now with more empathy, human interactions with nature in Latin America. For instance, in pure developmental terms, the agreement signed in 2014 by China, Brazil and Peru to build a route that unites the Atlantic with the Pacific Oceans could be seen as a promising infrastructural megaproject that may bring prosperity to both South American countries. Yet today, one cannot help but wonder what ecological disasters and other dire consequences may also bring for Indigenous communities. In fact, in 2011 there were a series of Indigenous protests in Bolivia over the planned Villa Tunari–San Ignacio de Moxos transoceanic highway that was going to cut through their ancestral lands in the Territorio Indígena y Parque Nacional Isiboro-Sécure (Isiboro Sécure Indigenous Territory and National Park, TIPNI), inhabited by more than 12,000 residents from the Chimare, Yuracaré and Mojeño-Trinitario peoples. The government's crackdown on the Indigenous protests on 24 September 2011 resulted in four deaths.

The same can be said about another megaproject in the region: the Tren Maya (Mayan Train), a 948-mile railway project, in part through the jungle, whose construction began in June 2020. Its objective is to connect historic Mayan sites, conceived as tourist destinations, in the Yucatán Peninsula. So far, more than 8,000 ancient artefacts and buildings have been unearthed during construction. Regarding environmental concerns, the National Alliance for Conservation of the Jaguar is worried about the adverse effects that the train may have on these endangered animals and has requested the construction of twelve wildlife corridors. Likewise, the Centro Mexicano de Derecho Ambiental (Mexican Center of Environmental Rights) has condemned the deforestation that is taking place, which was not accounted for during planning. Deforestation leads to localized climate change and a reduction in rainfall, which may end up turning the jungle into a savannah one day. On the other hand, urbanized touristic infrastructure takes large amounts of water and produces concentrated wastewater.[4]

In this context, Matilde Córdoba Azcárate, in her chapter 'Colonial enclaves: site-specific indigeneity for luxury tourism', included in *Stuck with Tourism. Space, Power, and Labor in Contemporary Yucatan* (2020), studies tourism's effects in connection with Indigenous culture. As she states, 'tourism pervades the region's landscape, transforming social relations and household dynamics by erasing potentialities and displacing habitual ways of doing, living, and imagining. But simultaneously, they show how tourism opens up unexpected collaborations, spaces of hope, and opportunities for well-being that previously did not exist' (3). Tourism does have its dark side in the way in which it adversely affects both the environment and local Indigenous cultures.

The environmental humanities can therefore be instrumental in changing how we interact with nature, leading us to think about the more-than-human world beyond the concept of 'resource'. As is well known, although ecocriticism began mainly with the analysis of the descriptions of nature in literary writing, it now engages approaches coming from feminism, decolonial and postcolonial studies to envision the natural world. Ecocriticism, which concentrates on literary and cultural representations of nature, the relationship between literary writing and the more-than-human world, and between human beings and the environment, together with the environmental humanities in general, are part of what is sometimes called 'the spatial turn'. One of our most exciting, relatively new subfields (along with the digital and medical humanities), the environmental humanities, has echoed these concerns since the 1990s. Kusserow, in his *Picture Ecology*, has aptly defined ecocriticism in the following terms:

Ecocriticism might be described as analysis of cultural artifacts, literary and material, that, against the usual anthropocentric mode of the humanities,

attends to environmental conditions and history and to questions of ecology –
the study of living beings in relation to their surroundings – exploring how
humans have differently construed and been inflected by these things across
time and cultures. Ecocriticism acknowledges the existence, standing, and
agency of the great diversity of life on earth, giving a moral purchase to other
kinds of life in the analysis of culture. (11–12)

The environmental humanities typically acknowledge the inherent value of all living
things without assigning an inherently superior moral or ethical status to humans.
Kusserow also explains how the environmental humanities can complement (and
lead, I would argue) approaches coming from scientists and economists:

Scientists excel at providing critical information, economists at rationalizing
fiscal behavior; but neither can explain our failure to act upon what we know,
or, it seems, engender such action. Here the lessons of history, morals,
and ethics, and the tools of persuasion, empathy, and the imagination, are
required. These are the purview of the humanities, and in the last decade
or so, recognizing that the ecological crisis is also a social and cultural
crisis, environmentally oriented pursuits in anthropology, philosophy, history,
literature, and now art history and visual culture have coalesced under the
rubric of the environmental humanities. (10)

Likewise, Elizabeth DeLoughrey, Jill Didur and Anthony Carrigan, in the
introduction to their 2015 *Global Ecologies and the Environmental Humanities.
Postcolonial Approaches*, argue that the humanities and the interpretative social
sciences can tell stories and create the necessary narratives to communicate
scientific facts to a broader, non-specialist audience, thus facilitating a global
response to climate change. They also present the humanities (postcolonial
studies in particular) as a valuable complement to the environmental sciences,
as they reveal how the current ecological crisis is entangled with colonial
practices, imperialism and globalization, all the while offering decolonial modes
of resistance.

Along these lines, the volume *The Natural World in Latin American Literatures:
Ecocritical Essays on Twentieth Century Writings* (2010), edited by Adrian Taylor
Kane, blends ecocriticism with postcolonialism, feminism and Marxism, among
other critical approaches. One of the sections, titled 'Environmental Utopias and
Dystopias', engages ecofeminism and feminist utopianism. Likewise, the section
'Ecology and the Subaltern' focuses on environmental justice ecocriticism as
affected by class and race, addressing the relationship between the environment
and marginalized groups such as migrant workers in the US–Mexico border,
Indigenous communities in Mexico and Guatemala, and the migrants from the
Brazilian northeast.

Conclusion

As part of the structural, systemic violence of late capitalism, this ecocidal extractivism that contributes dramatically to climate change can, therefore, be conceived of as an immoral and unethical mode of political jouissance that goes against social solidarity and transgresses socially acceptable interactions. This obscene enjoyment, seemingly devoid of any restraint coming from the superego, belongs to the political domain of neoliberal market ideology that uses deregulation of the private sector and privatization of the public sphere to allow predatory corporations to over-extract natural resources, contaminate the environment and destroy ancestral ways of life. There is a cynical political jouissance in the market-oriented policies of these neoconservative doctrines that trump ethics and social responsibility for profits and conceive of citizens as mere consumers: in the elimination of environmental and social protections; in mining companies' appropriation and contamination of water supplies; in the privatization of public services related to water, energy health, education, the prison system and transportation; in the stimulation of consumer demand and unchecked economic growth at the expense of the environment; and in all the other neoliberal projects that have catapulted current the climate crisis.

What can be done about it? As Jorge Alemán explains within his deliberations about neoliberalism's 'perfect crime', 'power not only oppresses, but also creates consensus, establishes the subjective orientation and produces a symbolic plot that works in an "invisible" way, naturalizing dominant ideas and where always, and its definitive success consists in this, it hides its act of imposition.'[5] I contend that the conceptual frameworks offered by the environmental humanities can help defamiliarize these power-environment relations and these self-defeating, ecocidal policies for the wider public.

Notes

1 As is well known, according to Sigmund Freud, the pleasure principle is the instinct of avoiding pain and seeking pleasure to meet our psychological and biological needs, which drives our id.

2 For additional information on the contribution of the hydrohumanities, see my essay 'From thought to praxis: the hydrohumanities and hydrocriticism as socio-environmental approaches in Latin American Studies', in LASA Forum. See also the 2021 volume *Hydrohumanities: Water Discourse and Environmental Futures*, co-edited by Kim De Wolff, Rina Faletti and Ignacio López-Calvo.

3 'La apropiación de recursos naturales impuesta con violencia y quebrando el marco de los derechos humanos y de la Naturaleza' (11).

4 For a longer study of the hydrohumanities and the struggle for access to water in Latin America, see my essay 'From thought to praxis: the hydrohumanities and hydrocriticism as socio-environmental approaches in Latin American Studies'.

5 'El poder no solamente oprime, sino que fabrica consenso, establece la orientación subjetiva y produce una trama simbólica que funciona de modo "invisible", naturalizando las ideas dominantes y donde siempre, y en esto consiste su éxito definitivo, esconde su acto de imposición' (13).

References

Alemán, Jorge (2016), *Horizontes neoliberals en la subjetividad*, Buenos Aires: Grama.

Córdoba Azcárate, Matilde (2020), *Stuck with Tourism. Space, Power, and Labor in Contemporary Yucatan*, Oakland, CA: University of California Press.

DeLoughrey, Elizabeth, Jill Didur, and Anthony Carrigan (2015), *Global Ecologies and the Environmental Humanities. Postcolonial Approaches*, New York: Routledge.

DeSombre, Elizabeth R. (2022), 'Refuge and Environmental Responsibility', in Ignacio López-Calvo and Marjorie Agosín (eds), *Refugees, Refuge, and Human Displacement*, London: Anthem.

De Wolff, Kim, Rina Faletti, and Ignacio López-Calvo, eds (2021), *Hydrohumanities: Water Discourse and Environmental Futures*, Oakand, CA: University of California Press.

Gudynas, Eduardo (2013), 'Extracciones, extractivismo y extrahecciones. Un marco conceptual sobre la apropiaión de recursos naturales', *Observatorio del desarrollo* 18: 1–18.

Hook, Derek (2017), 'What Is "Enjoyment as a Political Factor"?', *Political Psychology* 38(4): 605–20.

Kusserow, Karl (2021), *Picture Ecology: Art and Ecocriticism in Planetary Perspective*, Princeton: Princeton University Press.

Lacan, Jacques (2006), *Écrits: The First Complete Edition in English*, 1st edn, trans. Bruce Fink in collaboration with Héloïse Fink and Russell Grigg, New York: W.W. Norton and Company.

Lacan, Jacques (1991), *Le séminaire, livre XVII; L'envers de la psychanalyse*, ed. J. A. Miller, Paris: Seuil.

López-Calvo, Ignacio (2022), 'From thought to praxis: The hydrohumanities and hydrocriticism as socio-environmental approaches in Latin American Studies', *Dossier: Climate Change as a Cultural Problem: Transdisciplinary Environmental Humanities and Latin American Studies*, LASA Forum 53(2): 40–5.

Moore, Jason W. (2015), *Capitalism in the Web of Life. Ecology and the Accumulation of Capital*, New York: Verso Books.

Polanco Rodríguez, Ángel G. and Kata Beilin (2019), 'Toxic Bodies: Water and Women in Yucatan. Environmental Cultural Studies Through Time: The Luso-Hispanic World', *Hispanic Issues on Line* 24: 168–93.

Taylor Kane, Adrian (2010), *The Natural World in Latin American Literatures: Ecocritical Essays on Twentieth Century Writings*, Jefferson, NC: McFarland.

Verhaeghe, Paul (2006), 'Enjoyment and impossibility: Lacan's revision of the Oedipus complex', in Justin Clemens and Russell Grigg (eds), *Reflections on Seminar XVII. Jacques Lacan and the Other side of Psychoanalysis*, 29–49, Durham: Duke University Press.

Žižek, Slavoj (1997), *The Plague of Fantasies*, New York: Verso.

Zupančič, Alenka (2006), 'When Surplus Enjoyment Meets Surplus Value', Justin Clemens and Russell Grigg (eds), *Reflections on Seminar XVII. Jacques Lacan and the Other Side of Psychoanalysis*, 155–78, Durham: Duke University Press.

Chapter 5

Hyper-royalism

A Thai modality of political jouissance

Pavin Chachavalpongpun

God save the king

In June 2006, King Bhumibol Adulyadej celebrated the Diamond Jubilee on the occasion of his enthronement for sixty years. Week-long celebrations were held throughout Thailand in an extremely jubilant atmosphere. Thais were deliriously happy to commemorate the kingship of Bhumibol who was perceived as the pillar of political stability in the kingdom. Portraits of Bhumibol were everywhere, at traffic intersections, on flyovers and plastered on billboards across cities. Thai's love for their king was overflowing. It was a kind of jouissance – their physical delight or ecstasy in being the subjects of the king. King Bhumibol was crowned in 1946 following the mysterious death of his brother, King Ananda Mahidol. His enthronement took place more than a decade after the end of the absolute monarchy in 1932 in Thailand. Hence, Bhumibol's kingship began on shaky ground. But Bhumibol successfully re-established the royal hegemony, by co-opting with the military in dominating Thai politics. From the late 1950s onwards, the monarchy as an institution became the country's most important and powerful institution.[1] In this process, Bhumibol transformed himself into a god-king replete with *dhamma* or Buddhist teachings, and who was devoted to the well-being and happiness of Thai people. After all, Thailand is known as the 'Land of Smiles', supposedly because people are happy. And the monarchy is one reason for the Thai jouissance.

On the flip side, however, disrespecting the Thai monarchy is blasphemous. Thailand is the country with the harshest lèse-majesté punishment. Lèse-majesté, or the crime of injury to royalty, is defined by Article 112 of the Thai Criminal Code, which states that defamatory, insulting or threatening comments about the king, queen or regent are punishable by three to fifteen years in prison. Ironically, this is a country where most Thais are said to possess immense love and respect for their king for his benevolence, compassion and forgiveness. The Thai conservative royalists have employed the lèse-majesté law to counter growing criticism of the monarchy.[2] Since the coup of 2006 that overthrew the government of Prime Minister Thaksin Shinawatra, cases of lèse-majesté have surged, negatively affecting the state of human rights in the country. The law has been used as a political weapon undermining political opponents. For decades, the monarchy-military partnership had ruled over Thai politics. But the arrival of Thaksin in the premiership in 2001 shifted the political equation, prompting the monarchy and the military to defend its position in the bluntest way. As the Thaksin threat intensified, the monarchy's supporters unleashed a new ideology – hyper-royalism as an antidote against Thaksin.[3] Hyper-royalism is a belief, a self-expression and a political device designed to enshrine, promote and protect the monarchy for ultimately the protection of an individual's own interests. But it is not just an ideology found elsewhere in the polity. It has to be excessive, limitless, hegemonic and so surreal that it rationalizes even the most diabolical actions as long as they take place while protecting the monarchy. I define hyper-royalism as a modality of political jouissance – a fantasy that has been created around the royal institution in Thailand.

In 2016, Bhumibol passed away, ending the authoritative reign that had lasted for seven decades. State media built emotive anticipation of the looming death of the king, and on that day, 13 October, the Thai nation entered a period of protracted mourning. The happiness of living under Bhumibol might have ended, only to be replaced by another kind of jouissance, an obsessive nostalgia for the old days under the king. The news of the king's death was televised nationwide. Thousands of loyal subjects of the king, wearing yellow t-shirts (yellow is the colour of Bhumibol who was born on Monday), lined the streets leading to Siriraj Hospital where Bhumibol had been hospitalized. Nights before, people held candlelight vigils, praying for a miracle which would lift the king from his sickbed. News presenters described the death of the king as a calamitous event for Thailand. Scenes of loyal subjects crying wretchedly were something similar to the manipulated scenes in North Korea where the people were forced to display boundless affection for their dear leaders. This is not to doubt the sorrow of the Thais. But it was so surreal that it seemed exaggerated.[4] Yet again, this is a kind of political jouissance that all the great philosophers talk about.

Bhumibol might have been departing from the political scene. But hyper-royalism à *la* Bhumibol remains. Indeed, it has dangerously intensified. The succeeding king, Vajiralongkorn, son of Bhumibol, lacks the charisma and moral authority of his father. But like his father, Vajiralongkorn is politically ambitious.

Both have trumped the constitution and directly intervened in politics. But 2022 is different from the Bhumibol era. Today's young generation is not only defying the monarchic institution that has long violated the constitutional boundary, but it is also contesting the mainstream political jouissance long defined by the royalists. In the middle of 2020, the young generation staged months-long protests calling for immediate monarchic reform, hoping to remove the monarchy from politics. As an anachronistic institution, instead of adapting itself to change, the Thai monarchy has continued to defy modernity. Through its resistance, the ideology of hyper-royalism has been further disseminated on the basis of defending the monarchy in order to maintain 'Thai happiness'. Since the protests, many young Thais have been arrested, mostly under the draconian lèse-majesté law for defaming the monarchy and for disrupting the nation's happiness. Recently, the Thai Constitutional Court even ruled that a call for monarchic reform could be regarded as seditious. While this has caused a huge impact of democratization in Thailand, some Thais have encouraged the government to eliminate enemies of the monarchy. They legitimized the harsh approach of the government vis-à-vis the young protesters, citing that they wanted to keep Thailand as the 'Land of Smiles'.

Political jouissance in Thailand

French psychoanalyst Jacques Lacan developed the concept of jouissance that combines politics with the pleasure principle (instinctive seeking of pleasure to satisfy biological and psychological needs).[5] Intended not to be translated into English to convey its specific usage, jouissance as a concept compels one to constantly attempt to transgress the prohibitions imposed on one's enjoyment to go beyond the pleasure principle. The result of the transgression of the pleasure principle is however not more pleasure, but instead pain. There is only a certain amount of pleasure that one can bear. Beyond this limit, pleasure becomes pain. And this painful principle is what Lacan framed as jouissance. This refers to the earlier work of Marquis de Sade, which focuses on the emancipation of pleasure from the tyranny of civilization. Sade believed that jouissance was transgressive in nature because on its way to satisfaction, jouissance knows no boundary and remains indifferent to the price to be paid by the person. Sadomasochism is the giving or receiving of jouissance from acts involving the infliction of pain. From this view, jouissance is suffering but also pleasure at the same time.

Slavoj Žižek said that modern society is defined by the lack of an ultimate transcendent guarantee, or, in libidinal terms, of total jouissance. There are three main ways to cope with this negativity: utopian, democratic and post-democratic. The first one (totalitarianisms, fundamentalisms) tries to reoccupy the ground of absolute jouissance by attaining a utopian society (of harmonious society) which eliminates negativity. The second, democratic, one enacts a political equivalent of 'traversing the fantasy': it institutionalizes the lack itself by creating the space for political antagonism. The third one, consumerist post-democracy, tries to neutralize negativity by transforming politics into apolitical administration: individuals pursue their consumerist fantasies in a space regulated by expert social administration.[6] The Thai case or hyper-royalism seems to fit with the fundamentalist setting. Royalism is so hegemonic and pervasive that it has become the only source of political jouissance, as a result of creating a happy society under the direction of the monarchy which is intolerable vis-à-vis the others. Happiness is sustained by love and respect for the monarchy. There is no room for critics/enemies of the monarchy. Royal subjects could go to an extent in causing pain to critics/enemies of the monarchy in order to maintain a society of jouissance.

Hyper-royalism is a kind of political jouissance. Its characteristics fit in with the description of political jouissance popularized by Lacan. There are at least four characteristics of Thai hyper-royalism as political jouissance. First, jouissance has a tendency to be excessive, be it by virtue of the thrills of transgression, or simply by means of its indulgence in what is 'too much', beyond the bounds of what is healthy, reasonable or ordinarily permissible.[7] It is an elevation of desire. Sade's despotism of the passions could be explained as an attempt to maintain the greatest distance between law and jouissance, between what universalizes, as an absolute particularity, resists all universalization.[8] The happiness gained from the love for the Thai monarchy has been excessive, exceptional and even irrational, to the point of leaving no room for dissent. The Thai monarchy must not be violable, thus creating an enforced affection among Thais vis-à-vis their kings. Thai monarchs must be forever extolled and permanently projected in a positive light. There were cases of Thai historians being arrested for criticizing a sixteenth-century king under the lèse-majesté. A man was also arrested for criticizing a dog of King Bhumibol. This is exactly the case of excessiveness.

Second, hyper-royalism is an ideology designed to manipulate the soul of the people, control their faith and instruct their actions. It is conscious and intentional. Hyper-royalism, as a mode of intensity, is a type of arousal – a thrilling twist – that takes place when affect moves beyond the bounds of what is reasonable or satisfying.[9] Accepting the idea of happiness as a means for maximizing pleasure means accepting the will submitted to contingency. Ultimately this would mean acknowledging that there is only the relativity of the ethics of pleasure which is no ethics at all.[10] Royalists exploit the monarchy to manipulate the public so as to strengthen their own political position. They inculcate an extremist version of affection towards the monarchy – hyper-royalism – and explain it away as a kind of political jouissance. Third, hyper-royalism involves make-believe politics and fantasy. Like sexual enjoyment, hyper-royalism is necessarily structured by fantasy. It is organized by fantasmatic scenarios designating who or what is desirable or undesirable. Hyper-royalism does not occur in a vacuum. It is never simply a spontaneous individual psychological reaction. Nobody would feel excessive affection towards the monarchy had it not been for the incessant propaganda from the state that promotes the supernatural qualities of monarchs. Hyper-royalism is shaped by precise historical, political and symbolic conditions. For example, the fact that Thailand has never been colonized was historically explained in the context of the bravery of Thai monarchs. It has become a symbolic value for national independence which was built on the greatness of the monarchy. To be loyal to the monarchy, on this basis, is jouissance. It is something the society is willing to live and die for, a reason behind the symbolic labour of consolidating a (royalist) community or ensuring a kind of identity.

Fourth, hyper-royalism contains an element of pain, be it the pain of the ideologists or that of the non-believers. For the former, when love for the monarchy is made unconditional, hyper-royalists are willing to sacrifice everything for the existence of the high institution. They are obliged to protect and defend the monarchy even if this means destroying the non-believers in the meanest way, including killing or imprisoning them. It is a feeling that the monarchy is perceived as endangered, about to be snatched away by intruders.[11] In protecting and defending the monarchy, it renders jouissance. As for the non-believers, or indeed critics of the monarchy, the pain of being categorized as the other can be immense. They are constantly harassed by the hyper-royalists. The lèse-majesté law has become one of the most brutal weapons in penalizing critics of the monarchy. The more they are critical the more intense the punishment becomes. For hyper-royalists, to see their counterparts suffer is pure pleasure – negative pleasure. As Jean Jacques Rousseau said, 'The pleasure of someone who, when watching a suffering fellowman, says: "You may perish for aught I care, nothing can hurt me"'.[12]

Punishment as pleasure

Thailand's leading historian, Thongchai Winichakul, coined the term 'hyper-royalism' to explicate a prominent political ideology formed under the reign of King Bhumibol. As alluded to earlier, the rise of royal hegemony came as a result of the strengthening of Bhumibol's political position even though the monarchy was supposedly constrained under the constitution. Royalism re-emerged as a public culture and proliferated like wildfire. Bhumibol was placed at the centre of national life, symbolizing Thai happiness. Ancient royal rituals were restored to elevate the status of the king, including the once-obsolete practice of prostration. The king initiated a myriad of royal developmental projects to assist the poor, the result of which saw the surge of his popularity among Thais. His periodic interventions in politics, mostly to prevent the escalation of violence, made him/

the monarchy at the pinnacle of the Thai political structure. The monarchy has also been made a part of the country's holy trinity alongside the nation and Buddhism – the holy trinity is to represent Thai national identity. At the height of colonialism and the Cold War, the monarchy projected itself as being under threat of intruders, be they the colonialists or the communists. Royalism was aroused to protect the monarchy. Anti-monarchist elements inside the country were also treated like external enemies, which had to be annihilated. Indeed, it was because of the domestic threats to the monarchy that the royalist ideology was intensified. Hyper-royalism became apparent particularly at the peak of the Cold War when pro-democracy activist students were accused of being communists who strove to overthrow the monarchy.

According to Thongchai, hyper-royalism has four characteristics.[13] First, it is royalism with excessive intensity. The demand for expressive love and loyalty to the monarchy is massively increased. Public events and ceremonies related to the monarchy, old or new, were incessantly celebrated to return happiness to Thais. These events range from birthdays of the members of the royal family, coronations, marriages, funerals, Father's Day (Bhumibol's birthday), Mother's Day (Queen Sirikit's birthday), Golden Jubilee to the Diamond Jubilee. It can be said that the majority of national holidays in Thailand are related to the monarchy. Thailand has rarely celebrated the achievements of ordinary citizens. Second, hyper-royalism is full of aggrandizement, exaltation and hyperbole – a political jouissance that goes beyond normalcy. Members of the royal family are portrayed as supernatural humans. They have to be the best at everything, from able sportsmen, fashion icons, talented actors and singers, and excellent chefs to more serious occupations such as scientific researchers and academics, world-class artists or great philanthropists whose social services have included poverty alleviation, narcotic eradication, healthcare, irrigation and education. This was demonstrated through the numerous honorary doctoral degrees conferred upon King Bhumibol throughout his lifetime. His economic philosophy, known as self-sufficiency economy, to promote Thai life away from consumerism was extolled by the United Nations. People have been obliged to eulogize the monarchy's achievements. Yet when eulogies became truths, hyperbole became the norm. Thais were told that the royalty was of social caste. The existence of the monarchy was the nation's happiness.

Third, hyper-royalism operates through the means of extreme control of public discourse on the monarchy, including the discussion of public speech of the king, his thoughts and actions, with harsh punishment mostly with the application of lèse-majesté law for the non-believers. The fifteen-year maximum sentence for lèse-majesté is another kind of extreme borne out of hyper-royalism. Aside from the harsh punishment, this law allows anyone to file complaints against any others on the grounds of lèse-majesté, thus encouraging abuse in its application. It has been mostly used to silence critics of the monarchy on the pretext that it is imperative to keep society happy and peaceful. But hyper-royalism has made the bounds of lèse-majesté very blurry. What is considered lèse-majesté depends on who you are. The lack of clear boundaries of the lèse-majesté law has created a climate of fear. Ironically, this climate of fear runs alongside a climate of happiness under the rule of the king. To avoid prosecution, people speak highly of the monarchy regardless of what they might think privately.

Fourth, hyper-royalism is not solely about state propaganda but demands public participation. The aim is to integrate hyper-royalism into everybody's life – to make everybody happy. The propaganda is not only controlled by the state, or only in a top-down fashion. It has engaged with civil society organizations, non-governmental organizations and the academic community, as well as the mass media. Together, they strive to promote the exceptional quality of the king as someone who is devoted towards the people's happiness; meanwhile, critics of the monarchy are still suppressed. Social media has emerged as the latest battlefield in propagating the ideology of hyper-royalism. The government has set up 'cyber scouts' as a type of vigilante group to monitor social media users, to promote hyper-glorification of the monarchy, and to take legal actions against enemies of the monarchy. In the world of traditional media, the government broadcasts royal news at 8:00 p.m. every day. Royal activities are celebrated, with sanitized images of the family members. Thongchai said, 'Hyper-royalism is not simply a design or a project totally manipulated by a super state, or the Big Brother as imagined in George Orwell's 1984. It is indeed effective and enforceable, thanks to the Big Brother of the 21st century, namely the public.'[14] In recent years, love and loyalty have been extended to some other institutions surrounding the monarchy, including the military and the judiciary who demand total submission of the public for the sake of a happy society.

Bottom-up jouissance

The state may have prescribed what political jouissance is for the people as part of earning its legitimacy. But the people also have their own version of political jouissance. It is a bottom-up version that contests state-manipulated political jouissance. Žižek once said, 'Jouissance is an always sexualized, always transgressive enjoyment, at the limits of what subjects can experience or talk about in public'.[15] Because hyper-royalism constantly demands excessive royal extolment, anti-monarchy is thus outlawed and has to be expressed in secrecy. Disdain for the monarchy can only be expressed among trusted friends. Discussion on anything about the monarchy, particularly if it is of a critical nature, has to take place with great care. When open criticism against the monarchy cannot be made in the public space, it becomes gossip and hearsay. Lying about the monarchy is penalized; speaking truthfully about the monarchy invites heavier punishment. Despite the sanctions, people have continued to push the limits of what might be said about the monarchy, mostly in clandestine forms. They have done it through discourses, symbols, artworks, novels, songs and graffiti, among many others. These are the kind of political jouissance enjoyed among the non-believers – it is the feeling of liberation.

To understand today's bottom-up political jouissance, the political context in the past two decades in Thailand must be elaborated. The coup of 2006, in many ways, unleashed an unprecedented wave of anti-monarchism, simply because pro-democracy forces were convinced that King Bhumibol masterminded the overthrow of Prime Minister Thaksin who was perceived to be an enemy of the old establishment. By that time, Thaksin had already won the hearts and minds of many Thais who believed that his party, Thai Rak Thai (Thais Loves Thais), were serious about working towards lifting their livelihood. Democracy, not monarchism, was the key to opportunities in life. Overthrowing Thaksin was thus seen as the robbery of democracy. In the aftermath of the coup, a red-shirt movement was formed to counter the political intervention of the military (red was chosen to contradict the royal colour of yellow). From there, the movement grew in numbers. When the military launched a deadly crackdown on the red-shirt movement in 2010, leading to 99 deaths and over 2,500 injured, red-shirt members shifted their attention to the monarchy as the source of political violence. This political violence provided legitimacy for anti-monarchism to blossom.

At the same time, hyper-royalism was in full swing. It led to the collision of two kinds of jouissance – one supporting the existence of the monarch and the other seeking to abolish it. In the latter's camp, the political jouissance was expressed through new public discourses, which were essentially subversive. The new terminology, *ta sawang* [eye open], meaning the awakening from the royal propaganda, appeared so pervasively in red-shirt songs, poetry and graffiti. But because of the lèse-majesté law, red-shirt anti-royalism chose to hide behind metaphorical ambiguity, humour, vulgarity and absurdist parody, to get their messages across. A recent study on anti-monarchism explained this tactic – the process of desacralizing the monarchy involved creative skills which enabled red shirts to pick particular non-political themes and signs such as 'love', 'blind', 'smile', 'dinosaur' and others and politicizing them with additional and challenging meanings publicized through social media.[16] I call this tactic the defence of bottom-up jouissance. The hyper-royalists were aware of the hidden messages behind the usage of subversive signs and attempted to sweepingly criminalize such usage with lèse-majesté law.

The more the monarchy became involved in politics, the more intensified the tactics used by the anti-monarchists became. Following the funeral of a royalist who was killed in a clash with police in October 2008, the *ta sawang* phenomenon became more forceful. This was because Queen Sirikit decided to attend and preside over the funeral during which time Thai politics was fiercely divided. Her attendance at the funeral was perceived to be a political move. It was also regarded as the monarchy defending the royalists at the expense of the red shirts often identified as anti-monarchists. Because the queen often wore bright red lipstick, a subversive term of *e-pak deang* [red-lip woman] was adopted among the red shirts to signify her. These types of codewords reflected a transgressive enjoyment which exceeded the limits of conventionality in Thai society in regard to the monarchy. So when the deadly crackdowns took place two years later, the red shirts continued to use codewords, either as speaking words or graffiti, to express their grievances against the monarchy. The saying, *i-hia sang kha, e-ha sang ying* [the bastard ordered the killings, the bitch ordered the shootings], was understood as the king and the queen being behind the death of red shirts in May 2010.

The death of Bhumibol officially ended his authoritative reign and set Thailand on an unknown course. His son, Vajiralongkorn, was crowned shortly afterwards, further deepening the anxiety among the royalists and their nemeses equally. For the royalists, they became uncertain if the monarchy would continue to safeguard their political interests. For the anti-monarchists, the new flatly refused calls for monarchic reform but instead meddled in politics to enhance the royal absolutism. At this critical juncture, hyper-royalism, built on Bhumibol's charisma and authority, was challenged by its counterpart. It became time for anti-monarchist ideology to take root, particularly among the younger generation in Thailand. This explains why, in 2020, a group of younger Thais took to the streets of Bangkok to demand monarchic reforms with an aim to bring the monarchy strictly under the constitution. The protests have been on and off, partly because of the eruption of coronavirus and partly because of the legal measures put in place by the government to deter anti-monarchist elements. But Thailand has come a long way. A few years ago, nobody would have imagined that curses against the monarchy could be aired in public, despite the lèse-majesté law. Hyper-royalism, once a modality of political jouissance, seems to be dimming and instead replaced by the bottom-up jouissance promoted and supported by the younger generation. Today's Thai youths grew up during a time when the monarchy was seriously challenged by the Thaksin factor. With the shift in political ideology, they have adopted new ideas of power and legitimacy. These views are accompanied by a new modality of political jouissance, one which values equality, people-centricism and freedom of expression. They want to escape from the cult of happiness under the ideology of hyper-royalism.

Notes

1   Paul M. Handley, *The King Never Smiles: A Biography of Thailand's King Bhumibol Adulyadej* (New Haven: Yale University Press, 2006).

2 David Streckfuss, *Truth on Trial in Thailand: Defamation, Treason, and Lèse-majesté* (London: Routledge, 2010).

3 Pavin Chachavalpongpun (ed.), *'Good Coup' Gone Bad: Thailand's Political Developments after Thaksin's Downfall* (Singapore: Institute of Southeast Asian Studies, 2014).

4 Edoardo Siani and Matthew Phillips, 'Managing the Death of King Bhumibol', *New Mandala*, 16 October 2016, https://www.newmandala.org/managing-death-king -bhumibol/.

5 Jacques Lacan, *Livre VII: L'éthique de la Psychanalyse, 1959–1960*, ed. Jacques-Alain Miller (Paris: Éditions du Seuil, 1986).

6 Slavoj Žižek, *The Liberal Utopia, Section ı: Against the Politics of Jouissance*, https://www.lacan.com/zizliberal.htm.

7 Derek Hook, 'What is "Enjoyment as a Political Factor"?', *Political Psychology* 38, no. 4 (2017): 605–20.

8 Jelica Šumič Riha, 'Sadean Politics or a Tyranny of Jouissance', *Filozofski Vestnik* XXXIX, no. 3 (2018): 71–120.

9 Hook, 'What is "Enjoyment as a Political Factor"? , 9.

10 Riha, 'Sadean Politics or a Tyranny of Jouissance , 73.

11 Hook, 'What is "Enjoyment as a Political Factor"? , 11.

12 Riha, 'Sadean Politics or a Tyranny of Jouissance , 84.

13 Thongchai Winichakul, 'Thailand's Hyper-royalism: Its Past Success and Present Predicament', *Trends in Southeast Asia*, no. 7 (2016): 1–36.

14 Ibid., 24.

15 Matthew Sharpe, 'Slavoj Žižek (1949–)', https://iep.utm.edu/zizek/#Hc.

16 Anonymous, 'Anti-royalism in Thailand since 2006: Ideological Shifts and Resistance', *Journal of Contemporary Asia* 48, no. 3 (2018): 363–94.

Chapter 6
The joy circuit

Jens Schröter

Whosoever is able to hear or see the circuits in the synthesized sound of CDs or in the laser storms of a disco finds happiness. A happiness beyond the ice, as Nietzsche would have said. At the moment of merciless submission to laws whose cases we are, the phantasm of man as the creator of media vanishes

wrote Friedrich A. Kittler in his famous study *Gramophone, Film, Typewriter* (Kittler 1999, xli). There is an enjoyment to see and hear the circuits, to pierce through the veil of surfaces. The enjoyment is to not stick to the surface of the visible or the audible but to 'hear or see' the machinery itself. This enjoyment is at the same time deeply political. The one who hears or sees the machinery hears and sees beyond the 'surface effects, known to consumers as interface' (Kittler 1999, 1). The operations below the interface are the diagram of computational power: 'The *diagram* is no longer an auditory or visual archive but a map, a cartography that is coextensive with the whole social field. It is an abstract machine' (Deleuze 1988, 34). Circuits are in a very literal sense diagrams as abstract machines. See, for example, this circuit diagram representing an analog circuit – in this case, a simple amplifier.[1]

This image shows the diagrammatic representation of a simple electrical circuit. Basically, (analog and digital) circuits are the base of all modern electronic devices, and these devices are today literally coextensive with the whole social field. The circuit can, in analogy to the diagram, become a metaphor for societal processes and their circulations: 'For example, the merchant bourgeoisie of the cities conjugated or capitalized a domain of knowledge, a technology, assemblages and circuits into whose dependency the nobility, Church, artisans, and even peasants *would enter*' (Deleuze/Guattari 1987, 221). Or: 'The introduction of monetary signs into certain commercial circuits in Africa caused those signs to undergo an analogical transformation that was very difficult to control (except when the circuits underwent a destructive transformation instead).' (587).

A computer is just a very big assemblage of circuits. The way they are structured and ordered decides on a deep level what is technologically possible and what is not – and even software in its algorithmc structure is formally equivalent to the circuit. Algorithms could, in principle, be represented in the same diagrammatic manner as circuits. To see beyond the veil of surfaces is an enjoyment because it seems to give us the technological real beyonc the imaginary of surfaces. But at the same time, it's a kind of narcissistic enjoyment since it also gives the new appearance of relating to a deeper truth of technology, but:

> There is no real option between a cybernetics of theory or a theory of cybernetics, because cybernetics is neither a theory nor its object, but an operation within an objective partial circuits that reiterates 'itself' in the real and machines theory through the unknown. (Land 2011, 295)

Land very often uses the metaphor of the circuit to describe the fundamental entanglement of technology and society – and insists on the opacity of the circuit. So, is it really an enjoyment to hear or see the circuit itself? If enjoyment is the '*jouissance* of transgression' (Lacan 1997, 195), is it to see and hear beyond the sur-interface a transgression? Kittler, as quoted above, speaks of the submission to the Law, which erases the phantasm of men as inventor of media. For Lacan, the enjoyment is related to transgression, and transgression is nothing without the Law. But that also means that transgression binds us to the Law:

> We are, in fact, led to the point where we accept the formula that without a transgression there is no access to jouissance, and, [. . .] that is precisely the function of the Law. Transgression in the direction of jouissance only takes place if it is supported by the oppositional principle, by the forms of the Law. (Lacan 1997, 177)

If we take the diagrammatic form of the circuit as the Law of technology with its very political implications, how can we then relate the political jouissance of transgression to it? Surely, in normal cases, we just enjoy the surfaces, but Kittler insists on the happiness of hearing or seeing the circuit. Doesn't that contradict the merciless submission to the Law? Interestingly, Kittler doesn't speak of – let's say – opening up the compact disc player, the laser gun or the computer and looking at the microchips (or other technology 'inside'), although this is a figure of thought which is very central to Kittlerian media archaeology: understanding technology, disrupting the interface, learning programming languages. It is easy to understand the enjoyment of the classical Kittlerian position – you open up the machine, you understand its inner workings and therefore its politics, and you enjoy your privileged knowledge as compared to the interface-bound users. You transgress the Law that says that you aren't allowed to open the black box. But Kittler speaks in the passage quoted above of hearing and seeing the circuit *in the effects of the circuit*. And wouldn't looking at the inner machinations of a CD player still be looking at surfaces? Well, you see the microchips, the circuits . . . but then you still don't see their inner workings. This is reminiscent of Heidegger's reading of the earthly thing:

> If we attempt such penetration by smashing the rock, then it shows us its pieces but never anything inward, anything that has been opened up. The stone has instantly withdrawn again into the same dull weight and mass of its fragments. (Heidegger 2002, 24/25)

Of course, especially in Heidegger, technology is different from things, but the problem is nevertheless similar: if we open up the black box, we just find smaller black boxes. Of course, we can understand the diagram of the circuit, and we can understand theoretically the physics and chemistry behind technology, but that is just similar to what Heidegger says about the thing:

> If we try to grasp the stone's heaviness in another way, by placing it on a pair of scales, then we bring its heaviness into the calculable form of weight. This perhaps very precise determination of the stone is a number, but the heaviness of the weight has escaped us. Color shines and wants only to shine. If we try to make it comprehensible by analyzing it into numbers of oscillations it is gone. (25)

So according to Heidegger, it seems, Kittler doesn't want us (against most of his other statements on this) to reduce the appearance of the circuit to its technological substructure. Hearing the circuit, the diagram of technopolitical power of 'precised [präzisierter] information technology' (Janke 1999, 183), *in the music itself*, is the source of happiness. But what could that mean?

It might be a hint that Deleuze, in his second book on cinema, *L'image temps*, explicitly speaks of circuits (the word in French is written as in English and basically means the same). In the table of contents, the third chapter, his 'third comment on Bergson', has in its subtitles the formulation: 'Les circuits de l'image optique et sonore' (Deleuze 1985, 375) – seeing and hearing. He writes: 'La situation purement optique et sonore (description) est une image actuelle, mais qui, au lieu de se prolonger en mouvement, s'enchaîne avec une image virtuelle et forme avec elle un circuit.' (66). Of course, 'circuit' does not directly denote a technical structure here – but as we have seen above, a circuit is an abstract machine, an abstract structure, even on the technological level, and an abstract, diagrammatic ordering can also appear on the level of higher forms ('circuit' can also mean a structure of circulation, like in a 'blood circuit' – and a blood circuit and a computer circuit are similar, when seen as abstract, cybernetic, machines). On page 65, Deleuze quotes Bergson in footnote 4, showing one of Bergson's models of memory, which is represented as a diagram and called a 'circuit'. Deleuze's formulation is echoed again by Land (2011, 327) and reconnected to the question of desire: 'Machinic desire is the operation of the virtual; implementing itself in the actual, revirtualizing itself, and producing reality in a circuit.' The circuits of the visible and audible are, although Land uses the notion in a different context, 'desiring-circuits' (332): joy circuits as Gary Numan sang.

Before I come back to the political jouissance of technology, I want to discuss two artworks. One of them is a weaving by indigenous artist Marilou Schultz, which was shown on Dokumenta 14, 2017, in Kassel. The accompanying text in the exhibition (documented by myself, using a camera) read:

> In 1994, the Intel Company in Rio Rancho, New Mexico, commissioned Marilou Schultz, a well-known Navajo weaver and teacher, to produce a woven replica of a printed circuit board. [. . .] Navajo weavings are made by hand on a plain upright wooden loom. [. . .] Fourteen years after the work for Intel, the Nerman Museum commissioned Schultz to weave another computer chip. Schultz is known for 'diversity weavings' in which non-symmetrical designs are featured. The computer chip fabrics commemorate the Navajo women workers who were employed in the manufacture of integrated circuits, diodes and other computer components at the Fairchild Industries factory in Shiprock, New Mexico, which operated on a Navajo reservation from 1965 to 1975. In early promotional brochures, the company invoked analogies between the skills and aesthetics of Navajo weaving and the manufacture of computer chips. (translation mine)

Computer chips are vast assemblages of circuits. This artwork reflects on the early conditions of the production of such circuits, as well as on the practice of weaving. Text and textiles are closely connected (Rooney 2000). Representing the core of a symbol-processing and, therefore, basically a textual machine like the computer in a weaved pattern reflects back on basic properties of integrated circuits on the level of the materiality of the artwork itself. Moreover, historically the Navajo Nation played an important role in the history of cryptography in the Second World War (Singh 1999, ch. 5) – it was their traditional culture and especially their little-known language that could be used as a coding device. The Navajo Nation was in that case itself a black box in the circuits of communication and therefore inherited the place that at that time, and up to today, computing machines had. Nevertheless, the weaved pattern reveals nothing about the inner workings of the chips, of the integrated circuits themselves. The weaved image lays bare, according to the discussion of Heidegger above, that looking at chips doesn't reveal anything about their inner machinations.

The next image I want to discuss is the above mentioned second weaving of a computer chip.[2] The accompanying text in the exhibition by Laurie White (documented by myself, using a camera) read:

> By 1965, the semiconductor division of Fairchild Corporation was operating a large computer chip manufacturing plant in Shiprock, New Mexico, on the grounds of a Navajo reservation. The chips were made almost exclusively by Navajo women, who, because of their skilled and experienced manual labour, became valued assembly line workers. In its advertising for the factory, the company emphasized the almost uncanny similarity of computer chips and Navajo weaving patterns, as if to suggest an inherent connection between the two ways of working. The factory closed its doors in 1975, only ten years after its occupation by protesters from the American Indian Movement (AIM), who were trying to draw attention to unfair working conditions and layoffs. Although the role of indigenous peoples in the early stages of American computer technology is poorly documented, it is possible to conclude that the outsourcing of electronics manufacturing to women of colour in Asia was first tried on US soil, namely on the Navajo Reservation.

Again, the historical ground of circuit production is thematized – along with an 'uncanny' similarity between the look of integrated circuits and Navajo weaving. These artworks critically reflect on the circuit and its social and historical grounding and show, moreover, reflexively that mapping the structure of technology into the visible realm does not grant us access. Getting 'beyond the ice' as Kittler put it, under the spell of a merciless Law, would require additional steps: 'Matter as the intensity of the circuit, not the adequacy of the representation' (Land 2011, 438).

In his useful and concise presentation of *jouissance* as a political factor (following Lacan and Žižek), Derek Hook describes five aspects. Number five is that '*Jouissance* [. . .] takes the form of contravention (is transgressive) inasmuch as it pushes the subject painfully (enjoyably) beyond the law or socially prescribed limits' (2017, 612). As we already noted, the Kittlerian jouissance might be to open up the black boxes (against the socially prescribed limit of letting the black box closed) – but the intensity of the circuit will be discovered in another way. Is it an accident that Kittler speaks of the 'synthesized sound of CDs' and 'laser storms of a disco'? Is he not talking explicitly of the transgressive dissolution of the self in very loud dancefloor music in clubs? Is it not painful to be immersed in synthetic sounds at very high volume, being immersed in flickering lights and synthetic fog that make seeing difficult? Don't we lose control in this environment, swept away by pulsing rhythms of 'manically dehumanized machine-music' (Land 2011, 392) that take over bodily control? Seen in this way, a possible political jouissance of technology is precisely not the opening of the black box but inserting oneself into it, becoming the 'meat circuit' (Deleuze/Guattari 1987, 152). In many films of David Cronenberg, especially in *eXistenZ* (1999), this is re-enacted (Bukatman 1993). But isn't that an escapist movement? Not insofar as we embed ourselves into the technological pulse, into the abstract machine, and use this energy to disrupt our stabilized subjectivity. To dissolve in the 'synthesized sound of CDs' and 'laser storms of a disco' can be a political jouissance to transgress the subject form and see and hear the abstract machine of which we are part: '[B]eyond ice, beyond death – our lives, our happiness' (Nietzsche 2005, 3). The joy circuit is one way to go there.

Notes

1 Image of common base amplifier, *Wikimedia*, 16 May 2023. Available online: https://de.m.wikipedia.org/wiki/Datei:Common_base_amplifier.svg.

2 Marilou Schultz, Untitled, 1994, Wool on Wood, Nerman Museum of Contemporary Art, Kansas, Image available here: www.documenta14.de/en/artists/22610/marilou-schultz.

References

Bukatman, S. (1993), *Terminal Identity. The Virtual Subject in Postmodern Science Fiction*, Durham and London: Duke University Press.

Deleuze, G. (1985), *Cinema 2: L'image temps*, Paris: Les Éditions de Minuit.

Deleuze, G. (1988), *Foucault [1986]*, Minneapolis and London: University of Minnesota Press.

Deleuze, G. and F. Guattari (1987), *A Thousand Plateaus. Capitalism and Schizophrenia [1980]*, Minneapolis and London: University of Minnesota Press.

Heidegger, M. (2002), *Off the Beaten Track*, Cambridge: Cambridge University Press.

Hook, D. (2017), 'What Is "Enjoyment as a Political Factor"?', *Political Psychology* 38(4): 605–20.

Janke, Wolfgang (1999), *Kritik der präzisierten Welt*, Freiburg and Munich: Karl Alber.

Kittler, F. A. (1999), *Gramophone, Film, Typewriter* [1986], Stanford: Stanford University Press.

Lacan, J. (1997), *The Seminar of Jacques Lacan*, ed. Jacques-Alain Miller. Book VII. The Ethics of Psychoanalysis 1959–1960, New York and London: Norton and Company.

Land, N. (2011), *Fanged Noumena. Collected Writings 1987–2007*, Falmouth: Urbanomic.

Nietzsche, F. (2005), *The Anti-Christ, Ecce Homo, Twilight of the Idols [1888]*, Cambridge: Cambridge University Press.

Rooney, C. (2000), 'Deconstruction and Weaving', in N. Royle (ed.), *Deconstructions. A User's Guide*, 258–81, Houndmills, Basingstoke: Palgrave.

Singh, S. (1999), *The Code Book. The Science of Secrecy from Ancient Egypt to Quantum Cryptography*, New York: Anchor Books.

Chapter 7
Uncanny politics

Natalia Romé

The current conditions of our social life have proved to be particularly harmful to our mental health. Social studies have made use of various theories of the subject and subjectivity in an attempt to describe and explain these phenomena. The conjunction is not simple; a vast range of contributions is settled between more or less constructivist options of the subjective and more or less subjectivist versions of the social, with risks ranging from the extreme sociologization of psychic life – without rest or unconscious – to the psychologization of social life – without the capacity to identify the complexity of historical determinations that shape it.

In the 1960s, Louis Althusser developed his theory of ideology in order to theorize the complex mediations that connect the social historical with the unconscious psychic. The concept of ideology was, nevertheless, discarded in the following decades by various theoretical traditions that preferred to work with the categories of discourse, performativity and identity, among others.

However, these traditions have shown their limits when dealing with the current subjective configurations in which the dimension of unconscious affect is shown with particular symptomatic force. With the honourable exception of the developments carried forward by the Slovenian school, by Slavoj Žižek, Alenka Zupancic and Mladen Dolar, among others, and by certain critical and political readings of psychoanalysis, such as those developed by Ian Parker, David Pavón Cuellar and Jorge Alemán, among others, today there are relatively few theoretical tools capable of thinking about forms of social bonding increasingly characterized by rigid attachments to belief systems, reactionary segregationism and various forms of contempt for others and for oneself.

In this context, going back on Althusser's tracks does not seem a bad idea. In the following pages, I intend to explore some aspects of his work concerning the links between ideology, the unconscious and politics which, as I understand it, allow us to provide new elements and different nuances to those developed by the aforementioned perspectives.

The gravitation of psychoanalysis in Althusserian thought can be organized around two concepts: overdetermination and interpellation. With regard to the former, the explicit references to Freud in *Lire le Capital* and *Pour Marx* are connected to the materialist reformulation of dialectics and the problematization of the category of time. The relevance of psychoanalysis to this problem is of an ontological depth which would be difficult to reduce to a few theoretical questions because it is rather connected to the very conception of theory. However, the productivity of Althusser's encounter with psychoanalysis is often reduced to the concept of ideological interpellation, producing a 'regional' reading of his thought without considering important areas of his writing in which psychoanalysis plays a significant role.

Against these reductive interpretations, it is worth revisiting Althusser's reading of Machiavelli, where a detail comes to light: it is in the temporal interlude between Althusser's first manuscripts on Machiavelli in 1962 and the final writing of the volume *Machiavelli and Us*, written in 1972, that the substance of Althusser's reading of Lacan takes place.

I believe that Althusser's interest in Machiavelli must be taken seriously into consideration when reviewing his theoretical connections with Lacan because this opens up the possibility of an approach to the articulation between ideology and unconscious that opens the problem of politics considered rigorously, as a contradictory and overdetermined conception of class struggle and not in the reduced sense of state domination or sociological antagonism.

It is within this development that the instance of *jouissance* can be found in Althusser's thought in terms of an *impasse* – or a constitutive equivocity – in the structure of the ideological interpellation. In other words, the contribution of this Lacanian problematic to Althusser is not only the clue to think about the unconscious dimension of ideological attachment but also the relation between unconscious and political struggle.

Reading Machiavelli, Louis Althusser renews the old Marxist question: How do ideas become active? And this is because there is something in Machiavelli's writings itself that disturbs him, as it had disturbed Gramsci, decades earlier. In the dark night of fascism – Althusser writes – Machiavelli 'speaks' to Gramsci about the future.

Machiavelli's theoretical discourse is organized in a quite peculiar scheme. *The Prince* develops an undeniably rigorous political theory, in which, nevertheless, everything is built around a central point that 'endlessly escapes detection', Althusser poses. Machiavelli elaborates on a theory 'presented in the form of fragments of a whole that has been deemed "unfinished" (Croce), but instead seems absent' (1999: 15).

This 'central point' around which the incompleteness of the discursive whole is structured and which pushes theory into a paradoxical conceptual discursive dispositive is the (necessarily vacant) space for the political task, or in Althusser's terms, the place for *the fact that has to be done*. How can theoretical discourse deal with the future of political action which is somehow its main concern?

Machiavelli's theoretical dispositive offers a practical answer to this question.

A void space is located within discourse for the unpresentable of concrete political practice, which presupposes the position of the singular 'case' – that, by definition, resists the form of judgement – and opens up theoretical discourse to certain indeterminacy.

This space of the political in the theoretical is conceived by Althusser as an 'internal distance' that makes place for a double and complexly articulated temporality. First, we can find there the delicate question of the materialist dialectic, understood by means of the Freudian category of *overdetermination*, considered by Althusser as the clue to understanding the specificity of historical necessity: a *necessity of contingency*. This dialectic constitutes the disjunct-unity between theoretical practice and political practice, as a temporal knotting of two moments: the moment of the reading of history – the reading of a *fait accompli* – and the 'current situation' of political thought, which is the question about what is to be done.[1]

The presentation of the *unpresentable* – and not the non-represented – is the core of political theory, which appears always necessarily displaced, as a *décalage* or a dislocation in theoretical discourse. And the point where discourse shows an *impasse* is perceived by the reader as a 'familiar strangeness', to pose it in Freudian terms.

This kind of interrupted closure of the writing allows us to identify the heterogeneous coexistence between ideas and political action. The *impasse* works in the text as a practical interpellation which operates in absence – as if it was elided. It is the interpellation formulated to a (political) subject that will not exist if it does not consist of an effective gathering of real forces. But, of course, this condition surpasses the text, so it could only be formulated in the text as a void or an inner distance of discourse.

One of the great questions of the Marxist tradition, since the famous Thesis XI, is the question regarding how ideas can become active. This question can be read by Althusser in Machiavelli, as I have shown, but points towards Freud. In 1977, Althusser noticed that whoever opens *The Prince* and the *Discourses*, both texts that are more than 300 years old, finds themselves trapped by what Freud called a 'familiar strangeness' or *Unheimlichkeit*. Without knowing why, these ancient texts challenge us, while 'their thinking continues in us, in spite of us, disrupting what we think, and catching us by surprise, *like an infinitely proximate thought*' (Althusser, 2006: 469).

The 'place' of this affectation of theory by the otherness of theory can be encircled in the structure of its discursive forms as the space of a rarefication of the experience of time: there, where discourse offers us an anachrony that coincides with political power and contours the loop of a rupture and a redoubling.

This suspensive place is the place of the subject in the structure, understood as a reinscription of the limit from its own unpresentability (Balibar, 2005). Of course, to speak of 'subject' and 'structure' in these terms is only conceivable if one assumes an internal displacement, an immanent movement in the so-called 'structuralist' tradition. The movement that coincides with the Lacanian development of Freud's psychoanalysis and from which the structure, as Jacques-Alain Miller says, has an action (Miller, 1968: 94); that is to say, the correlative subject of this structure is not transported in the chain but inserted within it (Miller, 1985).

Althusser is interested in the double – historical and discursive – concern implied within the tension of Machiavelli's encounter between fortune and *virtu*; that is, between the contradictory articulation of the conjuncture – its determined contingency, the 'weakest link of the chain' – and the *libido* understood as a driving force. Machiavelli is not interested in 'the truth of things' in general, but in the Thing (*das Ding*): 'The "thing", in its singularity, the singularity of its case. And the "thing" is also the cause, the task', Althusser remarks (1999: 16).

The movement that makes of objectivity, fortune and contingency, virtue, constitutes the current pulse of a discourse that materializes in its device the staging of that decentred and transindividual *topique* in which the space of a strange encounter of times is drawn.

A *topological approach* enables the practical conception of ideas as *thesis*, which to say, positions in an occupied field, active practices.

The political efficacy of Machiavelli's discursive dispositive rests precisely on its singular *topique*. It is the disposition – *disposition* – of the elements in the discourse that explains, as Althusser suggests, its interpellatory and, at the same time, disidentifying efficacy.

The disposition of significant elements in discourse explains the 'uncanny familiarity' – *Unheimlichkeit* – that disturbs the reading. And this is the only way in which a thought can intrude on us by disrupting what we think, 'catching us by surprise' (Althusser, 2006: 469). A place is thus made, Althusser says, in this theory that thinks and maintains an immanent *distance* for political practice, through the gap between the definite and the indefinite, between the necessary and the unforeseeable. This mismatch, thought and unresolved by thinking, is the presence of historical objectivity and of the future of political practice in theory itself (Althusser, 1999).

The Freudian notion of *Unheimlichkeit* was taken up by Lacan in his 1962–3 seminar, 'producing an inflection in the reading of Freud, in order to recover the libido-rest in relation to desire and its cause' (Consentino, 1998: 101, my translation). Lacan introduces the Freudian *Unheimlichkeit*, in relation to anguish, to indicate a point of the drive irreducible to imaginary investiture (Lacan, 2006: 55). He locates the turn that goes from desire (of the Other) to the field of *jouissance*, where anguish, as part of the real or as a nomination of the real, is what will give meaning to the nature of jouissance (Consentino, 1998: 115).

> The *Unheim* is poised in the *Heim*. [. . .] if this word has a meaning in human experience, we have here man's home, his house [. . .]. Man finds his home at a point located in the Other that lays beyond the image from which we are fashioned. This place represents the absence where we stand. Supposing that, which does indeed happens, it shows itself for what it is namely, the presence that lays elsewhere which means that this place is tantamount to an absence – then it becomes the queen of the game. It makes off with the image that underpins it, and the specular image becomes the image of the double with what all the radical uncanniness it bring. (Lacan, 2004: 47)

Wondering about the experience of a 'familiar strangeness', underlining the connection with *Unheimlichkeit*, is to question the relation between discourse, desire and fantasy. This enables us to think of politics at the boundaries of ideology (i.e. as an exteriority immanent to the tendential ideological enclosure and homogenization of discourses). This problematic operates practically with regard to ideological struggle, as a double problem: that of the constant siege of the ideological capture of politics and that of the inherent politicity of every ideological discourse.

The ideological struggle is the resistance to one's own storytelling. Narrative structures offer the paradigmatic scene for the solidarity between Subject and Meaning 'evidences' (cf. Althusser, 1988: 53). This is, in other words, the field of the phantasm: 'Freud doesn't insist just for the sake of it on the quintessential dimension that the field of fiction imparts to our experience of the *unheimlich* [. . .] since this effect allows us to see the function of the fantasy' (Lacan, 2004: 49).

The scenic condition of the structure of the subject's interpellation can be considered as a theoretical reconstruction of a figure 'at once religious and police' that allows us to appreciate the 'theatre of consciousness (I think, I speak, I see you, I speak to you)' from behind the scenes (Pêcheux, 1982: 105).

> The power of *mise en scene*, the 'poetic' effect that takes you right to the scene, thus depends on the implicit condition of a displacement (*decalage*) of origins (of the 'zero points' of subjectivities), a displacement from the present to the past, coupled with the displacement from one subject to other subjects, which constitutes identification. (Pêcheux, 1982: 119)

As we read in Laplanche and Pontalis: just as collective myths attempt to provide a representation that dramatizes it as a moment of emergence or as the origin of a history, the origin of the subject is represented in the *original scenes* (1968: 145). Similarly, Slavoj Žižek (1997) stresses that every historicization, every symbolization must represent this *gap*, this transformation of the Real into history which psychoanalytic clinical experience testifies, as a continuous struggle for secure entry into the terrain of historicity. It is impossible not to recognize in Žižek's idea the tacit evocation of Althusser, who placed the contingent temporality of the beginning – the absolute prior question – at the basis of his definition of the object of psychoanalysis, as a struggle for survival or 'long forced march': the *'nâitre ou n'ettre pas'* of the subject (cf. Althusser [1964] 1993).

The consideration of the scenic (phantasmatic) consistency of the interpellation allows us to recognize the mystifying/demystifying force of the theatrical metaphor, which can be helpful for a critique of the Philosophies of Consciousness, in solidarity with a critique of political philosophy, where it has undoubtedly played a very important role.

Not by chance, Althusser has devoted himself extensively to the question of the link between the materialist critique of philosophy (Marx) and the problematization of theatre, especially in Brecht's notion of 'distancing effect' (*Verfremdungseffekt*), appealing to the idea of the unconscious as a determination *à la cantonade* of a scene (cf. Morfino, 2014: 95–122).

Thus, the strictly real and not merely symbolic condition of Althusserian overdetermination allows for a densification and complexification that demands the account of the political problem in a differentially articulated relation with the ideological – and neither immediately subsumed in it nor as its ultimate truth.

The expository value of a topical approach to discourses as this one consists in its capacity to expose the interstitial space 'between' instances. Of course, only in the framework of a complex consideration of structural causality as real immanent causality (that is, as the efficacy of the structure in its effects), can this be possible.

Hence, an important nuance can be understood between Žižek's work on the relation between *jouissance* and fantasy as a way of thinking about the efficacy of subjection to power and the materialist perspective that weaves from Althusser to Pêcheux, as a question of a politicization of the bond between *jouissance* and fantasy that, far from consecrating domination, opens up its pulsation to ideological struggle. However, it should also be noted that, through the fidelity of his reading, Pêcheux in fact goes a step further than Althusser with regard to the relations between *jouissance* and politics, taking the game of *décalage* between instances of a *topique* to the extreme.

In his later works, Pêcheux moves beyond what we might call a 'materialism of the imaginary' (cf. Montag, 2013) where the real is registered from the notation of its effects – considered as an extimate relation between split subject and signifier – towards a materialism of the real that traverses the regime of signifying materiality in order to interrogate the materiality of the *letter* or of the *spoken* which Lacan tried to identify with the neologism *lalangue*.[2]

It thus opens up an instance that complexifies the materiality and temporality regimes which the encounter between Marxism and psychoanalysis makes possible, in order to locate 'a "pulsation" by which the unconscious non-sense endlessly returns in the subject and in the meaning which is supposedly installed in it. There is no cause save for something jarring (Lacan)' (Pêcheux, 1982: 217).

The detection of unconscious non-sense in discourses makes it possible to identify a constitutive *impasse* in the ideological ritual, the failure of the dispositive of interpellation that makes metaphor and equivocity coincide in the signifying materiality of discursive processes. Therefore, it turns possible to grasp ideological interpellation in its ritual condition, which 'in all its implications presupposes recognition that there is no ritual without disruptions, lapses and flaws: "one word for another", that is the definition of metaphor, but it is also the point at which a ritual fractures in the slip' (Pêcheux, 1982: 217).

By detecting *décalage* as an oscillation of the unconscious immanent to the metaphorical constitutive condition of discourses, M. Pêcheux poses the question of the *chance* of resistance, a chance that is connected to the functioning of the *real* in the dominant ideology.

The force of the equivocal indicates the place of a split in the subject which is not a 'void' but an excess, a heterogeneous *plus* at the intersection of the symbolic and the imaginary.

This discovery calls for a singular type of analytic operation because it connects with another material instance of language, no longer understood as the field of the word but as *letter* (and discourse).

This instance discovered by Lacan in his later writings and named with the notion of *lalangue* points towards a transition from Freud's energetic consideration of *jouissance* towards a 'political economy' of *jouissance*, which relies on the analogy with Marx's *surplus-value* [*Mehrwert*] to define *plus-de-jouir* [*Merlust*] (2006 [1968–1969]: 17–19)

This diversification of *jouissance* introduces a new type of analytical intervention. The first one is oriented to produce a critique of the imaginary sense of discourse; the second one is intended to catch non-sense as the real of discourse.

In the first sense, the identification of *jouissance* leads to a kind of critical intervention which is oriented to cut the link between signifiers to contravene the compulsion to signify (imposed by the phantasm) and the *jouissance* of phantasmatic sense' and to unsettle the imagination of plenitude in which ego and meaning coexist.

In the second one, the political-economic consideration of *jouissance*, the intervention is oriented towards encircling the symptomatic jouissance that points to the unconscious real by 'conceiving the letter as a border between knowledge and *jouissance*' which consists of 'breaking, by means of equivocation, the signifier that sustains the symptom' (cf. Arenas, 2017: 38).

Thus, the ambivalence of the disjunct-unity of sense and non-sense in the materiality of the letter is captured as a regime of materiality connected to an irreducible poetic instance of language beyond meaning.

This poetic function – which Lacan notes as *lalangue* – is revealed as a notation of the limits of prosaic language, to recognize that the subject is the ground of a schism or a *chance*.

> [the] punctual, fading subject is divided between two contradictory tensions, one to hold on to what represents it, the other, on the contrary, to escape it. In the end, it would be a question of giving an account of the spring of what can push one to look for a signification or a meaning each time that '*ça parle dans le monde*', to use Lacan's formula [. . .] The subject's recollections can be the occasion as much of the reinforcement of a subjugation as, on the contrary, of an opening. (Henry, 2012: §28, my translation)

Lacanian development of the connections between *jouissanse* and *non-sense* enables Pêcheux to place a constitutive ambivalence in the core of ideological interpellation.

The equivocity of the ideological ritual thus takes on its real dimension as a failure of linguistics understood as an effort to formalize language, including the subject in the singular and unrepresentable of its enunciation, which involves an unconscious instance that is irreducible but apprehensible through the notation of its effects (cf. Milner, 1968: 347).

This surplus connects with what, inspired by the concept of surplus value, Lacan calls *plus-de-jouir*, while indicating, at the same time, that *plus-de-jouir* is only a part of *jouissance*. This is why, Pêcheux insists that,

> The reason revolt in human history is coeval with the extraction of surplus labor is that the class struggle is the motor of that history. And the reason, on quite another plane, that revolt is coeval with language is that its very possibility rests on the existence of the division of the subject inscribed in the symbolic. The specificity of these two 'discoveries' will not allow them to be fused in any theory whatsoever, even a theory of revolt. But a glance at the price paid for their foreclosure forces us to admit that they have something to do with each other politically. (Pêcheux, 1982: 217)

Given this, I understand that the location of the equivocity of ideological rituals can be read as an opportunity for the politicization of the *surplus-jouissance*. But this is not in itself identical to an ethics of emancipation. The ambivalent condition of *jouissance* must be taken seriously. The equivocity of ritual as a force of ambivalence immanent to the devices of subjection is precisely that unguaranteed terrain on which phantasms or, why not, spectres circulate.

The word 'spectre', says Pêcheux (1982), can be understood in several senses: the phantasmal figure of the spirit of the dead returning to haunt the living; the religious or mystical images of glorious bodies, turned into terrifying visions of scarecrows running through history; or the old trick of phantasmagoria, intended to produce, for the spectators, the illusion of an unreal presence, trading on stage with the actors of flesh and blood.

This irreducible real ambivalence of discourses supports the efficacy of spectres of any kind. Under given historical conditions, discursive constitutive equivocity could open to the chance for emancipation from dominant meaning or to the experience of the uncanny, the originary fear of disintegrity. The concrete efficacy of spectral abstractions such as 'the people'; 'the multitude', inscribed in the very practice of every language, is marked precisely by the displacements and transfigurations that affect the real of the unpresentable immanent to the work of representation of any political process.

> no discourse actually spoken by humans can be completely separated from the conditions of possibility (or the antecedents) that haunt it: the Nietzschean aphorism, according to which men will not get rid of religion as long as they continue to adhere to grammar, suggests that a society totally free of religion, whether that of a god, of a people or of a nation, of the Working Class or of mankind, of Science or of Method, or of its own Subjectivity, is perhaps impossible. Thus, if in the revolutionary space, it is a question of the passage from one world to another, the relation to the invisible inevitably arises there, as it does in the historical forms of the counter-revolution: the whole constitutes a single, contradictory process in which the relations between language and history are woven. (Pêcheux, 1982, 67, my translation)

Abstractions such as 'the masses', 'the proletariat' and 'the class struggle' cannot be represented (painted, filmed or televised) in a state of concepts without transfiguration [*travestissement*] – as happens with the Freudian unconscious – suggests Pêcheux.

This leads us to a final conclusion: if with Pêcheux we can say that the relation between phantasm and jouissance is not necessarily an enclave of domination – which distinguishes his understanding from Slavoj Žižek's (1997) reading of the matter – neither can we believe that in this ambivalence of the equivocal of *lalange*, it inevitably anchors the politicity of resistance as seems to be the perspective deployed by Judith Butler (1993), among others.

On the contrary, the opportunity of politics as active resistance to oppression, or as ideological struggle, demands reinscribing the links between the unconscious real and the real of history in the contradictions of an overdetermined conjuncture, that is, a case in which repetition finds its singular transfigurations. These transfigurations in which the spectres 'incarnate' take their materials from the historical conjuncture and, therefore, their contradictory condition.

> It would not be the first time that the ruling class has anticipated its adversaries by understanding what resistance and revolt displace in the established order, to take political advantage of it [. . .] From the *medium* in trance who made himself visible through his voice in radio Germany in 1933, to the audiovisual *spectrum* of contemporary media, what a progress in the art of making the masses walk, producing the invisible for them! (Pêcheux, 1982: 66, my translation)

Inversely, the equivocity immanent to all interpellation is the constitutive precariousness of all political representation; not only the precariousness of its duration but also the ambivalence that can turn, at every instant, love into hate and power into impotence.

This statement is crucial for the political efficacy of discourses in ideological struggle, and it returns us to Machiavelli. Machiavelli's political theory points out towards the empty centre of power.

In the place where the typically narrative political discourses place the Subject of the drama (the *hero*) as the centre of the scenic artifice of History and of the theatre of consciousness, Machiavelli places a void. But this void is not pure negativity but a play of mirrors and redirections without a centre or nucleus of truth, which indicates the unequal relationship of *transference* between the Prince and the People.

Machiavelli discovers the force of power as a connection of *jouissance* and phantasm, while he wonders how to guide *virtú*, in order to produce a real conjugation with fortune, being *virtú* the capacity to maintain, *in a lasting way a*, favourable conjuncture 'well beyond the moment when the "feminine" fantasy of fortune is offered to her conqueror' (Althusser, 1997: 15).

The (imaginary) power of the Prince in relation to his people lies in 'the emptiness of a distance taken' with respect to himself, in control of his own passions. It is a game of transference and counter-transference with no guarantee, constitutive ambivalent.

> The mastery of the passions in Spinoza, far from being able to be interpreted as an intellectual liberations of a negative efficacy of the passions, on the contrary consists in their subsumption united with the internal displacement of the 'sad passions' to the 'joyous passions'. Just as later in Freud no fantasy ever disappears but – and this is the effect of the cure – is displaced from a dominant position to a subordinate position [. . .] for this conatus torn between sadness and joy, what is it there by anticipation if not the *libido* torn

between the instincts of dead and life, between the sadness of *Thanatos* and the joy of *Eros*? (Althusser, 1997: 18–19)

This development of the relation between *phantasm* and *jouissance* is translated by Althusser into a consideration of the relationship between ideology and politics, both as an exercise of domination (the question of subjection) and as a process of practical transformation within the (political) struggle in the ideological.

The splitting of the subject, which Balibar read as a constitutive tension of interpellation (better expressed in the French *as(sujet)isement*), allows us to think of the place of a contradiction or internal tension in the very *topique* of the signifier. *Assujetisement* precisely points out, with all the force of ambivalence, the question of the 'place' or the home of the (unconscious) subject in (ideological) subjection. So, politics *qua* autonomy exhibits its aporetic condition insofar as it finds its place in the very core of heteronomy and deploys its heterogeneity (and its resistance) not as inversion but as a paradoxical *immanent exterior* (Balibar, 2005: 159).

Read by Althusser, Machiavelli reveals to us as a reader of Lacan *avant-la-lettre*. In an ironic and beautiful text, full of apocryphal quotations, Althusser jokes:

It has not been insisted enough that counter-transference is still transference (Freud, unpublished, recently published in German. *Nachlass* . . .). (1993: 171, my translation)

It has not been insisted enough that counter-revolution is still revolution (Machiavelli, *Discorsi*, II, XVIII. Mao Tse tung not quoting Machiavelli. Apocryphal works . . .). (ibid.)

Read under the light of ideology theory, the concept of *jouissance* conceived as an overdetermined core of discourses, not a pure negativity but a material *décalage*, a minimal ambivalence pulse of the structure, enables us to open a question about the conjunctural current conditions under which revolt discourses have turn into the so-called 'hate speeches', without reproducing a positivist or constructivist conception or subjectivity but opening the field for new research concerning the uncanny fibre of politics. This unit junction of sense and non-sense can be touched by a deep commitment to emancipation and justice as well as a conspiracy theory of apocalypse and catastrophe.

Notes

1 'about what makes it possible to act on History from within the sole history present, about what is specific in the contradiction and in the dialectic, about the specific difference of the contradiction which quite simply allows us, not to demonstrate

or explain the "inevitable" revolutions *post festum*, but to "make" them in our unique present, or, as Marx profoundly formulated it, is to make the dialectic into a revolutionary method, rather than the theory of the *fait accompli*' (2005: 179).

2 'To use this notion of *lalangue* is to accentuate the elementary, indeed atomist, idea that the phoneme constitutes the materiality of spoken language, just as the letter is the real of writing. Here, there is an essential point in the Lacanian conception of language: if the era of primacy of the Symbolic situated the signifier at the degree zero of the unconscious, the topological return to the Real makes the signifier a consequence of babbling, that is to say, it is tantamount to its objectal constitution' (Rassial J-J., Guérin, N., Petit, L, 2014: 12).

References

Althusser, L. (1993), *Écrits sur psychanalyse: Freud et Lacan*, Paris: Stock-IMEC.

Althusser, L. (1997), *Écrits philosophiques et politiques*, Paris: Éditions. STOCK/IMEC.

Althusser, L. (1997), 'The only materialist tradition', in W. Montag and T. Stolze (eds), *The new Spinoza*, Minneapolis and London: University of Minnesota Press, 3–20.

Althusser, L. (1999), *Machiaveli and us*, New York and London: Verso.

Althusser, L. (2006), 'Machiavelli's solitude', *Economy and Society* 17(4): 468–79.

Arenas, G. (2017), *Hacia una economía de los goces*, Buenos Aires: Gramma.

Balibar, E. (2005), 'Le structuralisme: Une destitution du sujet ?', *Revue de Metaphysique et de Morale*, número especial 'Repenser les structures', janvier.

Butler, J. (1993), *Bodies That Matter*, New York: Routledge.

Cosentino, J. C. (1998), *Angustia, fobia, despertar.Bs.As*, Eudeba.

Henry, P. (2012), 'Tirer lalangue', *Essaim* 2 (29): 97–109.

Lacan, J. (2004), *Anxiety. The seminar of Jacques Lacan Book X*, Cambridge: Polity Press.

Lacan, J. (2006), *D'un Autre à l'autre- 1968-1969. Le Seminaire, Liver XVI*, Paris: Seuil.

Laplanche, J. and J.B. Portalis (1968), *Diccionario de psicoanálisis*, Barcelona: Labor, 1981.

Miller, J.-A. (1968), 'Action de la structure', *Cahiers pour l'analyse* 9: 94–105.

Miller, J.-A (1985), 'Struct'dure', *Pas tant*, 8–9.

Montag, W. (2013), *Althusser and his contemporaries*, London: Duke University Press;

Morfino, V. (2014), *El materialismo de Althusser*, Santiago de Chile: Palinodia.

Pêcheux, M (1982), *Langage, semantics and ideology*, New York: St Martins Press.

Pêcheux, M. (1982), 'Délimitations, retournements et déplacements', *L Homme et la société* 63–4: Langage et révolution. 53–69.

Rassial, J.-J., N. Guérin, and L. Petit (2014), 'The Lapsus, Lalangue and Adolescence', *Recherches en psychanalyse* 1(17): 46–53.

Žižek, S. (1997), *The plague of fantasies*, New York and London: Verso.

Chapter 8

Necro-society and jouissance

The acrobat, Lilith, and the Romantic machine

Obed Frausto

Introduction

For Sigmund Freud, the death drive is one of the opposite and inverse forces that exist in the depths of our culture. This force can be expressed in the sexual desires and aggressions that are fighting in our unconsciousness. The death drive reflects what exists in nature. Forces of death are present in all species, in their interrelation within the environment and in their micro-macro, bio-chemical natural processes. The death drive is a destructive energy that manifests in humans as a natural predisposition to commit evil acts.[1] Freud states that the unconsciousness, or the psyche, is a machine or apparatus that allows the encounter of two antagonistic forces: life and death, or in other terms, *Eros* and *Thanatos*. Psyche is a mechanism or a dispositive, very similar to Foucault's biopolitics in which biological-social life is controlled and produced by technological mechanisms manipulating individual bodies and social groups. While Foucault describes a social conglomeration, Freud describes in order to understand the individual psyche. Freud conceives the psyche as virtual, which means a metabolic mediation 'in between' the body and the world, similar to an image being captured by a telescope. Contrary to Galileo Galilei's telescopic observation of sunspots in which he locates a specific time and space in the universe, Freud's virtuality is not located in any biological or organic position.[2] Yet virtuality makes the interaction between dreams and fantasies possible, which allows mental disorder in the psyche to be manifested. While Freud used the metaphor of the apparatus to express the human need to expel destructive forces or alterations produced by the death drive from the psyche or the culture,[3] Lacan uses the metaphor of the mirror stage to separate desire from the structure of the ego and thus he discovers the illusion of Freudian narcissism,[4] which focuses on the idea of a hermeneutical and imaginary perception of the ego. Lacan believes that the notion of narcissism is a dual imaginary expression between the ego and the other.[5]

In this interaction between the ego and the other, the human language that expresses life appears, because it is living people who articulate their language and it continues to live thanks to the objects, artefacts, devices and manuscripts passed down from generation to generation. This process creates the impression that life vanquishes death. Human beings have evolved in such a way that the pleasure principle has overcome the destructive forces of the psyche. However, in the end, the death drive defeats the pleasure principle because there is a predominance of death due to the biological tendency for all human bodies to experience loss of vital functions. Similarly, cultures, communities and societies tend to die over time. In different cultures and societies, the same antagonist logic is replicated in human culture as linguistic symbols and signs that represent the act of living and the act of dying. Impulses are the bridges between nature and culture. They are symbiotic and are intertwined. This is the advantage of crutches that allow humans to perceive the world. The purpose of this chapter is to understand the connections within organic and biological forces that are located in the instincts and comprehend how capitalism extrapolates these forces to allow capital accumulation to continue while maintaining social order and motivation among individuals. I have been reluctant to accept the idea that neoliberalism, the current phase of capitalism, might be better explained by Foucault's conceptualization of biopolitics,[6] even though the notion of biopolitics is focused in order to grasp an organic and biological concept that signifies the force of life within its social restrictions and control. It is unable to capture the other dimension: the impulse of death. Foucault sustains that biopolitics is a pacific process in which violence inflicted by the state is a result of it abandoning the public space. By contrast, violence is incited by the subjectivity located in moral containments. Foucault argues that the institutional configuration of the state has been transformed, power cannot be located any longer, and the violent mechanism of the legal system is disappearing given individuals' moral imperative for freedom. Also, over the past several hundred years, science and technology have been undergoing modifications in terms of how human populations are controlled, that is, paradoxically by allowing more mobility of individuals but tracking them with artefacts and devices. The perception of violence has been transformed by the technological and scientific social process of modernity. Violence used to be more visual and more visceral, performed in public spaces.

Modern biopolitical technology is civilizing and refining violence making it more private and more tolerable. I believe that technology has always had a double edge, as posited by necro-political theories. In this chapter, I will not focus on the theory of sovereignty and the conformation of power that are explicit in the concept of necro-politics. Instead, I would like to understand necro-politics from the perspective of jouissance and desire based on recognizing the forces of death in the process of indulging individual pleasures through consumerism. I would agree with some arguments that suggest the existence of an explicit connection of neoliberalism with jouissance and desire.[7] However, what is missing is the acknowledgement of how the forces of pleasure idealized by neoliberal capitalism are producing the death of the population and the planet. In other words, neoliberal society favours a type of consumerism in which there is more attachment and more human awareness of market commodities than of exploited human beings. The purpose of the chapter is to provide several metaphors to help understand how neoliberalism is combining a nihilistic attitude with the acceleration of pleasure, accepting somehow the moral command of cynic hedonism and its effect that is producing death everywhere. Neoliberalism is an ideology that elevates market-driven behaviour over any other aspect of human conduct. Therefore, neoliberalism is commercializing and profiting from human and planetary death. In other words, death produces profit or there is an accumulation of death in favour of the pleasure of some. In what follows I discuss three archetypes of the subjectivity of neoliberalism: Nietzsche's acrobat, the first woman, Lilith, whom God created, and the romantic machine.

Nietzsche's acrobat

One of the archetypes of the subjectivity of neoliberalism was explained in Peter Sloterdijk's book *You Must Change Your Life*, in which the author posits that modernity has produced a new existential form of life that Nietzsche described in *Thus Spoke Zarathustra* using the figure of the acrobat. Sloterdijk uses the notion of the acrobat as an example of his idea of socio and psycho-immunological methods that create a *homo immunologicus* that is perfecting the anthropotechnics of living.[8] I would like to try another approach. In *Thus Spoke Zarathustra*, Nietzsche explains that Zarathustra's first disciple was an acrobat, whom Zarathustra considered to be an example of the noblest spirits after the acrobat's mortal fall. The prophet was inspired by the acrobat's death to explain a new form of enlightenment, wondering at the outset why this trapeze artist was not afraid of anything, not even the devil or the demon who would make him suffer after his death. The acrobat used to say that he was not much more than a tamed beast, taught to dance, receiving blows for a few crumbs. This metaphor explains the transition towards a modernity where there is no longer a community of saints following God's call, but of travellers or acrobats who belong to an organization whose members ive on the precipice of danger. Nietzsche's notion of the acrobat moves the frontier between the impulses of life and death. Survival is the acrobat's code: surviving danger balances the pleasure principle with death. This juxtaposition is accelerated within a logic of capital accumulation that has no limits to the fulfilment of pleasure and jouissance. However, the two driving forces of life and death are not synthesized, like the Hegelian dialectic where differences are transcended but are deformed or transmuted and fall back on various concrete levels of the real world. Social contexts deform the ambivalence of the impulses of life and death. With respect to the impulse of life, the acrobat encodes an expression of life based on the struggle for survival but magnifies danger. The modern hero is Goethe's Faust who abandons the ascetic call of 'the beginning is the verb' and converts to a new dogma, the principle of action without borders and limits of his own will. The archetypal figure of the acrobat allows us to understand that his way of acting superimposes his enjoyment and pleasure of danger on all things, even to the limit of his own existence and the existence of everything else. The acrobat, by putting his own life in danger, has no limit, no restraint on putting others and nature in mortal danger. Perhaps the figure of the business gambling addict perfectly exemplifies this archetype of the acrobat. Parasitic capital is extremely prevalent in our society. Thus, stockbrokers who buy and sell shares do not mind taking risks with them, nor do they mind making financial manoeuvres to increase profits with the immediate securitization of the credit portfolio through the sale of derivatives. It hardly matters if this acrobatic trick produces crisis, unemployment and poverty for the majority of the population.

Foucault's notion of life is overtaken and disrupted because it is no longer the same Foucauldian notion of life that is controlled by science and technology that bifurcates into a notion of biological life based on hygiene and health for the purpose of prolonging and intensifying life. However, this notion of life in its biopolitical form no longer adheres to the neoliberal form of life and death. The figure of the acrobat is a better analogy for understanding the life and death drive. The acrobat's gymnastics intensify the danger of life to the extreme. Only a few survive the danger of an extreme act. A dangerous manoeuvre represents the acceleration of death, of the acrobat's death. There is a devaluation of death, so it is easy to intensify the death of the population and of nature. An acrobatic act contains a level of uncertainty and randomness that is captured by cybernetic logic, although its form of power is still technified in a mechanistic way as if the act were a war against the wildness of nature, life and society. In addition, an acrobatic act also touches the dimension of criminality, since the acrobat performs criminal acts, risking his own life, without fear of death, not unlike other great criminal activities such as drug trafficking, human trafficking, forced prostitution, illegal animal trafficking, illegal fishing, money laundering, cybercrimes, corruption and evading taxes in offshore tax havens. The sum of all the profits from these activities could easily reach 40 per cent of the world's GDP. *Homo economicus* is a human who embraces a nihilism that assumes that there is nothing morally wrong and, because there is no moral limitation, there is a transmutation of the values that strike an equilibrium of the forces of life and death. Nihilism has been exceeded by a cynical hedonism. Instead of limiting desires or pleasures as ethical hedonism proposes, cynical hedonism involves intensifying pleasures and desires in order for us to be satiated. However, the sensation of jouissance is momentary, and *homo economicus* has a compulsion to waste his/her pleasure in consuming commodities. The consequence of this pleasure is, paradoxically, death afflicted on other areas or regions of the world.

Lilith, the first woman

That nihilistic, cynical, hedonist acrobat very nicely describes *homo economicus*. Yet, there are other dimensions that are missing, especially those that are gender related. To include these missing dimensions, I first discuss how women are demeaned and degraded in our current capitalist system. I explain how neoliberalism is becoming a libidinal and sexual force that traps individuals in a pleasure syndrome to consume and enjoy life through the figure of a sexualized woman. Women have a sexual-desire power that was overtaken by the accumulation of capital forces. Women's sexual desires are objectivized, and the sexual desire for women forces individuals to be obsessed and compelled to consume market commodities. Just as when Christianity became predominant and expunged women's sexual desire in order to maintain moral control over their bodies, now neoliberalism is doing the opposite. It is exacerbating sexual desires for women to maintain the motivation to consume and exult in market commodities. But at the same time, capitalism is producing a system in which dishonoured, poor and tormented men are raping, killing and murdering women in zones or areas of exclusion and banishment. Impoverished women are disposed of in a system in which the death drive has intensified. The accumulation of sexual desire for women has increased the pleasure drive in society, but it has also raised the level of violence and sexual aggression against women. In our contemporary society, we have witnessed the proliferation of femicides; in other words, capitalism propagates zones of high-intensity violence in which women are in danger most of the time.[9] The metaphor that I would like to use is the story of the first woman created by God in the Garden of Eden. There are two different stories of the creation of the first woman in the book of Genesis. The first one says a man and a woman were created at the same time from sand. The second one says that a woman was created from Adam's rib after the animals and plants were created. The first creation was the first woman whose name has been erased from the manuscript. Her story appears in heterodox narratives of the Jewish tradition. Her name is Lilith. Lilith was a rebellious, antagonistic and dissident woman of colour. She is tired of having sex with Adam in the inferior position. So, she insisted that because they were both made of the same material, she had the right to have sex on top of him. There was a fight between Adam and Lilith in which both realized they were powerful. Lilith decided to leave Eden. I believe that this story is very inspiring because Lilith represents an empowered woman who is capable of using her sexuality to challenge the hierarchical structure of religion and patriarchy. Religion created another story of a submissive woman who is blamed for the fall of human beings in a world dominated by men.

Marx's notion of capital accumulation has a connection with his ideas of religion as alienation. Alienation is a process in which there is a loss of meaning in the sacred or *sacer*. Sacrifice has its etymological root in *sacer* and *facere* which means making sacred. However, as Feuerbach explains, the sacred in God is constraining human necessities in order to satisfy God's laws and commandments. Marx argues that capitalism has a spiritual power that constrains human capacity. In other words, human beings are dominated and controlled by the products they build. It also implies a transmutation of values in which humans used to have possession of land and their own labour. With primitive capital accumulation, however, there was a violent process of dispossession of peasants and serfs from their lands who were then forced to undertake wage labour. This is why human beings have become commodities. Now they depend on material economic forces that they are unable to control. Silvia Federici points out that Marx's notion of capital accumulation does not consider women's role specifically vis-à-vis commodification through the exploitation of women and their sexual reproduction.[10] Yet Marx developed the concept of surplus value and surplus profit. Marx's main argument is that surplus value originates directly from workers' surplus labour and not from capital. Federici argues that Marx overlooked women's role in the process of accumulation in two ways: one in which the imperial elite used women's bodies to force them to have more children and thus increase the population of workers by eliminating contraception methods, forbidding abortions and limiting sexual relations to reproduction. The second method forced women to perform domestic duties without receiving a salary or compensation.

Marx believed that the real motivation for alienation was necessity, which connected to the material resources of physical labour. However, Lacan points out a different motivation which is pleasure and desire. Lacan recognizes that capital accumulation is not only material or economical but rather that there is a symbolic connection represented in surplus jouissance in which speech and language are material, and goods and services are embedded within the structure of the mind, called the *object petit a*.[11] This Lacanian concept refers to a non-obtainable desire that makes it impossible to get rid of the master, that is, capitalism. Two important concepts are needed to understand the notion of women and how it is articulated in the narrative of cynical hedonism. (1) Patriarchy is a structure in which women are possessed and dominated by men. One of its manifestations is the predominance of male sexual satisfaction, achieved by stimulating the penis, and an insistence that women's bodies satisfy men's sexual pleasure to the point that women's bodies are objectivized. (2) Capitalism and neoliberalism, as economic and ideological structures, are forcing human bodies, especially women's, to the point of exhaustion and a silent death in a process of alienation and exploitation. Women are unable to reclaim their own bodily desires.[12] There is also a dimension of death in capital accumulation that we can see from women's perspective. The consequence of accumulation under capitalism is that impoverished women are utilized for men's sexual satisfaction. All human desires are subsumed to the capitalist mode of production and consumption, and women are used to sell goods and services, and to maintain patriarchy in place. My perspective is neither religious nor moral against sexuality. I agree that Christianity has established forms of control and dominion over women, specifically with its discourse in which sexuality has been transformed into a taboo. Nobody is allowed to speak about sex and, because of the stigma, women's power is restricted. Also, Christianity has forced women to conceive children through anti-abortion legislation and has also denied them contraception because there is an explicit belief that sex is only performed for reproduction and not for satisfaction or pleasure. The capitalist system used women's sexual liberation to increase the labour force and thus reduce salaries, to subsume women's bodies to the machines of production and to seduce with their sexual power to consume.

The Romantic machine

Another aspect of capital accumulation is the prominent relationship that we have with artefacts. Using the concept of commodity fetishism, Marx revealed how humans attribute magical powers to inert artefacts because, according to Marx, real human relationships are hidden. However, since the nineteenth century, there has also been an opposite tendency to attribute moral and spiritual powers to machines. This movement had romantic inspiration because there is a relationship in which human feeling and organic forces are interrelated with artefacts and machines. Romanticism usually has an interpretation of prophetic connection with nature which criticizes modern society and its technology and industrialization. However, the prophetic dimension was seen by some French philosophers as an expression of a romantic machine.[13] Here prophesy has to do with increasing imagination that produces power to transform society.

In the same way, machines were perceived as charismatic objects capable of awakening dark forces that come from nature and emanate from the machine as living beings with dynamic forces. Walter Benjamin understands this passage with his concept of a work of art's aura, described in his 'The Work of Art in the Age of Mechanical Reproduction'. Aura is nearness at a distance. The death of aura is expressed by the reproductivity of art techniques by photography and film based on destroying the uniqueness of art creations that come across in the here and now. Traditionally, art was a symbolic connection with the religious ritual which is distant, sacred and hidden. In other words, it represents the death of metaphysics. There is a transmutation of values and the loss of aura is manifested by the process of mechanization whereby industrial production transforms humans into machines; also, camera-based arts perceive humans as mere objects. Benjamin argues that the technique becomes art or, in other words, the machine becomes humanity. However, the humanity that was captured in the machine is one-centric or narcissistic. The reason why the mechanism abandoned any spiritual connection with nature is because Cartesian physics overtook Leibniz's physical theory. In Descartes's world, there are two situations: one is the static, illustrated by the lever and balance, and the second is a coalition between bodies. In this static model, it is hard to capture velocity, in addition to the fact that velocity is not caused, but given. The collision of two bodies shows conservation, that is, the product of mass times velocity. Descartes conceived a closed and determined system that is losing connection with other dimensions and other aspects of life. In contrast, Leibniz conceived the universe as contradictory points in which everything conspires. Leibniz thought that the whole universe is constituted by noncommunicating monads. The perceived world is no more than an illusion that is constructed by the defined monads. The force is what brings together whole elements and different points of view. Force is not solely measured by instrumental reason or artefacts. Each measurement depends on the specific situation of interacting physical forces and metaphysical assumptions. Any measurement is always a fiction but it has to be a well-constructed metaphysical fiction. Where bodies collide, Leibniz sees the live force as a type of motion that was freed from its restraints. The acceleration of such a body would result in increasing velocity or a live force (*vis viva*). Equilibrium does not mean zero velocity after the collision, but rather an embryonic velocity in an indeterminable magnitude of measurement. The fact that a falling body gains live force shows that there is independence at the time of the fall. This is why Leibniz argues that it is impossible to imply that we can judge the state of cause and effect. In Leibniz's conceptualization of the machine, the relationship between cause and effect is related somehow to human choice. The machine is a synthesis with human beings. This is easier to see by means of the concept of labour: in a way similar to how humans tend to tire, machines reduce their efficiency due to friction. The creation of value is always occurring thanks to the combination of machine and human. For Karl Marx, however, this dialectical contradiction occurs only through human will. He did not give machines the potential or capacity to have will or desires. This is why his conceptualization of emancipation is always produced by human beings. Leibniz's notion of live force grants machines some form of will, given by God in this case. Machines are not only objects on which human will is based or the means by which humans act. Machines themselves are agents that produce social actions and use humans as a way to act. The production of value is made by labour during production. However, an important part of the commodity trading chain is consumption. Products are enjoyed by us, the buyers. But humans are enjoyed by machines, the products. Commodities are nonhuman artefacts and humans. In the same manner that Langdon Winner asked, 'Do artefacts have politics?',[14] I would ask: Do artefacts have desires? From a posthuman perspective, it is possible to conceptualize desire or jouissance as an unconscious desire of the other human; on the other hand, we should consider the assembling of humans and machines. Humans and machines are intertwined in a sophisticated and complex network and interact in the immaterial production and accumulation of pleasure. The game of jouissance is co-produced by other humans and other machines. Humanity and its tools will soon become cyborgs or hybrids. Humans can never again be separated from technology and, because of this imbrication, artefacts and machines are becoming subjects of desire. In this necro-society, the ensemble of non-human machines and humans is producing death. Modern technoscience is producing unintended consequences within various forms of human life. It may lengthen forms of life and death for humans, but simultaneously, it has been increasing risks that negatively affect human lives, for example, by increasing human exploitation, widening human-death zones, polluting the planet and provoking climate change.

We are living in a necro-society in which the death drive increases among the general population and the planet, and life as a cynical hedonism satisfaction is only exclusive for the few. I used three metaphors to capture this modern phenomenon: the acrobat, the expelled woman and the romantic machine.

Notes

1   Sigmund Freud, 'Formulaciones sobre los dos principios del acaecer psíquico' (1911), in *Obras completas de Sigmund Freud, vol. xii*, trans. José L. Etcheverría (Madrid: Amorrortu Ediciones, 2013).

2   Rosaura Martínez Ruiz, 'The Psychic Machine: An Economic Phenomenon of Life death', *Mosaic: An Interdisciplinary Critical Journal* 48, no. 4. (December 2015): 137–52.

3 Sigmund Freud, *The Ego and the Id*, trans. John Riviere (London: Hogarth Press, 1927).

4 Jacques Lacan, *Four Fundamental Concepts of Psychoanalysis,* ed. Jacques-Alain Miller, trans. Alan Sheridan (New York: W.W. Nort, 1973).

5 Robert Samuel, *Between Philosophy and Psychoanalysis. Lacan's Reconstruction of Freud* (New York and London: Routledge, 1993).

6 Obed Frausto, 'Biopolítica, necropolítica, mortispolítica y neoliberalismo', *Acta Sociológica* (accepted for publication).

7 José Luis Villacañas, *Neoliberalismo como teología política. Habermas, Foucault, Dardot, Laval y la historia del capitalismo contemporáneo* (Ulzama: NED Ediciones, 2020).

8 Peter Sloterdijk, *You Must Change Your Life* (Cambridge and Maiden: Polity Press, 2013).

9 Rita Segato, *La crítica de la colonialidad en ocho ensayos* (Buenos Aires: Prometeo libros, 2015).

10 Silvia Federici, *Caliban and the Witch. Women, the Body, and Primitive Accumulation* (New York: Autonomedia, 2014).

11 Ali Chavoshian and Sophia Park, 'A Body Without a Head: Lacan's Understanding of Body and its Application', *Body and Religion* (December 2020), doi:10.1558/bar.17782.

12 Beatriz Preciado, *Manifiesto Contra-Sexual* (Barcelona: Anagrama, 2011).

13 John Tresch, *The Romantic Machine. Utopian Science, and Technology After Napoleon* (Chicago and London: The University of Chicago Press, 2012).

14 Langdon Winner, 'Do Artefacts Have Politics?' *Daedalus* 109 (1980): 121–36.

Chapter 9

Jean-Luc Nancy

A philosophy for a transformative sexistence

Francesca R. Recchia Luciani

Preamble: s/objects of desire beyond biopolitics

Thanks to entertainment and social networks, the overexposure of bodies is disproportionately expanding in the media and communication society. What is the role of sex in the contemporary hypersexualized and objectified system? The practices of contemporary biopolitics unfold the modes of control in multifarious forms, exercising power over every aspect of human life. On the one hand, these practices reveal the exercise of domination and disciplining; on the other hand, they trigger reactive mechanisms of opposition, rejection, resistance and resilience – of course, including *sexual politics*. This implies that in the present age, in the totalizing sphere of communication, everything is invested with a biopolitical valence and sex cannot be an exception to this rule. Nevertheless, the sexual sphere can be sociologically investigated: for example, it can be understood as a space of inter- and intrasubjective connection and as a mirror of human vulnerability to otherness; indeed, sex can be analysed in the light of its implications for affectivity, or in the light of its implications for the market. In line with this research path, sex can be analysed in connection with the planetary and pervasive diffusion of mass pornography: phenomena which seem to announce the liquefaction of erotic and amorous relationships (Bauman) or even the death of Eros (Han). However, sex can be intended as a philosophical object among others, as Jean-Luc Nancy intends to do, so to say, as a theoretical target worthy of the attention that Western philosophy has scarcely reserved for it in its millenary development. Following the path taken by the French philosopher, in this contribution, we intend to shift the centre of gravity of biopolitical observation in a direction that goes beyond it. For several decades, Nancy has devoted his careful theoretical reflection to the body and corporeality in its transcendence of pure physicality. Then he has moved to a radical questioning of sex and the sexual relationship itself. Indeed, Nancy's philosophical question is authentically ontological because it goes beyond the sociological critique of the sexual inclusion – or exclusion – policies. His latest philosophy understands sex as a human relationship that refers to nothing but itself, a way of being in and of itself, where the occurrence of sexual practices illuminates the inseparable and essential link that exists between animal and divine, intimacy and exteriority.

On closer inspection, Nancy does not divert from biopolitical discourse; instead, he walks an alternative path, illuminating certain aspects and meanings overlooked by biopolitics. As is well known, biopolitical representation has vigorously changed contemporary thought, focusing on the perception/ conception of the body within the historical, social and cultural processes. More specifically, this theoretical turn takes place in parallel with Foucault's rewriting of the 'history of sexuality' from the eighteenth century onwards through the 'four great strategic unities which [. . .] formed specific mechanisms of knowledge and power centering on sex. 1. *A hysterisation of woman's bodies* [. . .]. *2. A pedagogization of children's sex* [. . .]. *3. A socialization of procreative behaviour* [. . .]. *A psychiatrization of perverse pleasure* [. . .]'.[1]

As Foucauldian theory illustrates, these extended strategies and practices of domination indiscriminately involve, control and subjugate the absolute majority of subjectivities, depriving them of the essential freedoms and the principle of self-determination. The adult heterosexual male – and only if he is incorporated within the socially relevant dimension of the procreative couple – remains the only subject who is barely or partially touched by these strategies and practices. Consequently, he is the only subject who is capable not only of *sexual* but also of *ethical* and *aesthetical* self-determination – as taught by Foucault. This fringe of Foucault's biopolitical analysis represents inescapable support for a battle for the liberation of bodies from their social role and hierarchization. Furthermore, thanks to the support of the feminist critical deconstruction of androcentrism and the postcolonial critical deconstruction of the mythology of race, this theoretical perspective unequivocally explains why such a poststructuralist biopolitical vision constitutes the theoretical foundation of a radical rethinking of the role of gendered bodies, as well as of the practices related to 'self-care' that run through them, within the common social and political space. However, as Lévinas explained, the '*enchaînement*' (*être rivé: being bound*)[2] that inextricably binds us to our corporeal nature is insurmountable, and this is true both when it is observed from the side of sexuality – for example, in the form of openness to desire, pleasure and love – and when it is understood in the sense of the vulnerability ontologically inherent to the transient and distinctive nature of the human – that is, the immanent exposure of the body to pain, suffering and death. As *embodied* – and, therefore, also *sexed* – *bodies*, human beings are all indistinctly subject to this double constraint, which represents the social-relational nature of their vulnerability and a peculiar trait of their being in the world.

Therefore, subjectivities qualify themselves above all as bodies in relation, and this relational interconnection binds, connects, 'chains' subjectivities to each other that must be plumbed. This relational interconnection constitutes a substratum circumscribed both by the logic of domination/subjection relations and the emancipator/liberating potential that can unhinge those power relations. This fundamental turning point is a historical achievement of feminism. It is also the starting point for any possible evolution of every theory interested in analysing how – and why – the body occupies a liminal position between nature and culture: a margin from which not only all 'gender issues' are inevitably redrawn but also the terms of our relationship with desired, lived and practised sexuality change. This observation allows us to overpass the personalistic essentialism and/or the mythical ontology of the single monadic individual – understood as the epicentre of an isolated and independent agency. Rather, protagonists are those subjects who – based on the relationality, including the sexuality of their bodies – break those rules of 'coherence and continuity' that the very idea of a 'person' acting within the social context would imply; those subjects who identify themselves with the communities and groups determined by sexual gender, as happened first for women and then for sexual minorities.

What does this imply? First, it implies that 'sex, gender, sexual practice and desire' no longer establish a logical *continuum*[3] defined by nature or biology; on the contrary, they are invested and overwhelmed by the revelation of their very socio-cultural rootedness, which prevents them from being conceived as symbolic or functional equivalents of social or biological roles or as segments of a predictive causality established in a priori based on a physiological-causal determinism based on pure and simple anatomy. Instead, they become the mutant forms that the desiring body of an embodied subject acquires, whatever sexual orientation it takes on as its own; through those mutant forms, that subjectivity establishes its relations and creates its vital interconnections: in this way, sex, gender, sexual practice and desire become free determinations of the *subject of desire* rather than functions of the social body.

From here, where in the social-political sphere, biopolitical practices of resistance-resilience or the deconstructive activism of feminism are initiated, Nancy's thought creeps in to conceptually dismantle the *already given* and philosophically interrogate those practices that make us embodied subjects in a sexed body. These subjects tread the paths of their search for jouissance, subjects-in-relation, s/objects of desire.

Sex as a philosophical object: 'Sexistence' before Sexistence

Jean-Luc Nancy's recent production around the theme of sex and a philosophical exploration of it, in particular a conference titled 'Sexistence' of 2015 and a book with the same title, published in 2017, *Sexistence*, testifies to an intense questioning around the meaning for human beings by the intimate relation that takes place in the sexual encounter.

Following the grammar of relation and difference, Nancy poses the question of how the body manifests itself in sexual practice; in this way, he transforms sex into a proper philosophical object. From such a perspective, Nancy returns dignity and conceptual relevance to an unmentionable taboo of Western thought: the meeting between sex and philosophy, a meeting that – as Anne Dufourmantelle has written – 'was scheduled [. . .] three thousand years ago. Officially, at least. Since then, it has been continuously postponed'.[4]

Nevertheless, Jean-Luc Nancy has no more extended patience for further postponements. Indeed, in his latest production, he tackles the question that had ardently appeared on the scene of his theoretical reflection in 'The "There Is" of Sexual Relation'; in this essay, he engaged in hand-to-hand combat with Lacan, programmatically overturning his assertion that 'there is no sexual relation'. In a later essay, 'There is Sexual Relation – and Then',[5] Nancy develops the discussion with the philosopher-psychoanalyst, taking note of the theoretical consequences that develop around a nucleus in which sex is brought back to intercourse; on the contrary, it is 'sexual relation [that] represents the incommensurability of relation on its own terms – isolated and played out for itself' and that shows us 'the absolute incommensurability of relation in general'.[6] In a conference entitled 'Sexistence', given in 2015 for the first time, and in the homonymous book of 2017, the French philosopher elaborates a true philosophy of sexed existence, that is, the explication of a philosophical theory which takes seriously the role of sex – and the critical consequences of this experiential-relational dimension for human beings.

Echoing, in his way, the 'pleasure of the text' which Roland Barthes already conceived as a sharing between the writer and the reader, a reciprocal fulfilment that we also find elsewhere, Nancy explains: 'We speak in order to come, and we come in order to speak – which is also to say that each one, both sex and language, substitutes for the other, and also excludes the other, exhausts and excites the other'.[7] We can find fulfilment in the pages that Nancy dedicates to the body and eroticism, in the pleasure of reading a text that makes sex its object without objectifying it. Moved by the shamelessness of the inexhaustible questioning, Nancy faces the inescapable dimension of the relational nature of humans whose stake is their corporeity and the sexual encounter: a dimension which connects bodies, creating horizontal links, affective nexuses and interdependencies. Even before *Sexistence*, he addresses the same themes in some short essays, places where bold thought and writing cross the crossroads, where the body has sex, and sex has the body. Texts that do not aspire to description/explanation, nor to an analytical understanding of what is happening: instead, they long for the knowledgeable entertainment of thought on that happening. They burst forth from that enchanted language game that philosophy has always and everywhere engaged in; a game that springs from the Platonic-Aristotelian *thaumazein*, that is, from the dismayed wonder in front of the things that happen in the world, a game that gives rise to the interweaving of *phileîn* (to love) and *sophía* (wisdom). From such a perspective, philosophy creates an argumentative space about sex – understood as an elective human activity – revealing an unconfessed and intimate affinity between Eros and Logos.

Sex and incommensurability

These 'sexistencial' writings make love to sex and eroticism. Paraphrasing Plato ('Philosophy, the object of my love', *Gorgias* 482a), it can be said that here Eros is not so much the subject of study of Jean-Luc Nancy's philosophy but its object of love. What is this love-loving philosophy? It is the exercise of a 'loving thought', as he calls it. Eros, indeed, has long been on Nancy's horizon of meaning, and he has developed several precise reflections and many generous digressions to this topic in books and lectures; nevertheless, in *Sexistence*, his gaze and attention to erotic love and sex reach the fusion point, investing his object of love with an action of deconstruction/extension of meaning. Nancy penetrates the nature of sex with the weapons of thought, focusing on the immense power of sex and how it acts on us. These texts do not aim at structuring an exhaustive depiction of eroticism; instead, they follow eccentric directions, questioning the sexual action and focusing on some of its characterizing traits. Sex and eroticism are placed under a magnifying glass to detect their invisible, hidden meaning and open new research paths.

For instance, in his confrontation with Lacan, Nancy overturns his negative statement that 'there is no sexual relation' into a positive assertion: underlining that the 'relation [*rapport*] is neither being nor becoming', Nancy focuses on the semantic and ontological value of the expression 'there is' of sexual relation, utilizing its performative quality. Furthermore, he suggests that the being of classical ontology 'must, on the contrary, appear as what we get to by subtracting from relation. Someone, someone withdrawn from all his relations – what is left of him? [. . .] he remains "one", always indefinitely withdrawing further away'.[8] Nevertheless, since we are dealing with Eros and the 'consequences of love', we could comment on these words by Nancy referring to Derrida's *Cinders* (*Feu la cendre*): what remains after the fire, the ardour, the amorous combustion is only cinder – 'il y a là cendre', 'there is cinder' – the dust of fire, but still – as in the verses by Francisco de Quevedo quoted by the philosopher – 'I am cinder that darkens in the flame / nothing that remains to consume the fire / that in amorous conflagration' [is dispersed], and 'will be cinder, but will remain sentient / will be dust but amorous dust'. ('*Yo soy ceniza que sobró a la llama; / nada, dejó por consumir el fuego, / que en amoroso incendio se der rama [. . .] serán ceniza, mas tendrán sentido; / polvo serán, mas polvo enamorado*').[9]

If some distancing from the ontology is inevitable because here *being* is 'off-screen', the 'there is' of sexual relation can tell us something else about the fire of erotic passion. Since in sexual relation there is proximity or intimacy or, as Nancy writes, some order 'of superlatives: the closest, innermost, what penetrates most deeply into these areas, into these nooks and crannies, into the secret (the sacred?) of the "one" as well as the other', the category that the 'is' – of the expression 'there is' – calls into question is with all evidence an 'approach. It is not a matter of a state but rather a movement [insofar as] the approach carries within itself both advance and recoil, taking up the approach again and again'.[10] In this case, 'there' has to be understood as a reiteration, a rhythmic, a compulsion to repeat that cannot be avoided; because the logic of 'there' consists in giving oneself again and again, in desiring the reproduction of an unsatisfied desire.

According to Nancy, 'the practice of this approach is called attention'. In this regard, we can refer to what – in a somewhat different context – Simone Weil writes to the mystical poet Joë Bousquet (among many other things, also the author of a Sadian-inspired erotic book, *The Black Notebook*) in the spirit of an authentic, intimate and intense friendship that unites them in their appeal to the supernatural: *attention* 'is the rarest and purest form of generosity'.

On the other hand, Nancy does not overlook that 'charity and lust are certainly opposed, but the one cannot be entirely unrelated to the other, [. . .]. Two underlying tendencies – which both bring together and splinter – have therefore governed and divided Christianity: an infinite diffusion of *eros* and an absorption of every desire and pleasure into an originary cherishing.'[11] Both attention towards the other on a supernatural level and attention towards the other in the intimacy between the living are gestures united by generosity: gestures establishing – once again and on another threshold – a kinship between sex (as the immanence of desire) and the sacred (as a flight towards the transcendent) always suspected of profanation: 'for it is indeed necessary in some way to love what one desires and to desire what one loves'.[12]

However, there is more in Weil's letter: 'Attention is the rarest and purest form of generosity. It is given to very few spirits to discover that things and beings exist'.[13] The reality of what is other than the Ego is not already given in itself; the interested practice of attention generates a fruit that cannot be taken for granted: the involving ascertainment of the existence of others. Such an involvement occurs, whether attention is sublimated in *agapē* – that is, in Christian compassion – or (beyond Weil's intentions) attention coincides with the care lavished on the other in the 'rooms of Eros', that is, in love and sexual relations. Therefore, an intimate connection between selfless attention and the caring and participatory propensity towards the other is manifested in the erotic relationship. In this latter case, the generous and oblative, profuse and unproductive attention towards the other is the key to the relationship, its sense and its meaning. Moreover, sexual relation is a unique condition in which the subject and the object of attention overlap, merge and combine horizontally in the same incommensurability, cancelling the vertical hierarchical order of the economic. An idea that leads us to Bataille, who exalted – in line with (and beyond) Mauss's theory of the gift – the ideal of *potlàc* without return understood as unlimited freedom, a freedom from the sphere of interest and, at the same time, the way to full individual sovereignty. By exalting the *potlàc*, Bataille celebrates eroticism and the sacrificial aspects of religious cults – sex and the sacred – as *dépense*, waste, dissipation and unproductive expenditure, 'pure energy' without limitations or ends but also as an 'accursed share' of human experience.

In Nancy's words, we can say 'that *the sexual in all relation* (linguistic, social, affective, aesthetic) resides in the dimension of unaccomplishment. There is sex where there is no production, no result, and no positing of any sort of term.'[14] A place littered with the 'infinite entertainment' of bodies, the limitless play and exchange of roles between incommensurable singularities. As Rainer Maria Rilke would say: 'Let one sink into the other to resist.'

Sex and vulnerability

Are we talking about a 'metaphysics of sexual love'? – 'Metaphysics' here is understood as the intensification of the originating physics of sex rather than its transcendence. Nancy does not mention the Schopenhauerian stigma of Eros; indeed, Schopenhauer condemns Eros to the eternal damnation of the monotonous serial reproducibility of specimens of the human species. Indeed, Nancy is not interested in the biological fact of generation, with its productivist-poietic côté ('Making love does something other than make a baby, even when it does that'[15]); instead, his philosophical interrogation starts from the realization that 'Sex is an abyss and a form of violence: through the latter, we submit to and fall into the former, where we understand nothing'.[16] If anything, this assumption echoes Kant's astonished and disclosing exclamation, who recoils before the possible – but equally inadequate – explanations about that 'abyss' and that 'violence'. On the contrary, Nancy contrasts those explanations with the need – neither explanatory nor analytical but coherently philosophical – to 'consider sex in terms of existential value – of a disposition inherent to the very exercise of existing'.[17] If, as Nancy writes in *Corpus*, 'love is the touch of the open',[18] love-making is an unconscious positioning of oneself, an unstable placing 'to the border of a "making" that essentially touches at the same time the dual beyond of the animal and the divine, two names that articulate nothing but existence as its own dehiscence, a sexistence'.[19]

'Dehiscence' has to be understood as a spontaneous opening, an unfolding of a 'dis-enclosure' (*déclosion*) – as the earlier Nancy would say: 'The eclosure of the world must be thought in its radicalness [as] the eclosure of eclosure itself and the spacing of space itself. [. . .]. Dis-enclosure confers upon eclosure a character that is close to explosion, and spacing confines it to conflagration.'[20] Understood as *sexistence*, this dehiscence exposes us, time and time again, to the violence and abyss of intimacy with the other, which can only take place in the 'world of bodies': 'the nonimpenetrable world [. . .] where *bodies initially articulate space*'.[21] This means that our condition of being single and contiguous bodies constitutes the only possibility of knowing each other. Our bodies allow us to expose ourselves to each other and reveal ourselves reciprocally: 'I will always know others as bodies. *An other is a body* because only *a body is another*'.[22]

Thus, the *Nude Body* (it is the title of a conference held by Nancy in 2011) takes centre stage, not as a natural fact but precisely as a body re-semantized by its nudity, which in contact (approach, proximity, contiguity) with the other's body changes sign and meaning to open itself up to the relationship – through a dehiscence, a *disclosure* – in the sphere of intimacy. 'Intimacy always corresponds to nudity in one way or another. The nude body is the intimate body.'[23]

There is assonance, a refractive effect between nudity and intimacy that recalls 'the interminable aspect of desire'.[24] Moreover, in this game of mirrors, in this *mise en abyme* – the abyss, again – the game of sex is played out; once again, sex has not to be understood as an entity, but only and always as a relationship: more specifically, as that polymorphous nexus between intimacy and exteriority that represents its cypher in the order of desire, repetition, excitement, enjoyment.

'Intimacy' – as Virginia Woolf wrote – 'is a difficult art'.[25] As everyone can see in his or her own experience: this difficulty depends on the fact that intimacy inevitably invokes the category of vulnerability, insofar as the price to be paid for nudity, intimate contact and carnal 'commerce' is the jeopardizing of one's privacy, of one's self as a reserved space, a protected place that becomes un-closed, open. In intimacy, everything is risked and revealed, including what rests in concealment: the secret – *secretum* means separated, set aside. Furthermore, the secret is brought to light in the revelation of the interiority that takes place in the relationship, including those egoic zones that are removed because they are too dry and uninteresting or compassionate and delicate or unbridledly creative and rebellious. *Vulnus* is the Latin word for wound, and *vulnerable* is everything that is exposed to the possibility of being injured, offended, hit and thus suffering; consequently, *vulnerable* is also everything that succumbs to the passions – a term that can be traced back to both the Latin verb *pati*, that is, to suffer, and the Greek verb *pathos*, in our tradition of thought always opposed to *logos*. Thus, the naked subject, who succumbs to intimacy in the relationship with the other, makes himself vulnerable to suffering and passion, pain and pleasure, absence and presence, death and love.

A philosophy that appeals to sex – and its power for human existence – leaves no room for moralistic and/or nostalgic discourse around an Eros agonized by the market and the postmodern/neoliberal logic of 'performance'. In the same way, this philosophy does not accept the considerations of a 'liquid' sociology that can only read contemporary eroticism through the hegemonic dynamics of the consumer society hinged on material possessions elevated here to a code of desire.[26] Sexuality does not admit to being reduced and circumscribed; it cannot be interpreted only through the linguistic codes of transgression or pornography, nor even less with the formalistic commodity-money scheme.

The transformative power of sex is immense, and this is something that feminism has long understood, pointing to sexuality as the revolutionary sphere par excellence: sexuality is the space of the 'erotic power',[27] as Audre Lorde – 'poet, feminist, Black, mother, warrior, lesbian' as she liked to call herself – would say. The 'erotic as power' is for her 'a well of replenishing and provocative force', the empowering feeling of joy that once experienced wants to renew itself continually and that can change people's lives, collectively and individually. It is the vital and irrepressible energy that, when released in a relationship, can trigger the change in each person's life precisely because, with Nancy, we must 'consider sex in terms of existential value' – as a 'sexistence'.

Sex is pure erotic energy, and the erotic is, therefore, that power that changes and transforms existence with its power.

Notes

1   M. Foucault, *The History of Sexuality 1. An Introduction* [1976], trans. R. Hurley (New York: Random House, 1978), 103–5.

2   E. Lévinas, 'Reflections on the Philosophy of Hitlerism [1934]', trans. S. Hand, *Critical Inquiry* 17, no. 1 (1990): 62–71.

3 J. Butler , *Gender Truble, Feminism and the Subversion of Identity* [1999] (New York: Routledge,2007).

4 A. Dufourmantelle, *Blind Date: Sex and Philosophy* [2003], trans. C. Porter (Urbana, Chicago, and Springfield: University of Illinois Press,, 2007).

5 J.-L. Nancy, *The 'There Is' of Sexual Relation' [2001] and 'There is Sexual Relation – and Then' [2005]* are both in J.-L. Nancy, *Corpus II. Writings on Sexuality*, trans. A. O'Byrne (New York: Fordham University Press, 2014).

6 Nancy, *The 'There Is' of Sexual Relation' [2001]*, 101.

7 Ibid., 103.

8 Ibid., 99.

9 J. Derrida, *Cinders* [1987], trans. N. Lukacher (Minneapolis and London: University of Minnesota Press, 2014), 55–7.

10 Nancy, *The 'There Is' of Sexual Relation' [2001]*, 99–100.

11 J.-L. Nancy, *Sexistence* [Article], trans. I. Goh. *Diacritics*, vol. 43 (Johns Hopkins University Press, 2015), 110–18, 114.

12 Ibid.

13 Letter to Joë Bousquet on 13 April 1942. S. Weil and J. Bousquet, *Correspondance*, Lausanne: Editions l'Age d'Homme, 1982, 18.

14 Nancy, *The 'There Is' of Sexual Relation' [2001]*, 101.

15 Nancy, *Sexistence* [Article], 117.

16 Ibid., 116.

17 Ibid.

18 J. L. Nancy , *Corpus I*, trans. R. Rand (New York: Fordham University Press, 2008), 29.

19 Nancy, *Sexistence* [Article], 117.

20 J. L. Nancy, *Dis-Enclosure. The Deconstruction of Christianity*, trans. B. Bergo, G. Malefant, and M. B. Smith (New York: Fordham University Press, 2008), 160–1.

21 Nancy, *Corpus*, 27.

22 Ibid., 31.

23 J.-L. Nancy, *Corpo nudo* [Italian version, 2011] in *Del sesso*, F. R. Recchia Luciani (ed.), (Napoli: Cronopio, 2016), 61–81, 73.

24 Ibid., 81.

25 V. Woolf, 'Geraldine and Jane', in *The Common Reader: Second Series* (1932).

26 Z. Bauman, 'On Posmodern Uses of Sex', *Theory, Culture & Society* 15, no. 3–4 (1998): 19–33.

27 A. Lorde, 'The Use of the Erotic: The Erotic as Power' [1978], in *Sister Outsider: Essays and Speeches* (Berkeley, CA: Crossing Press, 2007).

Inside and outside the psychoanalytic view of politics

Chapter 10

Daydream and emancipation

Against surplus-enjoyment, repression and their parallax of lack and excess

Nicol A. Barria-Asenjo, Slavoj Žižek, Brian Willems, Andrea Perunović, Ruben Balotol Jr. and Gonzalo Salas

Introduction

Throughout its thriving and turbulent history, psychoanalytic theory has influenced many different strands of thought in humanities and social theories. Moreover, as Alenka Zupančič rightfully remarks: 'psychoanalysis is also something that "happened" to philosophy and that philosophy cannot remain indifferent to.'[1] Therefore, psychoanalytic conceptual tools were and still are frequently used in diverse theoretical frameworks, in order to examine phenomena such as politics, ideology, society, culture, economics and so on. But maybe most importantly, and again according to Zupančič, psychoanalysis has 'allowed us to rethink and maintain the notion of the subject at the very moment when contemporary philosophy was ready to discard this concept as belonging to its metaphysical past'.[2]

Yet, the ways in which (Freudian-Lacanian) psychoanalysis has re-actualized the conception of subject provoked very different reactions: sometimes its reception was followed by approbation and exhalation, while other times it wasn't so warmly welcomed, and awakening scepticism and resentment. Moderate reactions to psychoanalytic discoveries concerning human subjectivity were much rarer, almost inexistent.

Arguably, the most ambiguous theoretical encounter that psychoanalysis had undergone with another discipline throughout its history, is the one with the postcolonial theory. The ways in which postcolonial thinkers relate to psychoanalysis still today carry a significant load of complexity and strong affective intensities – at least inasmuch as all the love-hate relationships do. Already in Frantz Fanon's *Black Skins, White Masks* published in 1952, one can feel the ambiguity taking place in the relationship between the two disciplines. In the first pages of his book, Fanon states that 'only a psychoanalytic interpretation of the black problem can lay bare the anomalies of affect that are responsible for the structure of the problem' (p. 12) (and further in the text uses abundantly terms like desire, narcissism, unconscious, neurosis, gaze, complex, etc.). At the same time, he states that his task is rather 'sociodiagnostic' and that 'the black man's alienation is not an individual problem' (p. 13). As Hook and Truscott (2013) observe: 'In this way it is more the pathological nature of society, "the neurotic structure of colonialism itself" (Fuss, 1994, p. 20) that is diagnosed [by Fanon], than an individual subject'.[3] It becomes clearly visible then, that the knot of Fanon's ambivalent relation with psychoanalysis is precisely pointing to the locus of the subject. In order to show that the 'individual approach' isn't suitable for the analysis of colonialism, Fanon will consecrate a whole chapter to Octave Mannoni's book *Prospero and Caliban: Psychology of Colonization*,[4] criticizing (to a large extent very rightfully, we could claim) the conception of 'dependence complex' of the colonized (Caliban) but simultaneously acclaiming (only in passing, though) the 'inferiority complex' of colonizers (Prospero).[5] So, again, the place of the subject happens to be the place of ambiguity. Further in the book, Fanon (1985) will claim that the Oedipus complex 'is far from coming into being amongst Negroes' (152), yet will keep considering (Other's) desire as universal. Anyhow, this ambivalent stance towards the psychoanalytic conception of subjectivity will be inherited by other postcolonial thinkers.

Gayatri Chakravorty Spivak (1993), for example, designated Freud as one of her 'flawed heroes', an 'intimate enemy'; and while rejecting his views on 'race, class and gender-specificity', she praised his 'vulnerability as a moral philosopher' (p. 18–19).[6] The views on the subjective and the socio-political aspects of psychoanalytic theory are somehow again here in an ambivalent correlation. Another example of this ambivalence is to be found in Edward Said's (2004) last book, entitled *Freud and the Non-European* – in which he reads closely Freud's last book *Moses and Monotheism*. This text represents Said's search for Freud's 'unresolved sense of identity' that casts light on something in Freud's thought that is 'actually more general in the non-European world than he [Freud] has suspected' (Said, 2004, p. 55) and that would help to elucidate political phenomena such as the Israel-Palestine conflict. Again, socio-political draws on the subjective and *vice versa*, leaving the readers perplexed about the precise relation between those two categories.

With this being said, we can announce that the question that this chapter addresses will not directly interfere with the already existent quarrels and debates between psychoanalysis and postcolonial theory, nevertheless keeping them in sight as the inherent metacontext of its own investigation. Our argumentation will not be driven by the intention to impose the psychoanalytic theoretical method as the master's discourse for an analysis of the political and ideological specificities of postcolonialism. Rather, we will explore some aspects of the present *neocolonial* political reality, by staying on our 'proper' terrain – namely, on the crossroads between psychoanalytic theory, critical theory and German Idealism – without a pretention of developing something that would be a postcolonial theory of our own.

We will thus start by exposing the paradox of 'surplus-enjoyment' (the Lacanian *plus-de-jouir*), showing that its parallax structure of lack and excess is also applicable to the phenomenon of (surplus) repression. With and against Marcuse, we will show the impossibility of something such as the 'non-repressive desublimation'. By doing so, the paradoxical structure of repression that resumes itself in the logic of 'less is more' will be brought to light as the main strategy behind symbolic castration which keeps the dominating ideological instances in power, bribing us with the misery of some form of surplus-enjoyment. The persistence of such paradoxical logics that mediate subjectivity and social domination, will be further explained by the contemporary predominance of a specific kind of the Hegelian *Aufhebung* understood as '*failed* negation of negation' or 'negation of negation' as *failure*. From that melancholic point of view of the 'living dead' that we have thus become, we will note that the time of liberation is over, or rather, that it has become impossible. In the second part of the chapter, we will start again with a critical reading of Marcuse's *Eros and Civilization* (1955) where he claims that liberation lies in the distant past, far from the constraints of contemporary civilization. In opposition to this mythical view of the past, we will propose that liberation lies in prohibition, in a kind of 'compulsive freedom' or 'unfree improvisation'. In this context, we will claim that the right tool for understanding temporal structures of oppression, and moreover for attaining liberation – particularly in the neocolonial political situations – is the one of daydream, as Freud has conceptualized it. The central example illustrating our theoretical positions will be found in Icíar Bollaín's film *También la Lluvia* (*Even the Rain*). It is by analysing its narrative structures addressing the neocolonial reality that we will tend to approach indirectly, by reading the medium of cinematic narration, the 'neocolonial question'. The aim of that analysis will be to propose the temporality of the daydream as an emancipatory strategy, following the destiny of the main character of the film, whose behaviour approaches closely to the one which Lacan (1974) used to attribute to a *saint*, who embodies 'what the structure entails, namely allowing the subject, the subject of the unconscious, to take him as the cause of the subject's own desire' (p. 15).

So finally, if postcolonial studies were somehow inordinately focused on 'interrogating the politics of symbolic difference' as Gautam Basu Thakur (2021) proposes, we should now move 'to exploring excess, surplus or lack that linger in the wake of exercises of self-representation' (p. xiv). Without high jacking the position of postcolonial studies, we shall approach its task from our own perspective regarding neocolonial politics, showing that the subject still plays a fundamental role in neocolonial processes and precisely because it is nothing else but a gap in the symbolic order.

The parallax of lack and excess

The basic paradox of jouissance is that it is both impossible and unavoidable: it is never fully achieved, always missed, but, simultaneously, we never can get rid of it – every renunciation of enjoyment generates an enjoyment in renunciation, every obstacle to desire generates a desire for obstacle and so on. This reversal provides the minimal definition of the surplus-enjoyment: it involves the paradoxical 'pleasure in pain'. That is to say, when Lacan uses the term plus-de-jouir, one has to ask a naive, but crucial question: In what does this surplus consist? Is it merely a qualitative increase of ordinary pleasure? The ambiguity of the French expression is decisive here: it can mean 'surplus of enjoyment' as well as 'no enjoyment' – the surplus of enjoyment over mere pleasure is generated by the presence of the very opposite of pleasure, that is, pain; it is the part of jouissance that resists being contained by the homeostasis, by the pleasure principle. Or, it is the excess of pleasure produced by 'repression' itself, which is why we lose it if we abolish repression. This is what Herbert Marcuse (1974), in his *Eros and Civilization*, misses when he proposes a distinction between 'basic repression' ('the "modifications" of the instincts necessary for the perpetuation of the human race in civilization') and 'surplus-repression' ('the restrictions necessitated by social domination'):

> while any form of the reality principle demands a considerable degree and scope of repressive control over the instincts, the specific historical institutions of the reality principle and the specific interests of domination introduce additional controls over and above those indispensable for civilized human association. These additional controls arising from the specific institutions of domination are what we denote as surplus-repression. (p. 37)

Marcuse enumerates as examples of surplus-repression 'the modifications and deflections of instinctual energy necessitated by the perpetuation of the monogamic-patriarchal family, or by a hierarchical division of labor, or by public control over the individual's private existence' (p. 37–8). Although he concedes that basic and surplus-repression are de facto inextricably intertwined, one should go a step further and render problematic their very conceptual distinction: it is the paradox of libidinal economy that surplus/excess is necessary for the very 'basic' functioning – why? An ideological edifice 'bribes' subjects to accept 'repression'/renunciation by way of offering as surplus-enjoyment (Lacan's plus-de-jouir), and this surplus-enjoyment is an enjoyment generated by the very 'excessive' renunciation to enjoyment – surplus-enjoyment is by definition enjoyment-in-pain. (Its paradigmatic case is the Fascist call 'Renounce corrupt pleasures! Sacrifice yourself for your country!', a call which promises an obscene enjoyment brought about by this very renunciation.) One thus cannot have only 'basic' repression without the surplus-repression, since it is the very enjoyment generated by the surplus-repression which renders the 'basic' repression palpable to the subjects. The paradox is thus a kind of 'less is more' we are dealing with here: 'more' repression is less traumatic, more easily acceptable, than less. When repression is diminished, the lesser degree of repression is much more difficult to endure and provokes rebellion. (This is maybe one of the reasons why revolutions break out not when oppression is at its worst, but when it diminishes to a more 'reasonable' and 'rational' level[7] – this diminishing deprives repression of the aura which makes it acceptable) (Žižek, 2013).

This is why we should also reject Marcuse's idea of a 'non-repressive desublimation' as the goal of sexual emancipation. If we follow Lacan's precise definition of sublimation, then Marcuse's idea of 'liberated persons' who are able to experience 'the non-repressive desublimation of resexualizing their polymorphously perverse bodies' is a utopian nonsense – why? For Lacan, 'repressive desublimation' cannot be opposed to non-repressive desublimation because desublimation is AS SUCH repressive, which is why perversion in which the subject actualizes its dirtiest fantasies is, as Lacan pointed out, the hidden part of any oppressive power. For Lacan, sexual drive as such relies on sublimation: sublimation elevates an ordinary worldly object to the level of the impossible Thing – this is how sublimation sexualizes an ordinary object. So when Johnston claims that 'Freudian sublimation is nothing other than the achievement of satisfaction in the face of aim-inhibition', we should NOT read this in the ordinary sense of replacing a direct sexual object or act with a desexualized activity. Lacan reads sublimation in the Kantian way: what is prohibited in sublimation is not the direct object but the impossible Thing – that's the basic paradox here: what is prohibited is already in itself impossible to reach. In sublimation, we shift from one to another object to catch the elusive Thing which eludes already the direct object.

To get the paradoxical logic of 'less is more,' it is crucial to distinguish symbolic castration from the real castration (a penis – or testicles – is actually cut off) and the imaginary castration in which the loss is just imagined (as in the case of a woman imagining she once had a penis and lost it). In the symbolic castration, nothing happens in (bodily) reality, all that happens is that the phallus itself (as the moment of bodily excess) becomes a signifier of 'castration,' of its lack/impotence. In this sense, social authority really is 'phallic' insofar as it has the effect of symbolic castration on its bearer: if, say, I am a king, I have to accept that the ritual of investiture makes me a king, that my authority is embodied in the insignia I wear so that my authority is in some sense external to me as a person in my miserable reality. As Lacan put it, only a psychotic is a king who thinks he is a king (or a father who is a father) by his nature, as he is, without the processes of symbolic investiture. This is why being-a-father is by definition a failure: no 'empirical' father can live up to his symbolic function, to his title. How can I, if I am invested with such an authority, live with this gap without obfuscating it through psychotic direct identification of my symbolic status with my reality?

And this is why, from the strict Freudian standpoint, the human finitude (symbolic castration) and immortality (death drive) are the two sides of the same operation, that is, it's not that the substance of life, the immortal Jouissance-Thing, is 'castrated' by the arrival of the symbolic order. As in the case of lack and excess, the structure is that of parallax: the undead Thing is the remainder of castration, it is generated by castration, and vice versa, there is no 'pure' castration, castration itself is sustained by the immortal excess which eludes it. Castration and excess are not two different entities, but the front and the back of one and the same entity, that is, one and the same entity inscribed onto the two surfaces of a Möbius strip. The unity of limitation and immortality can now be clearly formulated: an entity finds its peace and completion in fitting its finite contours (form), so what pushes it beyond its finite form is the very fact that it cannot achieve it, that it cannot be what it is, that it is marked by an irreducible impossibility, thwarted in its core – it is on behalf of this immanent and constitutive obstacle that a thing persists beyond its 'death.' Recall Hamlet's father: Why does he return as a ghost after his natural death? Because of the gap between his natural death and his symbolic death, that is, because he died in the flower of his sins, unable to find peace in death, to enact his symbolic death (settlement of accounts).

One of the determinations of modernity is that, in it, a specific form of the negation of negation arises:[8] far from the triumphant reversal of negativity into a new positivity, this 'negation of negation' means that even negation (our striving to reach the bottom, the zero-point) fails. Not only are we not immortal but we are even not mortal, we fail in that endeavour to disappear and we survive in the guise of the obscene immortality of the 'undead' (living dead). Not only do we fail in our pursuit of happiness, but we even fail in our pursuit of unhappiness; our attempts to ruin our life produce small unexpected bits of miserable happiness, of surplus-enjoyment. In old Yugoslavia, policemen were the butt of jokes as stupid and corrupted; in one of these jokes, a policeman returns home unexpectedly and finds his wife alone in bed, half-naked and aroused; he suspects a lover is hiding beneath the big bed, gets on his knees and looks beneath. After a couple of seconds, he gets up with a satisfied expression, just mumbling 'Everything OK, nobody is there!', while quickly pushing a couple of banknotes into the pocket of his trousers. This is how in our daily lives accepting failure is paid by the misery of some form of surplus-enjoyment.

In social life, not only do most of us fail to achieve social success and slide slowly towards some form of proletarization, but we even fail in this tendency towards the bottom of the social scale, to become proletarians who have nothing (to lose but their chains) and somehow maintain a minimum of social status. Perhaps therein resides the impasse of today's Western radical Leftists who, disappointed at the lack of a 'true proletariat' in their own country, desperately search for an ersatz proletariat which will mobilize itself as a revolutionary agent instead of 'our' corrupted and inert working class (the most popular candidate is lately nomadic immigrants). Is this weird 'downward negation of negation' really what escapes Hegel in his obsession with the forward march of the spirit? What if this 'downward negation of negation' is rather the true secret of the Hegelian dialectical process? It is along these lines that one should reread Hegel backwards, from the perspective of Samuel Beckett's late short texts and plays which all deal with the problem of how to go on when the game is over, when it has reached its end-point.[9] Hegel is not simply the thinker of closure, of the closed circle of the end of history in Absolute Knowing, but also the thinker of the terrible void of inertia when, after 'the system is closed', nothing (that we can think) happens although 'the time goes on'.

But what if the choice between finitude and immortality is false? What if finitude and immortality, like lack and excess, also form a parallax couple, what if they are the same from a different point of view? What if immortality is an object that is a remainder/excess over finitude, what if finitude is an attempt to escape from the excess of immortality? What if Kierkegaard was right here, but for the wrong reason, when he also understood the claim that we, humans, are just mortal beings who disappear after their biological death as an easy way to escape the ethical responsibility that comes with the immortal soul? He was right for the wrong reason insofar as he equated immortality with the divine and ethical part of a human being – but there is another immortality. What Cantor did for infinity, we should do for immortality, and assert the multiplicity of immortalities: the Badiouian noble immortality/infinity of the deployment of an Event (as opposed to the finitude of a human animal) comes after a more basic form of immortality which resides in what Lacan calls the Sadean fundamental fantasy: the fantasy of another, ethereal body of the victim, which can be tortured indefinitely and nonetheless magically retains its beauty (recall the Sadean figure of the young girl sustaining endless humiliations and mutilations from her depraved torturer and somehow mysteriously surviving it all intact, in the same way Tom and Jerry and other cartoon heroes survive all their ridiculous ordeals intact). In this form, the comical and the disgustingly terrifying (recall different versions of the 'undead' – zombies, vampires, etc. – in popular culture) are inextricably connected. (Therein resides the point of proper burial, from Antigone[10] to Hamlet: to prevent the dead from returning in the guise of this obscene immortality . . .) (Žižek, 2019).

So, again, the idea of the 'negation of negation' as a failure is not strange to Hegel. In one of the most famous passages in his Phenomenology, the dialectic of master and servant, he imagines the confrontation of the two self-consciousnesses engaged in the struggle to life and death; each side is ready to go to the end in risking its life, but if they both persist to the end, there is no winner – one dies, the other survives but without another to recognize it. The whole history of freedom and recognition – in short, the whole history tout court, the whole of human culture – can take place only with an original compromise: in the eye-to-eye confrontation, one side (the future servant) 'averts its eyes,' is not ready to go to the end.

Perhaps the ultimate form of the self-annihilating negation of negation is a certain mode of melancholy, a melancholy which arises when, say, I am leaving my home permanently: what makes the situation melancholic is not just seeing how the beloved home is disappearing from my life but the sadness of knowing that this disappearance itself will disappear: there will be a moment when I will no longer miss my home but simply stop caring about it, a moment when homesickness itself, not just home, will disappear.

The impossible time of freedom

The time of liberation is over, which is what still makes it possible. The time is over because the real time for liberation was in 1871, 1917 or 1968. Yet the idea that the possibility of true rebellion lies in the past is also a myth. There was no 'golden age' of freedom in belief or actions that are constrained today. Even the Greeks did not really believe in their own gods, which also indicates the obverse, that contemporary life is not so far removed from superstition. In the words of Paul Veyne, 'Daily life itself, far from being rooted in immediacy, is the crossroads of the imagination, and there people actively believe in racism and fortune-tellers' (Veyne, 1988, p. 117). This is true not only for the daily life of the past but also for the present. In this sense, they are both the same. Yet this sameness also indicates something more profound, since the crossroads of the imagination that Veyne mentions are a juxtaposition of prohibition and liberation which confronts the fantasy of freedom with its own limitation, a confrontation which is never truly understood, and yet impossible to escape.

For Marcuse (1966), true liberation is located in the past because that is when pleasure ran free, unfettered by the constraints of contemporary civilization: 'the deepest and oldest layer of the mental personality, is the drive for integral gratification, which is absence of want and repression. As such it is the immediate identity of necessity and freedom' (p. 18).[11] Hence the role of memory, which is 'to preserve promises and potentialities which are betrayed and even outlawed by the mature, civilized individual, but which had once been fulfilled in his dim past and which are never entirely forgotten'.[12] (This is why 'Regression assumes a progressive function. The rediscovered past yields critical standards which are tabooed by the present' (p. 21).[13] Marcuse indicates a fundamental change is the location of liberation. As Margaret Cerullo (1979) notes, Marcuse's 'insistence on the possibility of a new reality principle as the promise of a socialism which could no longer be understood as a change in social institutions, but had to be deepened to include a vision of change in consciousness'. The role of psychoanalysis is to engage with the personal, bringing forth this past freedom, or 'the memory of a time when individual and species were still one, of a prehistorical life prior to division' (Raulet, 2004, p. 121)[14] within the contemporary land of repression.

However, as was argued above, liberation lies in prohibition, a kind of 'compulsive freedom' or 'unfree improvisation' (Brassier, 2003), not the supposed unfettered freedom of the past. This is because complete liberation is impossible to reach, which is the same thing as saying it is prohibited. In other words, if the Thing is always elusive and denied direct contact, then dealing with the denial of prohibition and the shifting identities of sublimation can be taken as a strategy for approaching freedom, rather than its negation.

This is why we can take issue with another statement of Marcuse's from the same chapter when he says that only certain expressions of past freedoms fit his criteria for absolute freedom: 'Psychoanalytic theory removes these mental faculties from the noncommittal sphere of daydreaming and fiction and recaptures their strict truths.'[15] For Marcuse, the issue is that daydreaming and fiction are in no way independent since they are deeply rooted in the same kinds of repression and sublimation that affect adult lives. Freud (1959), in his 'Creative Writers and Day-Dreaming', first presented at the end of 1907, has a similar approach, but for a different reason. He begins by arguing that creativity in adults is tied to the play of children, since 'we can never give anything up; we only exchange one thing for another'.[16] One way creativity becomes manifest in the adult world is through daydreams, although daydreams are not unfettered spheres removed from reality. Similar to Marcuse, daydreams reflect the daydreamer's current life and struggles. They are marked by a 'date-mark'[17] (*Zeitmarke*) from the moment they take place so that the daydream of a woman about to lose her job is different from the daydream of a woman about to start college. So far it seems that Marcuse and Freud have a similar position regarding daydreams, but there is a difference. For Marcuse, daydreams are to be dismissed because they are infected by the date-mark of the adult's world. The future projections of critical theory 'are not to be idle daydreams, but an imaginative programme of social construction based on an analysis of tendencies in the present society' (Kellner, 1984, p. 123). For Freud, the 'freedoms' of one's childhood inform but do not predict the adult, and the date-mark of contemporary daydreams just helps make this impossibility visible. Therefore the limitations of the daydream are one way that we can access some kind of freedom. The manner this is done is through daydream temporality.

One expression of the political nature of the daydream is found in Icíar Bollaín's 2010 film *Even the Rain* (*También la Lluvia*), which first mirrors the parallax structure of castration and then complicates it. A Mexican director and Spanish producer go to Bolivia to film a historical production about Columbus landing in the 'New World'. The parallax structure of this process is shown in a number of scenes in which the line between fact and fiction, or actors and their roles, is crossed. '*Even the Rain* blends several cinematic tendencies, which at times clash to create a temporal short circuit' (Cliento, 2012, p. 245). In one such moment early in the film, the actors are in the garden of their hotel reading through their lines. 'Columbus' (Karra Elejalde, who is playing the actor Antón, who is then playing Columbus) is shown proof that his long journey has paid off: the natives are wearing the gold that the Europeans have come for. Columbus and his crew are being played by actors, yet in order to perform their scene, they turn to two local employees of the hotel who are outside of the game, serving their guests food and drinks. 'Columbus' approaches the female employee and, without her permission, takes her gold earring from her ear. The employee looks both amused and confused as the actor continues the scene, with him demanding ever more vehemently, 'Where is the gold? You know what I'm talking about. Gold! Where is it?!' During this exchange, she does not flinch, although she does look nervously over to the male employee at her side, who seems like he is about to jump in and defend her.

But this is all just a game. The actor playing Columbus eventually breaks the tension by coming out of character and being 'himself,' claiming, 'Who gives a shit about gold?' and, 'I need a fucking drink!' The actors laugh and the woman is offered an apology.[18] However, while at first it seems as if the contemporary film crew are making a movie to expose the colonialism of the past, they are actually perpetuating it, seen here in the actor's assumption that he can approach, touch and treat the employee in this way. The fact that the situation is fake, just a rehearsal, means nothing. The oppression of the real Columbus is not somehow negated when the actor appears from behind his mask. In fact, this supposed negation of Columbus is itself negated by the actual harassment the actor inflicts on the employee, with 'the positioning between the film-makers and the film-in-production's subjects serving as a recurrent point of reflection'.[19] Here the parallax structure of the film comes forth. The actor negates the colonialism of

Columbus by coming out of character, yet the separation of actor and role is itself negated by the film crew's continual mistreatment of the Bolivian natives. Oppression takes on an undead, monstrous form in this scene, made visible when the actor is not acting, or when the hotel worker is not working, but playing a part in a scene. The truth of the moment is created when no one is fulfilling their role to perfection when everyone misses the mark somewhat.[20]

Yet there is another figure in the film that complicates this reading by engaging in the temporal structure of the daydream. The first scene of the film shows the filmmaking crew arriving in Bolivia and a long line of locals waiting to be considered for roles. The filmmakers are inefficient. There is no way that they will be able to interview everyone. One man in line protests at being sent home. He says that they will all stay until they have each been seen, and he eventually gets into a fight with a security guard. This catches the eye of the film's director, and the man in line, Daniel (Juan Carlos Aduviri), is cast as Hautey, the famous Taíno chief who worked to warn other natives of the treacherous Spaniards, eventually fighting the invaders before being captured and burned alive (Barreiro, 1990). With Daniel, the relationship between actor and role is different. There is no separation to be negated. He *is* the role he is playing. despite the fact that Daniel is a contemporary Bolivian, while Hautey was from Haiti, and killed in Cuba in 1512, Daniel *is* Hautey in the sense that they share the same character traits: Daniel is also a fighter against oppression, although in a different guise. Daniel does not need to get in and out of character as the actor playing Columbus does. Daniel *is* the character. There is something different going on here. Something else is in play.

In the summer of 1999, the World Bank and the International Development Bank made the privatization of the water supply of Bolivia's Cochabamba region a condition for receiving loans (Olivera & Lewis, 2004). The title of Bollaín's film, *Even the Rain*, is taken from Law 2029, passed by the Bolivian government to satisfy these demands. This law prohibited the traditional distribution of water to rural areas beyond official jurisdiction, as well as banned the construction of collection tanks to gather rainwater or the privatization of rainwater. The character of Daniel is at least partially based on the real-world leader of the main opposition group *Coordinadora de Defensa del Agua y de la Vida* (Coalition in Defense of Water and Life), Oscar Olivera. In the film, Daniel's work defending the local water supply repeatedly takes precedence over his acting duties. In fact, he has only taken part in the film to obtain money to support the movement.[21]

But what is really so revolutionary about the character of Daniel? He illustrates the temporality of the daydream. For Freud, daydream temporality follows the endopsychic structure of id, ego and superego, in that the daydream is first triggered by a contemporary event, then it reaches back to the past when a similar wish was fulfilled, before finally stretching out to the future to imagine when such a wish could be fulfilled again. In *Even the Rain*, the current event of the Water War triggers the memory of the (at least partially) fulfilled wish of

Hautey's revolt in the past, which is then projected into the future wish for the film crew to change from maintaining 'the existing order but with a human face' (Žižek, 2020, p. 36) to owning up to their behaviour and doing something about it (which the film producer seems to do when he puts himself at risk to save the life of Daniel's daughter). Thus colonial oppression is contemporary Eurocentrism is World Bank neoliberalism. Yet the film also shows how this temporality makes the impossibility of the Thing visible. Hautey's life was cut short by being burned at the stake by the Spanish invaders. The representation of this scene in the film is supplemented by the police arriving to arrest Daniel for his role as a protester in the Water War. Yet there is another element in play. There is an impossible moment in this scene. Daniel, playing Hautey, is shown burning at the stake, but this is not mere acting. Real fire is shown to be actually burning the actors alive.

This scene, in which 'the film's intertwined temporalities are fully manifested',[22] does not make sense in the economy of the film. The fire should have been added post-production, or somehow done with special effects, while here it is being shown as actual fire, really burning the actors. Yet a moment later the police come, interrupt the shooting, arrest Daniel, and take him away, unburned and unscathed. This scene indicates the impossibility of the Thing itself in the way that the scene is impossible in terms of the structure of the film. Yet the manner that this impossibility comes forth is through the limited, repressive, disruptive time of the daydream, which is one of the few places where approaching the real becomes possible. Perhaps this is also why the last third of the film is the least successful. The European actors have supposedly 'learned' their lesson of being oppressors and are now inhabiting the role they thought they actually occupied before: as saviours. Yet this falls flat, since seeing themselves as saviours is the same sentiment that led Columbus to rationalize the occupation of the 'New World' with the thought of Christ rejoicing 'on earth, as he rejoices in heaven, in the prospect of the salvation of the souls of so many nations hitherto lost'.[23]

Conclusion

The French state-owned television network France 24 reported that some authorities in Ukraine encourage beating and tying people to poles who are caught stealing. It was reported as videos of accused looters emerged on the web, which took place in various parts of Ukraine. The Russia–Ukraine conflict resulted, for Ukrainians, in the deprivation of their basic commodities and particularly food shortages. Paradoxically, Ukrainians described the attack of Russia as evil without apathy particularly to civilians while looters who wanted to survive were tied and beaten to the poles without sympathy. Meanwhile, in England, Queen Elizabeth II, the longest-serving British monarch, celebrated a platinum jubilee, and despite the country's colonialist history, the event garnered tribute from world leaders and ordinary people for one of history's great acts of constancy that placed the British at the apex of power – in contrast to their failure to redress colonial-era land grabbing in Kenya.

Other issues around the globe have something to do with what Mannoni pointed out that the colonial is not looking for profit only, he is greedy for certain other – psychological – satisfaction, and that is much more dangerous, requiring adequate attention to the peculiar dynamics of desire that characterize the colonial situation.[24] Truly, we live in a time of uncertainty, confusion, suffering and trouble, and there emerges a weird phenomenon that points us to the idea that sometimes what is needed when confronted with uncertainties is not to search for solutions but a requirement to change our standpoint for one to see the false realities.[25] It demands a rereading and reanalysis of the hegemonic foundations of our society from the vantage point of psychoanalytic theory to colonial/postcolonial issues. Benjamin pointed out that those nations are not only forged by the pens and rhetoric of the intellectuals but also by the blood and cries of the marginalized. Thus, it is an important task for scholars to 'brush against the grains'.[26] In this regard, psychoanalysis plays an important role in the pursuit of Walter Benjamin's historical-philosophical thought. The psychoanalytic tradition of Sigmund Freud and Benjamin participate in Foucault's view on criticism, where Foucault pointed out that criticism is a matter of flushing out that thought and trying to change it: to show that things are not as self-evident as one believed.[27] In addition, Benjamin's perspective participates in Freud's concept of daydreaming, which is the desire to alter the existing and often unsatisfactory or unpleasant world of reality. The past and present are projected towards the future through the medium of art just like the 2010 film of Icíar Bollaín, *Even in the Rain*. In Icíar's presentation of her daydream (Even in the Rain) publicly, there arises an experience of great pleasure, thus making it emancipatory. According to Freud, the essential *ars poetica* of the film is in the technique by which the feeling of repulsion is overcome, and this has certainly to do with those barriers erected between every individual being and others. Icíar bribes the viewers with the offer of purely formal, that is, aesthetic, pleasure in the presentation of her phantasies. Freud further explained by saying that the increment of pleasure that is offered to us in order to release yet greater pleasure arising from deeper sources in the mind is called 'incitement premium' or, technically, 'fore-pleasure', which the enjoyment of film releases tensions in our minds.[28] Thus, this makes daydream emancipatory as an emancipatory strategy and effective compared to Marcuse's 'non-repressive desublimation'.

Notes

1   Alenka Zupančič, 'Answers by Alenka Zupančič', *European Journal of Psychoanalysis*, https://www.journal-psychoanalysis.eu/answers-by-alenka -zupancic/.

2   Ibid.

3   D. Hook and R. Truscott, 'Fanonian Ambivalence: On Psychoanalysis and Postcolonial Critique', *Journal of Theoretical and Philosophical Psychology* 33, no. 3 (2013): 155–69. ISSN 1068-8471.

4   O. Mannoni, *Prospero and Caliban: Psychology of Colonization* (Westport: Paeger, 1964).

5   This claim, as well as the more general history of the reception of Mannoni's book is nicely exposed in C. Lane, 'Psychoanalysis and Colonialism Redux: Why Mannoni's "Prospero Complex" Still Haunts Us', *Journal of Modern Literature* 25, no. 3–4 (2002): 127–50. doi:10.2307/3831859.

6   G. Chakravorty Spivak, 'Echo', *New Literary History* 24, no. 1 (1993): 18–19.

7   The line of thought from the chapter 'Parataxis', in: Žižek, *Less Than Nothing* (London: Verso Books, 2013).

8   The line of thought deployed by Aaron Schuster and Alenka Zupančič (private communication).

9   The line of thought deployed by Mladen Dolar (private communication).

10   The line of thought from 'Corollary 2: Circular Time', in *Sex and the Failed Absolute* (London: Bloomsbury 2019).

11   H. Marcuse, *Eros and Civilization* (Boston: Beacon Press, 1974), 13. (1966 Beacon Press Edition).

12   Ibid.

13   Margaret Cerullo, 'Marcuse and Feminism', *New German Critique* 18 (1979): 21.

14   G. Raulet, 'Marcuse's Negative Dialectics of Imagination', in *Herbert Marcuse: A Critical Reader*, ed. John Abromeit and W. Mark Cobb (London: Routledge, 2004), 121.

15   Marcuse, *Eros and Civilization*.

16   Sigmund Freud, 'Creative Writers and Day-Dreaming', in *The Standard Edition of the Complete Psychological Works of Sigmund Freud, Volume IX (1906–1908)*, ed. James Strachey (London: Hogarth Press and the Institute of Psycho-Analysis, 1959), 145. For further analysis on this same subject, see Brian Willems's review of Laurence Rickels's three-volume *Critique of Fantasy* (Punctum Books, 2020–1), forthcoming in the *Journal of the Fantastic in the Arts*.

17   Freud, 'Creative Writers and Day-Dreaming', 147.

18   At first glance this scene has structural similarities to the fantasy rape scene in David Lynch's *Wild at Heart* (1990) discussed in *The Parallax View*, although the scene in Bollaín's film is not, ultimately, about '*practicing* the love of one's neighbor' (Slavoj Žižek, *The Parallax View* [Cambridge: MIT Press, 2006], 70) but the opposite.

19   M. Hulme-Lippert, 'Negotiating Human Rights in Icíar Bollaín's *También la lluvia*', *Journal of Latin American Cultural Studies* 25, no. 1 (2016): 108.

20 There are a number of scenes in the film where the parallax structure of castration generates the true meaning of the film. Local actors refuse to re-enact a scene of drowning their children even though the director insists that 'I'm not making this up. It's what happened'. And a child actor, sitting in a movie theatre and watching her performance of watching her film father having his arm chopped off because he has not fulfilled his daily quota of gold for his masters, feels empathy with the oppression of her ancestors, a feeling which is worlds away from the congratulations for a good performance given to her by the director once the scene finishes.

21 In another connection between Olivera and the film, the passage cited above for information on the Water War, when reprinted in the 2018 *Bolivia Reader*, is given the title 'Even the Rain'. See Oscar Olivera, 'Even the Rain', in *The Bolivia Reader: History, Culture, Politics*, ed. Sinclair Thomson, Rossana Barragán, Xavier Albó, Seemin Qayum, and Mark Goodale (Durham: Duke University Press, 2018), 603–7.

22 F. Cliento, '*Even the Rain*: A Confluence of Cinematic and Historical Temporalities', *Arizona Journal of Hispanic Cultural Studies* 16 (2012): 255.

23 Paul Leicester Ford (ed.), *Writings of Christopher Columbus: Descriptive of The Discovery and Occupation of the New World* (New York: Charles L. Webster and Co., 1892), 50.

24 Derek Hook, 'Postcolonial Psychoanalysis', *Theory & Psychology*. SAGE Publications 18, no. 2: 269–83, doi:10.1177/0959354307087886.

25 S. Žižek, *Like a Thief in Broad Daylight* (New York: Seven Stories Press, 2018), 8, 182–208.

26 Walter Benjamin, *On the Concept of History*, 5–6, http://www.efn.org/~dredmond/Theses_on_History.html.

27 S. Freud, *Collected Papers*, vol. 4, trans. Joan Riviere (New York: Basic Books, Inc., 1959), 173–5.

28 Ibid., 173, 180–3.

References

Barreiro, J. (1990), 'A Note on Tainos: *Whither Progress?*', *Northeast Indian Quarterly* (Fall 1990): 66–77. http://www.hartford-hwp.com/archives/41/013.html.
Basu Thakur, G. (2021), *Postcolonial Lack*, New York: SUNY Press.
Brassier, R. (2003), 'Unfree Improvisation/Compulsive Freedom', *Mattin*, http://www.mattin.org/essays/unfree_improvisation-compulsive_freedom.html.
Chakravorty Spivak, G. (1993), 'Echo', *New Literary History* 24(1): 18–19.
Cliento, F. (2012), 'Even the Rain: A Confluence of Cinematic and Historical Temporalities', *Arizona Journal of Hispanic Cultural Studies* 16: 245–57.
Fanon, F. (1985), *Black Skin, White Masks*, London: Pluto Press.
Freud, S. (1959), *Collected Papers Vol. 4*, trans. Joan. Riviere, New York: Basic Books, Inc., 173–5.
Hook, D. and R. Truscott (2013), 'Fanonian ambivalence: On psychoanalysis and postcolonial critique', *Journal of Theoretical and Philosophical Psychology* 33(3): 155–69. ISSN 1068-8471.

Hulme-Lippert, M. (2016), 'Negotiating Human Rights in Icíar Bollaín's *También la lluvia*', *Journal of Latin American Cultural Studies* 25(1): 108.

Kellner, D. (1984), *Herbert Marcuse and the Crisis of Marxism*, London: Macmillan.

Lane, C. (2002), 'Psychoanalysis and Colonialism Redux: Why Mannoni's "Prospero Complex" Still Haunts Us', *Journal of Modern Literature* 25(3–4): 127–50. doi:10.2307/3831859.

Lacan, J. (1974), *Television*, New York and London: W.W. Norton & Company, 15.

Mannoni, O. (1964), *Prospero and Caliban: Psychology of Colonization*, Westport: Paeger.

Marcuse, H. (1974), *Eros and Civilization*, Boston: Beacon Press

Olivera, O. and T. Lewis (2004), *Cochabamba! Water War in Bolivia*, Cambridge: South End Press, 8–10.

Said, E. (2004), *Freud and the Non-European*, London: Verso.

Veyne, P. (1988), *Did the Greeks Believe in Their Myths? An Essay on the Constitutive Imagination*, trans. Paula Wissing, Chicago: The University of Chicago Press.

Zupančič, A. 'Answers by Alenka Zupančič', *European Journal of Psychoanalysis*, https://www.journal-psychoanalysis.eu/answers-by-alenka-zupancic/.

Žižek, S. (2018), *Like a Thief in Broad Daylight*, New York: Seven Stories Press, 8, 182–208.

Žižek, S. (2019), *Sex and the Failed Absolute*, London: Bloomsbury

Žižek, S. (2020), *PANDEMIC! COVID-19 Shakes the World*, New York: Polity Press.

Chapter 11

Perverted erotics in the political unconscious

Lacan and Bataille

Tim Themi

For a time it seemed Lacan was to follow up his *Seminar III* distinction of psychosis via the mechanism of 'foreclosure [*verwerfung*]' with a *Seminar IV* distinction of perversion via 'disavowing [*verleugnung*]'.[1] Thus, a catechism is formed of three clinical structures linked to three modes of defence: repression for neurosis, foreclosure for psychosis and *disavowal* for perversion.[2] For the latter Lacan links to the maternal phallus a child expects in the 'phallic phase' (SIV, 88) preceding the genital stage proper – as per the developmental path of Freud's 1923 'Infantile Genital Organisation' article, which led to the footnote on 'the phallic stage of organisation' being added to his 1905 *Three Essays On Sexuality*, where both male and female child 'knows only one kind of genital: the male one'.[3]

The discovery of difference is thence a shock, wherein it might be *disavowed*, the girl fearing hers has been taken, the boy his will be too. The issue then is the fetishistic substitutes created to whitewash the feared lack, from the mother's leg as phallus to the child itself as one – the *political* significance of which, as it extends into the adult's unconscious, instantly captured in Freud's 1927 'Fetishism' article regarding the 'panic' cried out when 'Throne and Alter are in danger' and 'illogical consequences will ensue' (SE21, 153). For it is not just commodities or pornographies that field our fetishes, like so many substitutes standing in for an original loss, but also, as Freud's capitalizations imply, our national empires, religious ideologies and identifications – the transferences of which are less obvious to handle, though no less explosive for all that.

Further examples in 'Fetishism' are the English patient whose partner must have a 'shine on the nose [*glanz auf der nase*]', a cross-lingual pun suggesting the phallus he expected a *glance* at was displaced to a nose of a certain shape or shine (SE21, 152); the *coupeur de nattes* 'pervert who enjoys cutting off the hair of females', to symbolically 'carry out the castration' that was disavowed; and the shrinking of a 'female foot and then revering it like a fetish', as smaller phallus, 'to thank the woman for submitting to being castrated' and again *re*-establish the disavowed difference (157). But Lacan's *Seminar IV* focus is also on how for a girl 'it's not simply a matter of lacking the phallus' but of fetishizing a child into a phallus, to *give* 'it or its equivalent to her mother, *just as the boy wants to*' (185).

Lacan cites Freud's 1931 'Female Sexuality' article to grasp this (SE21, 239), wherein a 'masculine', 'early, pre-Oedipal phase' of the girl's development is discovered from a predominance of 'the clitoris' over the 'vagina', with the 'mother' as corresponding 'choice of object' – all of which is likened by Freud to 'the discovery, in another field, of the Minoan-Mycenean civilisation behind the civilisation of Ancient Greece' (225–6, 228, 230). But when Lacan adds that 'nothing is conceivable in the phenomenology of the perversions' unless we 'start with the idea that what is involved is the phallus', where 'the child realises' their 'unfulfilled' yet 'all-powerful mother is fundamentally in want of something' (SIV, 185) – problems arise with the seeming reduction of *all* perversion to fetishism, as if ignoring Freud's other demarcations, which Lacan also uses. For when Lacan's *Seminar XXII* quips that 'neurosis is a failed perversion'[4] – or *Seminar IV* that neurotics with 'sadomasochistic' fantasies have 'great difficulty', 'even abashment', in 'wording these' (SIV, 106–7) – it is *not* in reference to any phallus but to how Freud would mark perversions as 'the positive' of neuroses which are themselves 'the negative of perversions'; or how 'unconscious phantasies of hysterics' and neurotics 'coincide' 'down to their details' with the 'clearly conscious phantasies', 'manifest behaviour' and '*action* of perverts'.[5] But these perversions for Freud were also demarcated by 'regression' to 'fixation' at the oral or anal 'pregenital' stages *preceding* the phallic, where 'one of the components' of libido has 'withdrawn from the later processes of development' – to sado-masochism, and the 'function of micturition or defaecation'.[6]

Such confusion would threaten Bataille's *analyst*'s desire, expressed in *Accursed Share* after the war, that more 'consciousness of erotic truth' – of the 'most deeply rooted desires in the penumbra' of a 'condemnable semidarkness, which psychoanalysis named the *unconscious*' – is required so that politics becomes more 'objective' and less 'irrational', 'distorted' by an 'unconscious subjectivity' bent on the 'hypocrisy' of a 'generalised' pursuit of 'rank and war' destined to 'become the *fraudulent* bankruptcy of the human race'.[7] For regarding perversion, psychoanalysis no longer seems clear on what we should be conscious about, a lack compounded by Freud's final observation that 'disavowals' or the 'splitting of the ego' said to distinguish fetishist perversion occur 'very often' in neurosis, if not also psychosis.[8] This chapter, then, analyses Lacan's seemingly counterintuitive *Seminar IV* articulations of perversion in response to Freud's ostensibly incomplete treatments, to further elucidate Bataille's notion of a distorting political unconscious. For fetishist disavowals of the phallus may well still intrude, as unconscious *jouissance*, and perverted erotics in politics today.

Concerning the original phallic loss, as Lacan's *Seminar IV* marks from Freud's 'Infantile Genital Organisation' – 'at this moment there is no realisation of male and female' only 'what is endowed with the phallic attribute and what is not', the latter 'deemed equivalent to having been castrated' (SIV, 88). Such is the typical failure characterizing our early research, where it is not just 'unawareness of the fertilising role of male semen', or the 'existence as such of the female organ' (SIV, 88) but also, Freud notes, unawareness even of scrotums, 'the little sac with its contents', as if the entire genital organization had not 'consisted of anything more than the penis' (SE19, 142n). This 'primacy of the *phallus*' (SE19, 142; SIV, 88), as Lacan and Freud call it, is how the clitoris is seen as a smaller-absent-castrated one, an assumption so at odds with later adult consciousness. But this assumption is what contributes to the *unconscious* formations that go onto plague adults' relationships with themselves and others, making their smooth governing impossible.

There is forever the envy, anxiety, the demand for more fetishes to compensate for this unconscious loss marring all with what Lacan calls those 'possessive or destructive reactions at the moment of the phallic crisis' that are 'so problematic', as always some 'imaginary object, as a substitute for this missing phallus' is *re-sought* – the 'supervalence' of which 'only finds its point of impact retroactively' (SIV, 91). Impacted here is everything from child rearing and the 'stuffed' attempts to signify our 'sexual relations' to what Freud-Lacan saw as our interminably 'impossible professions' of 'governing, educating, and analysing'[9] – making the ideal of a rational political seem utopian as the metempsychosis myths dominating from the Orphic-Pythagorean parts of Platonism into a later Christian form, the 'predestination' fantasy of Calvinist-Capitalism and so-called 'work ethic' of today.[10] But the latter is fetishism *par excellence*, as if the primal greed *hoarding* such sums of money establishes the selfless purity of an immortal soul for an afterlife imagined as home, disavowing all the losses strewn as corpses along the way.

With the *retroactivity* of such *possessive-destructive reactions* to the original *phallic crisis*, we see how Lacan finds the phallus central to the perversions at the seeming expense of other markers. For regression to pregenital perversions pertaining to oral, anal, scopic and invocatory component drives – with aggressions and dejecta – still, for the adult, must traverse back *through* the phallic-genital stages that followed and thus coloured them. This is how in a beating fantasy the whipstick bearer stands in as maternal or paternal bearer of the phallus, pacifying the other to a castrated position while punishing via incest taboo; or how the urethral stream is the golden *shine* of the missed maternal phallus.[11] It illuminates well Lacan's idea that perversion 'is just as structured as neurosis', and 'structured in relation to everything' pertaining to 'absence or presence of the phallus', which thus 'always bears some relation' to 'castration complex' (SIV, 243).

Such *retroactive* structuring is how 'perversion is a drive' that, too, is 'elaborated by the Oedipal and neurotic mechanism', rather than being 'a pure and simple relic, the persistence of an irreducible partial drive' (SIV, 113) – that is somehow, as 'negative of neurosis', 'out in the open' as 'state of freedom' (107). But Lacan gleans from Freud's 'Child is Being Beaten' how *retroactivity* means memorialized libido also flows forward, which is why, initially, 'pregenital relations come into play in the Oedipal dialectic' itself, from the 'anal level or the oral' (SIV, 116). For the 'child has no experience', and thus 'pregenital relations', Lacan cites Freud, '*can be more easily apprehended in verbal representations* [*Wortvorstellungen*]' (SE17, 188) – which Lacan explains is because the 'child can tell themselves more easily that what the father gives to the mother is his urine', as this is all they are 'acquainted with in use' (SIV, 116).[12]

Regarding this limited acquaintance, Lacan turns to Freud's 1920 'Case of Homosexuality in a Woman' (SE18, 145–72) to mark how the girl, discovering her mother's lack, turns to the father to receive a phallus to fill her own, as if the 'penis she desires will be received from the father in the form of a substitute, namely a child' (SIV, 116). But this is a child *fetishized* into a phallus, which from the start Lacan saw as how 'the fetish is the transposition of the imaginary' into 'a symbol'.[13] With Freud's homosexual woman, on entering her teens, it meant believing a boy from a 'children's playground' 'she took to' (SE18, 155) was the phallus given her, placing her in what for Lacan is the 'imaginary mother' (SIV, 117) position later disturbed when her 'father intervenes in the real' to give her mother a 'real child' (SIV, 125). This triggers her 'profound reversal' of 'sexual orientation' where she 'changes position' (SIV, 98), to a 'male position' (120), and 'identifies with her father' in a way that 'keeps his penis' (122) – to give to the lady she then begins courting, who, in the feminine position, 'does not have the symbolic penis' (120). But because the phallus took by paternal identification is as little real as the playground 'real flesh-and-blood child' (SIV, 116) is her actual phallus, it made for 'platonic love' (101), in what to Lacan is a 'perverse relationship' (125) because meant here 'to demonstrate to her father how to love' (139). Such charade is 'perversion', then, not just for its phallic disavowal but its 'metonymic function' of 'getting something across by speaking about something utterly different' (SIV, 137) – wanting to *castrate* her father as moralistic revenge for the alleged *non*-Platonic crime of giving a real child with his *real* phallus to her real mother.[14]

This revenge is also from the 'relationship cf jealousy' (SIV, 121) with the mother initially triggering her inversion – being, Freud notes, envious that her 'harsh' or 'neurotic' mother should Oedipally win out with a father whose 'treatment of his only daughter was too much influenced by consideration for his wife' (SE18, 149). It shows how ostensibly Platonic relations can not only have perverse traits but even perverse structures of fetishist disavowals of lacks that are better to acknowledge. For after being caught by her father, as she ultimately 'wanted' (SE18, 160), and *cast a furious look* (SE18, 161; SIV, 96) that led the lady to break it off, the young woman let herself 'fall [*niederkommen*]' (SE18, 162; SIV, 98), off a bridge, a suicide attempt that 'mimes a sort of symbolic childbirth' (SIV, 139) of *falling* pregnant 'through her father's fault' (SE18, 162). This *falling* is a final metonymy and 'demonstrative way of herself becoming this child that she has not had' (SIV, 139) but feels she should have to *bear* instead of her mother. For this was already a phallic mother who Oedipally refused to let a daughter's beauty blossom in the house, seeing but 'an inconvenient competitor' (SE18, 157) to remaining prize *object* for her husband (SE18, 149, 157), in the more typically feminine act of self-fetishizing or *being* the phallus.[15]

Lacan's *Seminar IV* focus on the phallic mother of Freud's 1909 'Little Hans' case is here pertinent, where this time it is a phallic-bearing child to fetishize into a phallus. But, Lacan recalls, 'this doesn't mean she has greater consideration for the child's phallus' (SIV, 217), for at the prompting by Hans to touch it, having been told by 'an aunt' how '*dear*' (350) it is and wanting to confirm if 'he is the one who's got the true phallus, the real penis', which can 'give her complete satisfaction' (200–1), 'she is seized by a sudden dread', beyond the call of incest taboo in exclaiming: '*That would be Piggish!*' (236). This speaks to Lacan's notion that 'we must take *Penisneid* as one of the fundamental givens of the analytic experience' *and* 'the mother's relationship to the child' as 'experience proves that there is no means of articulating the perversions in any other way' (217).[16]

In Hans's case, this causes a horse-phobia as symptom of the need for 'separation' (SIV, 236) from the mother's lack, phallic ambitions and co-dependency, 'a call for rescue' (50) to fulfil his own desire as bearer of the real phallus. Instead, Lacan notes, Hans is forced to his mother's desire, reduced to 'a fetish object' in a 'pacified position' (406), to *be* her phallus rather than *bear* his own. Such 'domination of the maternal phallus' means he 'takes its place, identifies with it, and certainly masters it' (406), meaning he 'is surely not to lose his penis because at no moment does he acquire it' (407). He is 'a metonymy of her desire for the phallus' that really, Lacan marks, 'she does not have and never will have' (235). Hans stays 'identified with the maternal phallus', which 'does not mean that he can thereby retrieve his own penis and take on board its function', for it 'remains on the margins, disengaged', as only 'reviled and reproved by his mother' (407). It leads to what for Lacan is impotence which, as 'his mother's ideal', as 'substitute for the phallus', finds him more 'nudged towards the priesthood', 'sainthood' or ascetic version of 'progressive' (406–7).

Regarding *identification*, there is further the trans phenomena Lacan records, where a boy dons female 'garments' not by identifying with the maternal phallus but 'with the phallic mother' herself 'insomuch as she veils over the lack of phallus' (SIV, 158). This is as if she were still *bearer* of the phallus and needed 'protection' through 'envelopment' or 'aegis' (154) against castration, difference or enjoying the father – signalling what Freud's *Three Essays* calls the 'sadistic' misinterpretation of the 'sexual act as a sort of ill-treatment' or 'subjugation' (SE7, 196), adding to the misinterpretation of difference as castration. A variety is also the 'male homosexuality' Lacan marks, where at stake 'is still his phallus' insofar as 'he will seek out his own phallus in another party' (SIV, 186), with a real one like him, to avoid triggering castration. Freud notes how 'disparagement' of women for 'being castrated' can fuel 'exclusive homosexuality' (SE21, 229) with contempt for the opposite sex, or orientation – which in female homosexuality can lead to 'envy'-based misandry, if not misogyny, through *repudiating* femininity 'to be boys themselves' (SE7, 195).[17]

In sum, this all shows that while perversion is more acted upon, it is still overlayed with the phallic significances of fetishist disavowals and complexes of castration, and also those Oedipal and regressions to pregenitality – rather than being pure nature or 'identity' as if nothing more to say. Further, it is not that the ubiquity of perverse traits thus reduces neurotics and psychotics to perverts who themselves are reduced to the fetishism that for Freud is only a subspecies 'as one of the perversions' (SE23, 202, 204; SE7, 195). Rather, as Lacan's *Object Relation* seminar finds, 'fetishism', with its clearest display of castration disavowal, is 'the perversion that has taken the role of exemplum in analytic theory' (SIV, 143), as 'the perversion of all perversions' (186), that 'actualises the question of the object in an especially keen fashion' (143). That is, fetishism is the most perspicuous place to see how the action of the phallus *recurs* through all possible clinical structures.[18]

Bataille's work can also show how disclosing such phallic disavowals is not simply a matter of accusing, confessing and renouncing but of finding them safer outlets in aesthetics so as to keep politics separate. As precedent for this is religion *before* Christian-Platonism's binary of *spirit* (as Good-masculine) and *matter* as (bad-feminine) – where previously religious aesthetics was a space to periodically re-access prohibited sexual-animal-bodily-materiality as a meaningfully satisfying erotic *jouissance*: with the Dionysian festivals, and their equally feminine deifications, serving as exemplum. This is not to suggest eschewing science to return literally to beliefs in a more vital polytheism exemplified by *Hellenismos*. Rather, it is that such myths today return as aesthetics where, Bataille notes, 'the opening of art', by *not* being religion, or politics, 'lies but without deceiving those whom it seduces', wherein it even uncovers in desire 'the only truth that counts' (ASIII, 256).

Science, moreover, was already well established in what Lacan's *Seminar VIII* calls the 'fertile period' and 'historic climax' of the 'sixth and fifth centuries' BCE – 'overflowing with intellectual creativity' – *before* Plato's later *fourth*-century enshrining of a 'metempsychosis' denigrating bodies with an ascetic ideal.[19] But the classical prime before him shows it better to have aesthetic outlets for erotic drives and play, *including* the perversions, where even Freud marks how converting the lost maternal phallus to contiguous forms 'almost deserves to be described as artful' (SE23, 277) and how pregenital fixations afford boosted energy to be 'transformed by sublimation' – granting creative satisfaction to drives through a propitious *distance* in a 'special process which would be held back by repression' (SE17, 182).[20] It means we are not seeking perverse enjoyment unconsciously instead in politics while whitewashing with empty moralism a sphere that should be kept fair and rational; perverse desires should be unveiled in art, instead of covertly acted out in politics. Thus, debates to make art conform to the ascetic purity of the *Bible* or Plato's *Phaedo* are misguided, such as in Plato's *Republic* where the great poets are banned in a way Lacan notes, via Plato's *Gorgias* and Nietzsche's *Birth of Tragedy*, merely demonstrates Socrates' 'profound incompetence' on the topic of tragedy (SVIII, 31–2) – to go with 'Yahweh's ferocious ignorance' on 'sexual knowledge' (SXVII, 116, 136), to which it was later spliced through the rise of Christianity.[21]

I conclude, then, that the ethico-political perversions of greed, violence and corruption are not symptomatic of lack of repression but of proper outlets for drives expressible in Bataille's *philo-erotic* renewal of aesthetics, augmented by Lacan's clarifications on perversion in response to Freud. Bataille's erotic works such as *Story of the Eye* and *My Mother* were even directly full of psychoanalytic knowledge, which did not diminish their appeal, with Bataille as analysand acknowledging the 'lewdest of meanings' as *lure* for overcoming our inherited amnesia – as per the 'secular advance of repression' Freud and Lacan mark between Sophocles and Shakespeare via incest-wish in Oedipus and Hamlet, and via feminine beauty in Helen and Ophelia.[22] Such renewal of aesthetics allows a separation of art from politics like the distancing from the mother's perceived lack that perverse structure needs, according to Fink.[23] It helps us sublimate to remain more objective in politics, consistent with the *symbolic* register of Lacan and prohibition in Bataille, and a role for paternal metaphor that distantiates without excluding the *real* desire of the mother, or daughter, together with the son, and those between – with a separate space allowed periodically for a *jouissance of transgression* of usual taboos in the phallic play of *re*-eroticizing aesthetics, guided by the wiser relations to the real enabled by the truths of psychoanalysis.

Notes

1   Lacan, *Seminar III, The Psychoses, 1955–56*, trans. R. Grigg (London: Norton, 1993), 321; *Seminar IV, The Object Relation, 1956–57*, trans. A. Price (Cambridge: Polity, 2019), 148. Repeat citations SIV, 148.

2   For examples of this see 'Perversion' chapter of Bruce Fink, *A Clinical Introduction to Lacanian Psychoanalysis: Theory and Technique* (Cambridge, MA: Harvard University Press, 1997), 166–7; and Stephanie Swales, *Perversion: A Lacanian Psychoanalytic Approach to the Subject* (London: Routledge, 2012), xiii. For critique see Danny Nobus, 'Perversion in the 21st Century: A Psychoanalytic Conundrum', in *Perversion Now!*, ed. D. Caine and C. Wright (London: Palgrave-Macmillan, 2017), 103–4.

3   Freud, 'Infantile Genital Organisation' (1923), in *Standard Edition*, trans. J. Strachey (London: Vintage, 2001), 19: 142. Repeat citations SE19, 142. Freud, *Three Essays on Sexuality* (1905), SE7, 199n2.

4   Lacan, *Seminar XXII, R.S.I, 1974–75*, trans. C. Gallagher, *Jacques Lacan in Ireland* (Dublin, 2011), 93, www.lacaninireland.com (accessed 31 March 2022).

5   Freud, '"Civilised" Sexual Morality and Modern Nervous Illness' (1908), SE9, 191; *Fragment of a Case of Hysteria 'Dora'* (1905), SE7, 50; *Three Essays*, SE7, 165–6.

6   Freud, 'Child Is Being Beaten' (1919), SE17, 189, 181; *Three Essays*, SE7, 196, 198.

7   Bataille, *The Accursed Share, Volumes II & III* (1952–3), trans. R. Hurley (New York: Zone, 1999), II: 190, III: 225–6, III: 429, 424, 427. Repeat citations ASII, 190.

8   Freud, 'Outline of Psychoanalysis' (1938), SE23, 202, 204; 'Splitting of the Ego in Defence' (1938), SE23, 277.

9   Freud, 'Analysis Terminable and Interminable' (1937), SE23, 249. *Lacan, Seminar XVII, The Other Side of Psychoanalysis, 1969–70,* trans. Grigg (London: Norton, 2007), 33, 166.

10   For critique of capitalist-ethic via Lacan, Bataille and Max Weber, see Tim Themi, *Eroticizing Aesthetics: In the Real with Bataille and Lacan* (London: Rowman, 2021), 35–9, 44–5, 101, 109–10, 116–17, 166, 175–6.

11   Freud notes how guilt over incestuous penetration fantasies causes need for censorship and punishment, and thus 'regressive debasement' to 'pregenital, sadistic-anal' stages in a beating fantasy that still symbolizes the 'forbidden' penetration; 'Child is Being Beaten', SE17, 185–9.

12   Freud attributed begetting-beliefs of 'micturating in each other's presence' to how this 'material' is 'more easily apprehended in verbal images' than other mysteries 'connected with the genitals' (SE17, 188).

13   Lacan's *Seminar V* notes this as mode three of '*Penisneid* [penis-envy]': i) is 'that the clitoris be a penis'; ii) where 'what is desired is the father's penis'; and iii) is 'having a child by the father', 'the penis in symbolic form' (260). See also SV, 329: 'inasmuch as the penis is initially a substitute', 'a fetish', 'the child [. . .] too, is, then', 'a fetish'; and SIV, 147: 'the fetish is a symbol', Lacan, 'The Symbolic, the Imaginary, and the Real', *Inaugural Meeting of SFP* (1953), in Lacan, *On the Names of the Father*,

trans. Fink (Cambridge: Polity, 2013), 47, 15. Lacan, *Seminar V, Formations of the Unconscious, 1957–58*, trans. Grigg (Cambridge: Polity, 2019).

14 Lacan's *Seminar X* re-stresses the courtly aspect, noting 'she behaves towards the Lady as a devoted knight, as a man, as one who can sacrifice for her what he has, his phallus', In courtly love this sacrifice is because the lady is wife of the King whose service the knight is under, Oedipally: King as father, lady as (forbidden) mother (needing rescue). Lacan, *Seminar X, Anxiety, 1962–63*, trans. Price (Cambridge: Polity, 2014), 123.

15 Swales notes *Seminar IV* refers '*not* to' object '*a*', as emerged from 'his sixth seminar', but to a 'hybrid' of 'Freud's lost object and the imaginary phallus'; for to make good her loss 'A mother always requires her child to have (or be) the phallus'. Cf., Lacan, SIV, 48, 62; and SV, 329: 'that she displays herself' as 'object of desire identifies her [. . .] with the phallus', 'with her femininity', Swales, 'Phobic and Fetish Objects', in *Studying Lacan's Seminars IV and V: From Lack to Desire*, ed. C. Owens and N. Almqvist (London: Routledge, 2019), 38–9.

16 Lacan's *Seminar X* also notes a 'type of mother that we call a phallic woman' where, 'as very precious as an object is for her' she is 'dreadfully tempted not to hold onto it in a fall' – invoking 'Greek tragedy' where 'Electra's deepest grievance against Clytemnestra is that one day she let her slip from her arms' (122).

17 Lacan also referenced one of his 'transexual patients' who depicted the 'harrowing' and 'painful surprise he felt' upon seeing 'his sister naked the first time' (SIV, 264).

18 As Freud notes, fetishism is not an 'exceptional case' but 'particularly favourable' regarding 'splitting of the ego', insofar as 'disavowals' occur 'not only with fetishists' (SE23, 203–4).

19 Lacan, *Seminar VIII, Transference, 1960–61*, trans. Fink (Cambridge: Polity, 2015), 170, 114, 208. See also Themi, *Eroticizing Aesthetics*, 102–3, 135–6.

20 For discussion of sublimation see Chapter 2 of Themi, *Lacan's Ethics and Nietzsche's Critique of Platonism* (Albany: SUNY, 2014); and *Eroticizing Aesthetics*, 7, 38, 85–6, 102, 137–42, 177–83.

21 For more on the art-politics relation see Themi, *Eroticizing Aesthetics*, 20–31, 115, 141–2, 175.

22 Bataille, *Story of the Eye* (1928), trans. J. Neugroschel (London: Penguin, 2001), 74. Freud, *Interpretation of Dreams* (1900), SE4, 264. Lacan, *Seminar VI, Desire and Its Interpretation, 1958–59*, trans. Fink (Cambridge: Polity, 2019), 244–5. See also Themi, *Eroticizing Aesthetics*, 84–5.

23 Fink, *Clinical Introduction to Lacanian Psychoanalysis*, 175.

Chapter 12

In the absence of politics

A matter of life and death drive

Daniel Bristow

Jouissance, jouissance everywhere

We shall take as our central theme the retreat from politics of the great psychoanalyst Wilhelm Reich (1897–1957). At one time one of the most remarkable practitioners within the Vienna Psychoanalytic Society, Reich started out as a committed Marxist and Communist, but became increasingly drawn to far more esoteric domains over his extraordinary life and career after outrightly rejecting Sigmund Freud's concept of the death drive. In exploring here the political ramifications of jouissance – the idea of its modality as 'the only discourse there is' politically, as Jacques Lacan implies – in its combinations with the death drive, this essay will revolve around the core question: what would be a psychoanalysis without the death drive?[1]

As two sober and sobering recent studies of the exponential and insatiable 'concept' and the unstoppable theoretical phenomenon of jouissance hammer home, it's prey to getting taken up and used within Lacanian circles to refer to, represent and even to *reify* almost any hint of enjoyment whatsoever. Indeed, *jouissance itself* is rather too *enjoyed*, and – to annex the Žižekian refrain – it's everywhere. In Darian Leader's *Jouissance: Sexuality, Suffering and Satisfaction* (2021), he patiently works through the uses and abuses of jouissance to (re)arrive at its embodiedness and enmeshments with(in) sexuality. As he puts it: 'the interpretation of bodily sensation – especially when it is difficult to localise – forms a part of early experiences of arousal, and may have profound effects on the shaping of sexualities.'[2] From this point of departure, he interrogates 'the popular formula, that jouissance is "that which doesn't stop"', and alights at the subjective sensation of engulfment: 'it is the feeling of being overwhelmed that generates the sense of the unstoppable, rather than the other way round.'[3] It is thus as if what is unstoppable in jouissance gets caught up in autointerpretativeness and feeds on this too-much or already-in-excess; in other words, that in it 'which doesn't stop' is put into motion when the subject is overflowing, and by something in its being-overwhelmed, and/or its being-without-conceptual-coordinates. Indeed, in Christian Fierens' exploration of jouissance in relation to pleasure in *The Jouissance Principle* (2022), he positions these psychical-libidinal phenomena within a schema of principles, as opposed to concepts, thus returning them to their original Freudian categorization. As he states:

> Pleasure and jouissance can only be approached because they determine how we act *without themselves being concepts* (which would offer us a theoretical grasp on what they are). They are always already working in tandem even before we are aware of it and, even more so, before we can theorise it. They can only be approached as *principles* (and not as concepts), as operating principles.[4]

This is to talk of how we operate, differentially; when regulated by the reality principle, revved up by the pleasure principle, or riven by the jouissance principle.

Orgone, orgone everywhere

Beyond the pleasure principle: death drive. Beyond the pleasure principle: jouissance. So go the psychoanalytic formulae so often, in Freudian or Lacanian moulds. In common they share this *beyond* itself. It is what we will return to after working through some of the intricacies of Reich's split with Freud over the death drive.

Reich's critique of the death drive is worth taking seriously and on its own terms; it will be elucidated here via his summations of the dispute with Freud as outlined in his autobiographical 1942 work, *The Function of the Orgasm*, towards the beginning of which he asserts: 'I am not a politician and I am not versed in politics' and argues that 'sex-economy has nothing to do with any one of the existing political organizations or ideologies'.[5] We're a long way from its beginnings in Reich's Sex-Pol movement (the organization of the German Society of Proletarian Sexual Politics, which he had founded in 1927). And so, it must be kept in mind that not only from this book – which was authorially revised in 1948 – but from nearly all of his latter endeavours almost any mention of Reich's political positions and activities becomes increasingly diminished, to the point of conspicuous absence.[6] Reich distanced himself from his leftist political commitments in his later years, in the wake of facing intense and sustained political repressions over the course of his lifetime, from his expulsion from the Communist Party and the International Psychoanalytic Association to persecution, exile and libricide at the hands of the Nazis, and later the Food and Drug Administration in the United States, who burned his books, before he was imprisoned by the American authorities for continuing to distribute his banned materials and orgone accumulators. He would go on to go back over his published works and largely omit allusions to his political stances – though not entirely – to which these had previously been integral.

His critique of the death drive does not – as many have taken it to – come from a stubborn revanchism launched from his having planted his flag so firmly and declaredly in the fertile ground of sexuality and the life tendencies from the earliest stages of his career: these in psychoanalysis encompass the libido and the 'life instinct', or 'Eros', and in Reich's subsequent forms of therapy – which started out in sex-economy and character analysis, and evolved into bioenergetic analysis, vegetotherapy and body psychotherapy – take the forms of the biophysical life energy, the electricality of sexuality and anxiety, the vesicles he named 'bions' – which were taken to represent a stage between the non-living and the living – and finally (and retroactively) the all-encompassing cosmic 'orgone'.[7] Rather, Reich was firstly concerned about how the introduction of the death drive would affect the practice of psychoanalysis. He comments: '[Theodor] Reik made me realize where Freud had begun to go wrong. Disregarding all Freud's precautions, Reik simply used his patient's death instinct to excuse his own psychotherapeutic inadequacies.'[8] The immediate subscription by the psychoanalytic set to the theory of the death drive Reich saw as an unthinking devotion to a dogma (albeit a speculative hypothesis in Freud, the fact of which Reich holds onto) that held the potential to excuse clinical waywardness and that reversed longstanding and foundational analytic insights. Concerning the question of masochism – which Reich staunchly held to be a phenomenon that came about in a subject secondarily, and corruptively (affecting its healthy functioning), even if very early on in its development – he saw what he construed as Freud's naturalizing a demand for punishment as an abandonment of sexuality proper. As he states:

> until this point [the introduction of the death drive], a neurosis was looked upon as the result of a conflict between sexual demand and fear of punishment. Now it was said that a neurosis was the result of a conflict between sexual demand and demand for punishment, i.e., the exact opposite of fear of punishment for sexual activities. This was a complete liquidation of the psychoanalytic theory of neurosis. It was at variance with every clinical insight.[9]

Reich also saw Freud's speculations on the death drive in *Beyond the Pleasure Principle* (1920) as heralding a psychologization of biology (the scientific field into which Reich had moved, however autodidactically), which he characterized as 'a metaphysical point of view'.[10] In his more politically engaged writings, Reich hits out more pointedly at what he took to be Freud's insufficiency in apprehending the social sphere and its ills in any way cogently (with aim taken especially at *Civilisation and Its Discontents* [1930]); here, he highlights how he sees Freud and his disciples – through the death drive theory – 'explain[ing] the chaotic and catastrophic nature of social conditions on the basis of a death instinct which wreaked havoc through society' and claims that through this, 'psychoanalysts contended that the masses were *biologically* masochistic'.[11] As Freud 'did not find his way into sociology', Reich sees his claim – 'that psychoanalysis could grasp not only medical problems, but universal problems of human existence' – as thereby hampered; for Reich, while 'in *Beyond the Pleasure Principle*, [Freud] had entered into important biological questions hypothetically and had deduced the theory of the death instinct[,] it turned out to be a misleading hypothesis'.[12] As a result of all this, Reich had penetrated into a political problem that has long plagued psychoanalysis, the possibility of the direction of its treatment entailing that 'rebellion against dictatorial authority, against the father, [be] regarded as neurotic, whereas conformity to its institutions and demands [be] regarded as normal'.[13] Reich's answers here are: 'first, that there is no biological masochism; second, that conformity to present-day reality, e.g., irrational upbringing or irrational politics, is itself neurotic.'[14]

This is not a bad blueprint at all for a functional psychoanalysis without the death drive, and its deep political insights should inform any psychosocially directed clinical practice. While 'we may not ever be able to free ourselves entirely from our desire for oppression', as Ian Parker and David Pavón-Cuéllar suggest in *Psychoanalysis and Revolution* (2021), 'we can know it, discern it when it intervenes, erupts, blocks us, and this knowledge can be the first step towards our liberation' – and Reich (and his takeup in the schizoanalysis of Gilles Deleuze and Félix Guattari, to which Parker and Pavón-Cuéllar are also referring) helps us in setting about this, from either side of the couch.[15]

Lacan – very much in his signature style – says in 'Variations on the Standard Treatment' (1955) of the International Psychoanalytic Association's decision: 'in ousting him not unjustifiably, no one ever really knew how to formulate why Reich was wrong.'[16] Earlier – in 'The Function and Field of Speech and Language in Psychoanalysis' (1953) – Lacan had put him in one of two groups of types of analyst who refused Freud's death drive, the group that, 'like Reich, take the principle of seeking an ineffable organic expression beyond speech so far that, like him, in order to free it from its armor, they might symbolize, as he does, the orgasmic induction that, like him, they expect from analysis'.[17]

Clearly Lacan does not expect the function of the orgasm so much from, or in, analysis as Reich does. In 'Variations', he spends several pages laying out his musings on Reich's praxis of character analysis, which he claims was 'rightly considered to be an essential stage in the development of the new technique' (albeit one departing from psychoanalysis' interpretative foundation).[18] Bruce Fink has summarized these reflections in his essay 'Lacan on Personality from the 1930s to the 1950s' (2008): he suggests there that Lacan's identification of the 'only mistake in [Reich's] character analysis' – that 'what he calls "character armor" and treats as such is actually but an armorial', or 'blazon' – is made through Reich's becoming erroneously tied up in 'the imaginary – that is, with the narcissistic image' and taking it for the symbolic; that is, confusing a coat of arms (an instance of 'display behaviour') for armour itself (a symptomatic defence mechanism).[19] Lacan's conclusion:

> Reich's error can be explained by his deliberate refusal of the signification that is tied to the death instinct, which was introduced by Freud at the height of his conceptual powers, and which is, as we know, the touchstone of the mediocrity of analysts, whether they reject it or disfigure it.
>
> Thus character analysis is only able to establish a properly mystifying conception of the subject on the basis of what proves to be a defense in that analysis, if we apply its own principles to it.[20]

That is, its defence against the death drive. Let's follow Lacan's arguments a bit further here. He states that Reich's primary therapeutic idea resides in that the 'imaginary function' of character armour – as well as 'the symbolic material of neurosis' – must always be seen to be being marshalled as 'a defense by the individual against the orgasmic effusion whose primacy in lived experience can alone ensure its harmony'.[21] He continues: 'the extremes this idea led him to are well known.'[22] Such a conviction in the existence of this achievable orgasmic harmony perhaps occluded for Reich any realization of his own being endlessly in search of it. In its perceived plenitude – once he had located defensive armouring completely in the body and its musculature – Reich ended up finding the cosmic orgone energy (its name in part incorporating 'orgasm') everywhere, as the fundamental constituent of all life, as the substance of the universe, blue in colour, hence the sky's hue, its accumulation possible through a machine made of alternating inorganic and organic materials, the orgone accumulator, which he had invited an intrigued Albert Einstein to conduct tests on, and which had left the latter miffed.[23] So unlimited did his research become that he pressed on further and further and was latterly convinced that he would be able to control the weather via his cloudbusting device, and went on to develop a keen interest in ufology, all the while only dwindling remnants of his original political ecstasies remained.[24] To give all this a Lacanian reading, in the spirit of the 1955 *écrit*: perhaps Reich was now headed full-pelt towards the Real, mistaking it similarly for the Symbolic as he had the Imaginary in his analytic development and innovations. But this would be to get ahead of ourselves, too.

For Reich, Freud's theory was too purely 'antithetical'; he saw it as a matter of life or death, which his functionalist approach (in which natural forces combine, and vie, with societal constraints and choices) sought to rectify.[25] But rather, for Freud, it was a matter of life and death drive, something that was not merely antithetical to the life instinct or process but inscribed within it. Despite his brilliance in the dialectical method, this is what Reich was unable to think: a *beyond within*; that is, *extimacy*. As Hegel himself had described in the *Phenomenology of Spirit* (1807): 'individuality has *also its beyond* within it, can go beyond itself and destroy itself.'[26] Accordingly, within the subject is a little bit of real, harbouring death (destruction) but also beatitude (beyondness), at once. Alain Badiou, in *Happiness* (2015), elucidates this latter affect:

> Anyone who has had the experience that, in the middle of the night, after many hopeless efforts and scribbled pages, the architecture of a demonstration and the sense it gives to an entire theory is suddenly illuminated, will know what I mean [by] beatitude[; it] is the name of the happiness that being *qua* being dispenses, once grasped in the writing of its purity.[27]

We will see it again in Lacan momentarily, but this is perhaps what Reich missed a little in the seeming limitlessness of endless discovery and discovering that he ended up in: a *little bit* of the infinite, or – as Badiou beautifully puts it in one of his definitions of happiness – '*a finite* jouissance *of the infinite*'.[28] Indeed, Reich's orgone theory goes off straightway to infinity, and becomes wildly unstoppable, but not from the position of *necessity*, of that which doesn't stop writing itself, even when overwhelmed; or, indeed, and especially, from within its engulfment. What is jouissance here? It is not, or not only, limitless enjoying, but limitless frustration also, and it is these inextricably entwined. What limitless enjoying would paradoxically be is mythical 'satisfaction' (never an unsatisfied moment), while it is the very limitlessness of jouissance that provides a limit, just as the death drive itself 'short-circuits' – as Freud put it – thereby providing the pulsion of life. To come up against a limit is to encounter a little bit of real, and the slow work of tussling with it is the stuff of life (which can also take the form of fidelity to an event).

Thus, what Reich doesn't or is unable to conceptualize is *constitutive unsatisfiability* – inscribed within the very fabric of libido or drive – and jouissance, themselves. It is this circulative unsatisfiability that makes the drives and libido *jouissant*, as their extimate beyond. To put the biological constitutivity *of the organism* to one side for the moment, Reich's conception of a libido-without-beyond, even of life-without-beyond, negates what is – in the Freudo-Lacanian psychoanalytic schema – constitutive *of the subject*: the inscription of its beyond, of that which is outside, *within it*. This is a unificatory/separatory inscription of the *without* (in both of its senses: of lacking, and of outside) *within*: a little bit of death in life.[29] While the late Reich fancied himself as operating with and from within nature, as Lacan relished in recounting, Freud was able rather to state of himself, in relation to his findings: 'I am right in the middle of what is outside nature.'[30] If we take all this back to the harmony that Reich's orgasm theory presupposed, we can transpose our core question into another key that Lacan knew well: For what is an orgasm without *a little death*?

But it may be that Lacan missed something in his 1955 reading, too: to put it simply – if suggestively – that Reich discovered the body (in psychoanalysis). If Lacan had somewhat hastily plopped Reich's theory too squarely in the imaginary because of its (over)concentration on the body then, he would later come to realize what this risks eliding: that the body is one of the poles of the materialist dialectic (of psychoanalysis), which Badiou sums up thusly: 'there are only bodies and languages, except that there are truths.'[31]

We will give the culminating word on this to Lacan's proclamation made in *Talking to Brick Walls* (in the 4 November 1971 session), and briefly explore its consequences:

> Where does jouissance reside? What does it require? It requires a body. To obtain jouissance, you need a body. Even those who promise eternal Beatitude can only do so by presuming that a body will be translated into it. Glorious or otherwise, the body has to be there. Why so? Because for the body, the dimension of jouissance is the dimension of deathward descent.[32]

The dimension of jouissance is the dimension of deathward descent, just as the discourse of jouissance is the discourse of politics: the death drive its constitution, the political its modality, the body their vessel. From the body, as from the body-politic, Reich eventually had to extirpate these constituents, in accord with his late theory. This led to his positing an incorruptibly healthy life-driven core in the human organism beset on all sides by malignant and perverse cultural encrustations that form a layer of sordidness over it the valences of which become evermore inexorable and exponential in Reich's descriptions and postulations of the 'Emotional Plague of Mankind', with its monstrous avatar 'Modju' (a name conjugated from Giovanni Mocenigo, the denouncer of Giordano Bruno – a philosopher Reich had come to love – to the Inquisition, which led to his seven-year trial and being burned at the stake in 1600, and Djugashvili, the original Georgian surname of Joseph Stalin – whom Reich had come to despise); his promulgations of 'red-fascism' and gravitation to American Republicanism and McCarthyism; his messianic identifications; and his paranoia of Muscovite plots: Modju, Modju everywhere.[33] In short, it entailed hell:

> All that Freud tried to subsume under the death instinct is in that middle layer. He thought it was biological. It wasn't. It is an artefact of culture. It is a structural malignancy of the human animal. Therefore, before you can get through to what Freud called Eros or what I call orgonotic streaming or

plasmatic excitation (the basic plasma action of the bioenergetic system), you have to go through hell. Just through hell! This is true for the physician as well as the patient. In this hell, there is confusion, schizophrenic breakdown, melancholic depression. [. . .] [W]hy bring the Life Force in here? There is only one reason: To show you why nobody wanted to touch it or to get at the biological core where I was working at the time. Before you can reach that core, you must encounter hate, terror murder. All these wars, all the chaos now – do you know what that is to my mind? *Humanity is trying to get at its core, at its living, healthy core. But before it can be reached, humanity has to pass through this place of murder, killing and destruction.*[34]

These notions, so eloquently conveyed, cannot be rejected outright; they might perhaps be seen (contra Slavoj Žižek's well-known analysis of Martin Heidegger) as wrong steps, in the right direction. But it must be shown how for all his championing of Freud's notion of 'polymorphous perversity', Reich's insistence on the fundamental hygiene of the orgonotic gene resulted in purifying notions that his exemplary early political work did wonders previously to dispel. From the beginning, however, Reich was a little too wrapped up in the idea of an ultimate sexual health and a full orgasmic potency, rendering him unaware of his own normitivizations in regard to what he considered healthy sexual functioning, and from which he warded off whatever he saw as warped, the criteria of which was based, fundamentally, on his own set of uninterrogated and unworked-through value-judgements, underwritten by his defence against the death drive and the limit-experience of jouissance, and their *petite-mort*; so vital was orgasmic potency for Reich that he explicitly stated: 'the pleasure of living and the pleasure of the orgasm are identical.'[35] Sadly, for Reich, these missteps conferred a degree of ostensible *necessity* on humanity's going through hell: war, terror, murder, destruction, which for Freud likewise represented 'a positively morbid state of things', as he stated in his letter to Einstein on the question: 'Why War?'[36] However heretically it might have been seen to be, he accounts in this for 'the origin of human conscience by [a] "turning inward" of the aggressive impulse', or death drive, from the discontents of which arises culture (which had become so accursed in Reich), and – Freud asserts – 'we may rest on the assurance that whatever makes for cultural development is working also against war'; thus, in Freud's view, of he and Einstein (and their assimilation, and assumption, of the death drive): 'pacifists we are, since our organic nature wills us thus to be.'[37]

Beyond the death drive?

In *Logics of Worlds* (2006), Badiou asserts that 'considered outside of any dependence on a supernumerary event, dying, just like existing, is a mode of being-there, and therefore a purely logical correlation'.[38] Like Reich, rightly, before him, Badiou doesn't make of death an 'event', demystifying it as a mode – simply – of being-there, in the world. Where he goes further is in his postulation of (the happy) life as the finite jouissance of the infinite, something that – while drive-driven – can go beyond the drives (as essential as they are to it):

> Ultimately life is the wager, made on a body that has entered into appearing, that one will faithfully entrust this body with a new temporality, keeping at a distance the conservative drive (the ill-named 'life' instinct) as well as the mortifying drive (the death instinct). Life is what gets the better of the drives.[39]

The *beyond* – and the *going-beyond* – *within*, as capacities *of life*: the disallowance of these seems to be what got the better of Reich. Yet, from the early political and revolutionary Reich – of the essays collected in *Sex-Pol* (1929–34), of *The Mass Psychology of Fascism* (1933) and *The Sexual Revolution* (1936) – there can still be gleaned political coordinates that can orient psychosocial and Freudo-Marxist practice; and should their unrevised editions appear in English, yet more so.[40] What the late Reich ended up positing was something like an *ineluctable modality* of the political, as an unnatural force, which was capacitated to take into itself, and send back out into the world, all of the odious and vicious facets of fascism, with its predicates in racism, sexism, ableism, homo- and transphobia, Islamophobia, anti-Semitism, capitalism, class hatred and economic division, and war and extermination machines; in short: death, with little life in it.[41] For all his vitalistic resistance to the deathly life that these entailed, his theory nonetheless became increasingly swallowed by the encroachment of said deathliness. His attempted foreclosure of the death drive became so fervent that it seemed to reemerge on the horizon of the real; monstrous, and incapable of being tolerated or incorporated. In his hyperconcentration on life, he forgot death, even as a correlative. Contra the excising of the political as an ineluctable modality, we might return to Reich's classic texts such as 'What is Class Consciousness?' (1934) and 'Dialectical Materialism and Psychoanalysis' (1929/1934) – writings electrically charged with his nominated socialistic principles and communistic politics – and uncover in these a counter-position, which we can formulate in the question: 'why not *elective affinities* instead of these *ineluctable modalities*?'[42]

It is well known how easily fascistic phenomena and oppressive discourses can attach to the viscera of jouissance (through their populist, nationalist, etc., mobilisations; in their manifestations of scapegoating, witch-hunts, smear-campaigns, collective punishment, etc.).[43] This is not to suggest, however, that their counter-discourses are somehow inherently devoid of excitability and doomed to doldrums of irremediable and irredeemable disaffection and decathexis. We must turn the tables on such an idea, and – through a tentative return to Reich – repropose, and choose, *life*: it has risen before and shall again!

Notes

1   See Jacques Lacan, *The Seminar of Jacques Lacan, Book XVII: The Other Side of Psychoanalysis [1969–70]*, ed. Jacques-Alain Miller, trans. Russell Grigg (New York: W. W. Norton, 2007), 78. Many of the reflections in this article were prompted by insightful and incisive questions from China Miéville in response to a talk Jaice Titus and I delivered to the Frightful Hobgoblins discussion group during the covid-19 lockdown. For the inspiration, I dedicate this essay to him.

2   Darian Leader, *Jouissance: Sexuality, Suffering and Satisfaction* (Cambridge: Polity, 2021), 124.

3   Ibid.

4   Christian Fierens, *The Jouissance Principle: Kant, Sade and Lacan on the Ethical Functioning of the Unconscious*, trans. Kieran O'Meara (Abingdon: Routledge, 2022), 2.

5   Wilhelm Reich, *The Function of the Orgasm: Sex-Economic Problems of Biological Energy* [1942], trans. Vincent R. Carfagno (London: Souvenir Press, 1983), 16 and 10. For a captivating popular appraisal of and engagement with Reich – and an experiential account of the process of Reichian body therapy – see Olivia Laing, *Everybody: A Book about Freedom* (London: Picador, 2022).

6   Nonetheless, Reich talks very interestingly on his remaining conviction that 'Russia's initial social democracy was the most human approach possible under the existing historical conditions and given man's structure', after the Revolution of 1917 – on which both he and Freud were also initially agreed – and how it lost its way in the slide into 'dictatorial Stalinism', in the chapter 'An Abortive Biological Revolution'. See ibid., 211. Thereafter, he rehearses his theory of the mass psychology of fascism, also.

7   Nor of course does Reich deny unpleasure, pain or struggle as constituents of human life. See ibid., 201–2.

8   Ibid., 127.

9   Ibid.

10   Ibid., 251.

11   Ibid., 259.

12   Ibid., 217.

13   Ibid., 260.

14   Ibid.

15   Ian Parker and David Pavón-Cuéllar, *Psychoanalysis and Revolution: Critical Psychology for Liberation Movements* (London: 1968 Press, 2021), 10.

16   Jacques Lacan, 'Variations on the Standard Treatment' [1955], in *Écrits: The First Complete Edition in English* [1966], trans. Bruce Fink, in collaboration with HéLöise Fink and Russell Grigg (New York: W. W. Norton, 2006), 284.

17   Jacques Lacan, 'The Function and Field of Speech and Language in Psychoanalysis' [1953], in ibid., 260.

18   Lacan, 'Variations on the Standard Treatment', 281.

19   Ibid., 284; Bruce Fink, 'Lacan on Personality from the 1930s to the 1950s', *European Journal of Psychoanalysis* 26/27 (2008), https://www.journal

-psychoanalysis.eu/lacan-on-personality-from-the-1930s-to-the-1950s/ (accessed 18 March 2022). Lacan's correcting here of Reich's 'misstep' nonetheless shows the influence of it in his work, in the adoption of the concept of armour as a final ego-function in 'The Mirror Stage as Formative of the *I* Function as Revealed in Psychoanalytic Experience' [1949], in Lacan, *Écrits*, 78.

20   Lacan, 'Variations on the Standard Treatment', 284–5.

21   Ibid., 284.

22   Ibid.

23   For the construction and use of the orgone accumulator, and the explanation of the blueness of the sky, see Wilhelm Reich, *The Orgone Energy Accumulator: Its Scientific and Medical Use* (Rangeley, Maine: Orgone Institute Press, 1951), and also *The Function of the Orgasm*, 384. For information on the meetings and correspondence between Reich and Einstein, see Wilhelm Reich, *History of the Discovery of the Life Energy (American Period, 1939–1952), Documentary Volume A – XI – E: The Einstein Affair* (Rangeley, Maine: Orgone Institute Press, 1953).

24   Reich's issues of the *(CORE) Cosmic Orgone Engineering* journal, put out between 1954 and 1955, and the *Contact with Space: ORANUR* report of 1957 cover these experiments.

25   Reich, *The Function of the Orgasm*, 251.

26   G. W. F. Hegel, *Phenomenology of Spirit* [1807], trans. A. V. Miller (Oxford: Oxford University Press, 1977), 342.

27   Alain Badiou, *Happiness* [2015], trans. A. J. Bartlett and Justin Clemens (London: Bloomsbury, 2019), 93.

28   Ibid., 95.

29   We might indeed here add another jouissant pun to Lacan's litany of them, and coin '*jouisans*' (thus incorporating the concept of lack, of 'being without' (*sans*), and 'outside' – the realm of being-without – and implying the death-driven state; and, moreover, the state of one's own(most) without-being: death itself).

30   Lacan states that Freud wrote this in a letter to Wilhelm Fliess (although it has proven difficult to trace in this exactitude); see Jacques Lacan, *The Seminar of Jacques Lacan, Book III: The Psychoses, 1955–1956*, ed. Jacques-Alain Miller, trans. Russell Grigg (New York: W. W. Norton, 1993), 194 [in italics in original].

31   Alain Badiou, *Logics of Worlds: Being and Event 2* [2006], trans. Alberto Toscano (London: Bloomsbury, 2013), 4 [in italics in original].

32   Jacques Lacan, *Talking to Brick Walls: A Series of Presentations in the Chapel at Saint-Anne Hospital* [1971–2], trans. A. R. Price (Cambridge: Polity, 2017), 22.

33   For reference, see the section 'The Emotional Plague', in Wilhelm Reich, *Selected Writings: An Introduction to Orgonomy* (New York: Farrar, Straus and Giroux, 1960), 467–515. Reich's expansive researches eventually even led to the necessitous reincorporation of the death drive into the orgone itself, as D.O.R. (Deadly Orgone Radiation), as the orgone snowballed further into its all-encompassing form as something akin to Spinozan Substance. See Reich's last theoretical essay, Wilhelm Reich, 'Re-emergence of the Death Instinct as "DOR" Energy' [1956], *Orgonomic Medicine* 2 (1956).

34 Wilhelm Reich, 'The Interview' [1952], in *Reich Speaks of Freud* [1967], ed. Mary Higgins and Chester M. Raphael, trans. Therese Pol (London: Pelican Books, 1975), 100.

35 Reich, *The Function of the Orgasm*, 161–2.

36 Sigmund Freud, 'Letter to Albert Einstein, Vienna, September, 1932', in Albert Einstein and Sigmund Freud, *Why War?*, trans. Stuart Gilbert (League of Nations: International Institute of Intellectual Co-operation, 1933), 46.

37 Ibid., 46, 57, and 53.

38 Badiou, *Logics of Worlds*, 270.

39 Ibid., 509.

40 My engagement with these works, which are fundamental to my theory and its practical implications, can be found in Daniel Bristow, *Schizostructuralism: Divisions in Structure, Surface, Temporality, Class* (Abingdon: Routledge, 2021).

41 To this effect, he diagnoses a general 'process of deterioration, which has destroyed every great social movement in history'. While maintaining the founding social and scientific value and validity of discourses he had been involved with, he claimed: 'just as the primitive Christianity of Jesus was transformed into the Church, and Marxist science became fascistic dictatorship, many psychoanalysts soon became the worst enemies of their own cause.' See Reich, *The Function of the Orgasm*, 125.

42 Jaice Sara Titus and I discuss the relevance of these essays to the historical picture of psychoanalytic clinical practice in our 'Towards a Political Psychology: Historical Materialism and Psychoanalysis', *Awry: Journal of Critical Psychology*, 3rd ser., 1 (2022). Our cues here for the counterposing of ineluctable modalities and elective affinities are of course taken from their appearances in James Joyce's *Ulysses* (1922) and Johann Wolfgang von Goethe's *Elective Affinities* (1809) respectively, with the latter's extension in Max Weber's sociological work also in mind.

43 A very brief selection of works that cover elucidations of how so – and how such cathexes may be combatted – might include: *Psychoanalysis in the Barrios: Race, Class, and the Unconscious*, ed. Patricia Gherovici and Christopher Christian (Abingdon: Routledge, 2019); *Lacan and Race: Racism, Identity, and Psychoanalytic Theory*, ed. Sheldon George and Derek Hook (Abingdon: Routledge, 2022); Kirsten Campbell, *Jacques Lacan and Feminist Epistemology* (Abingdon: Routledge, 2004); Patricia Gherovici, *Transgender Psychoanalysis: A Lacanian Perspective on Sexual Difference* (Abingdon: Routledge, 2017); Anna Mollow, 'Lacan and Disability Studies', in *After Lacan: Literature, Theory, and Psychoanalysis in the Twenty-First Century*, ed. Ankhi Mukherjee (Cambridge: Cambridge University Press, 2018); Lara Sheehi and Stephen Sheehi, *Psychoanalysis Under Occupation: Practicing Resistance in Palestine* (Abingdon: Routledge, 2022); Laura Sokolowsky, *Psychoanalysis Under Nazi Occupation: The Origins, Impact and Influence of the Berlin Institute* [2013], trans. Janet and John Haney (Abingdon: Routledge, 2021), as well as the contributions within the pages of this book.

Chapter 13

Synchronic interactions among discourse, knowledge (saber) and jouissance. Politibiology and/or biopolitics[1]

Alfredo Eidelsztein

Introduction

Even outside psychoanalysis, it is commonplace to consider that *jouissance* and the drives [*pulsiones*] are prior to and more primitive than discourse and knowledge (*saber*; Fr. *savoir*). It is then concluded that the former are a generating factor or source of ideologies and political views. In the philosophical tradition, this is asserted as the claim that *res extensa* has priority over *res cogitans*. In more colloquial terms, it is claimed that the biological body comes before thought and speech. And in the medical field the conviction, allegedly supported by scientific evidence, is that genes, neurons and hormones precede everything that is subjective in nature.

The latter has had an enormous impact on public opinion. Indeed, reports of scientific research allegedly supporting those claims have been widely published. Some of their titles – otherwise quite eloquent – include 'The Gene of Faith has been Found', 'Hormones Govern Confidence and Skepticism', 'Genes Determine Faithfulness', 'Altruism, Decisions Regarding One's Finances, and Political Ideas have a Genetic Basis', 'A Woman's Brain Prefers Love and Hope to Having Sex', 'The Brain Area Responsible for Kindness has been Found', 'The Brain Region Linked to the Fear of Losing Money has been

Discovered', 'Morality Lies in the Genes', 'Kisses are a Means to Chemically Evaluate Romantic Compatibility between Two People', 'A Gene Determines Male Monogamy', 'The Bigger the Brain Capacity is, the More the Tendency to Lie', 'Genes Determine our Way of Being', 'Genes Choose to Vote Left- or Right-leaning Parties', 'Scientists Find the Cerebral Location of Jealousy' and 'The Possibility of Irony Lies in the Brain'. The media covering international news has also published allegedly scientific research on the biological basis for having terrorist inclinations.

This kind of claim, supported by arguments presented as scientific and admitted by common sense since roughly the second half of the last century, was formerly (say, in the first half of the twentieth century) invoked to account for 'blood' and 'race' and, consequenty, responsible for perhaps the most abhorrent period in the history of humanity. In that time the opposition constituting the main topic of this chapter was conceptualized in terms of the opposition between nature and culture. Today, 'nature' has been substituted by genes, neurons and hormones. But it could well be the case – this chapter aims to warn about this danger – that the old 'instinct' is still alive under the notions of 'drive' and/or '*jouissance*'. Indeed, although the latter lacks a pre-given object, these notions have in common with the instincts that they all stem ultimately from the anatomical body.

Thus, biology becomes the fundamental science within the realm of the social sciences, including ethics and philosophy. This view has its own epistemology: a 'naturalized epistemology',[2] that is, a movement that purports to overcome the opposition between inductivist and hypothetico-deductivist epistemology.

The main consequence of these naturalized theories is that language, culture, society, ideologies, and politics are considered to be posterior and subordinate to the existence of the anatomical body and its constitutive properties. This way of thinking impacts the way time is conceived: as linear and evolutive in nature.

In the realm of psychoanalytic concepts and Freud's theory in particular, these ideas are reflected in several of Freud's main lines of reasoning, for instance, the progressions oral → anal

→phallic →→genital; auto-erotism → alo-erotism; narcissism → object-love and so on. But this way of thinking promotes other progressive series: primitive peoples → European peoples; women → men; clitoris → vagina and so on, all of which are quite problematic. The symbol '→' represents the arrow of evolutive time. These progressions propose that evolution takes place from what is inferior: if the biological body allows it and the socio-cultural medium does not become an obstacle, then maturation will take place and the superior will be attained.

For the Lacanian school, these ideas take a different form. For instance, alienation → separation (which reinforces individualistic ways of thinking, as maturation entails separating oneself from the Other) and real → imaginary → symbolic.

Consider the latter. Contrary to what Lacan argued, the Lacanian school holds that there is something real, originally belonging to the biological body, that is doomed to remain fundamentally inaccessible to the imaginary and the symbolic. All this paves the way for the justification of racist, xenophobic and misogynistic arguments, such as: if one is born with an African-descendant, Jewish or female body, there is something to these bodies that will remain the same, that is, something real, an essential core to which one should adapt oneself. Further, as these followers of Lacan also claim that *jouissance* is singular (unique) and originally pertaining to the anatomical body, they open the door for a sort of social Darwinism that, in our time, has not ceased to expand and shape the allegedly scientific approach to subjectivity and social relations. Let us make clear that Lacan never admitted the thesis of the singularity of *jouissance*, as he argued that the latter remains always particular in nature, that is, it is a modality of the Other.

The views criticized above tend to present themselves in opposition to the delusory character of all forms of idealism, proclaiming that they are 'materialistic' in nature and aspiring to be seen as genuinely real and true disciplines.

What follows is a series of arguments, ideas and theories that sustains the opposite stance.

1. If by 'prejudice' one means an idea that is presented as self-evident and, therefore, impervious to any criticism, then one should reject the 'materialist prejudice' that claims that in psychoanalysis, as well as in other fields of knowledge, concepts arise from personal experiences, be they the consequence of clinical experience or of field studies. Focusing on psychoanalysis, this prejudice can be refuted simply by enumerating some of Freud's fundamental concepts and showing how they did not originate in Freud's clinical practice but were taken from his reading of various authors: erogenous zone (from Bloch), ambivalence (from Bleuler), bisexuality (from Fliess), *Id* (from Grodeck), auto-eroticism (from Ellis), regression (from Jackson), infantile sexuality (from Moll), libido (from Krafft-Ebing), the ominous (from Schelling), the Nirvana principle (from Schopenhauer), the inertia principle (from Newton), free association (from Morelli), the unconscious' other scene (from Fechner) and repression (from Herbart). It is worth noticing both Freud's intellectual honesty – he himself referred his readers to all of these sources (as well as to many others not listed here) – and the impressive manner in which he was able to integrate so many theoretical contributions into a paradigm consistent enough as to create psychoanalysis as a new practical-theoretical discipline.

2. Another prejudice that must be rejected is that which claims that sexuality, the satisfactions and dissatisfactions linked to it, the drives and their amounts, and the modalities of *jouissance* are originally biological in nature, that is, originated in the anatomical body and its contents, something one is born with. Research conducted on these topics clearly shows that these claims are untenable: heterosexual love and extramarital passion are historical products;[3] the value and meaning of sexuality are socially and historically determined;[4] hysteria is an invention;[5] the subjective locus of sex has been constructed;[6] pain has cultural roots;[7] heterosexuality as a generator of a specific order of things is a cultural reality;[8] the ways in which humans eat, drink, sleep, have intercourse and so on, are socio-cultural techniques;[9] maternal love emerged within particular temporal and spatial coordinates;[10] sexuality is a device originated in Western technologies of power in the nineteenth century;[11] and the demand to attain *jouissance*, as well as the desire to possess the missing object, is derived from the command to consume intrinsic to Western postmodern society.[12] Thus, pain and love, passion and desire, so-considered 'normal' heterosexuality, and the usage of the body and its possibilities are historical, cultural and social facts. Even the significance conferred to sexuality as an ordering principle of one's subjective positions has a datable origin and is a socio-cultural reality.

3. To effectively resist individualistic prejudices, it is important to be aware of the many authors that, starting centuries ago, posit that thinking occurs without an I doing the thinking. Among them, let us mention D. Hofstadter, J.L. Borges, B. Latour, L. Fleck, Saint Agustine, Averroes, Lichtenberg, Schelling, Nietzsche, Lévi-Strauss, Rimbaud, P. Ricoeur, A. de Libera, M. Angenot, Foucault, Popper, Kuhn and Lacan. It is perhaps Lacan who developed this thesis most consistently. In *Seminar 17*, he claims that 'properly speaking, there is a perfectly articulated knowledge for which no subject is responsible'.[13] And here is a stronger formulation: 'In the unconscious, less profound than inaccessible to the conscious attempt to go deeper, *it* speaks'[14] (my italics). And also, finally: 'The unconscious, *it speaks*, which makes it a function of language' (my italics).[15]

It thinks and, with Lacan, *it* also speaks and *it* experiences *jouissance*; therefore, *I* do not think, speak or experience *jouissance* as an individual. Further, the biological body is not the antecedent of these actions: it is the Other (language, family, society, etc.).

4: As Lacan teaches, it is imperative to consider the Other as an instance that is always prior to the subject,[16] desire,[17] *jouissance*,[18] the unitary trait,[19] the unconscious,[20] S_1 and its rejection[21] and so on.[22]

Admitting Lacan's argument, one must accept that language exists prior to those who speak it. Lacan articulates this insight thusly: 'language has always been there since eternity.'[23] Along the same lines, in his teaching, he introduces the idea that 'in the beginning there was the Word'.[24] 'Since eternity' and 'in the beginning' do not mean that language comes first in an evolutionary line. Quite the contrary, it means that when one is studying the subject and society, all pure, causal, biological determinations must be deemed irrelevant as a consequence of the emergence of language. To clarify the nature of this way of reasoning, it is very helpful to have recourse to the Big Bang Theory.[25]

Lacan's position – one that entails the rejection of the idea that the anatomical body with its drives and *jouissance* is prior to the signifier, the Other discourse, and, especially, knowledge – is validated by the extensive list of all the simultaneous discoveries made along the history of modern science by scientists and inventors that ignored the work of their fellow researchers. The prejudice we are examining can therefore be challenged by presenting a list of discoveries or inventions simultaneously published by different authors: cytology, thermodynamics, the periodic table of elements, the meson, oxygen, the gas law, non-orientable surfaces, the evolution of the species, the telephone, electrons, Newton's laws, aluminium, Einstein's field equations, the XY chromosome system, the dynamo, the mechanisms of breathing, infinitesimal calculus, universal gravity, the quarks and so on. As all these discoveries, inventions, theories and techniques were made public around the same time by a plurality of authors who were not aware of the others' work, one must conclude that both knowledge and unknown-knowledge (what is about to become known or is about to be discovered – and even invented) exist in an epistemic field independently of the individuals that participate in these fields – fields that only a few of these authors have formalized and made public.

Lacan embraced a clear stance on this topic. Writing on Newton's laws, he writes that their discovery is 'the best example in the history of science showing the extent to which human discourse is universal',[26] and holds that 'inventions are produced . . . at exactly the same time . . . by *subjects* . . . who are at great distances from one another'.[27]

5: Along the same argumentative lines one should also stress the fundamental role that Lacan's reflections on the Borromean Knot play in his teaching. This knot is characterized by a specific property: in it, the symbolic, the imaginary and the real are intertwined in a Brunnian manner (the set is bound as a whole, but removing any loop entails the dissolution of the whole). This is a reasoning that rejects the evolutionary logic defended by most of Lacan's disciples: first there is the real (the biological body of the newly born baby), then the imaginary (the mirror stage when the child is around six months old), and, finally, the symbolic (when the infant learns a language, approximately in its eighteenth month). The Borromean Knot – R, S and I or S, R, I – firmly establishes a logic according to which all the loops exist together in a synchronic temporality and are intertwined in such a way that their interdependence is absolute.

As Lacan makes clear, synchrony is not the same thing as simultaneity. The former is a neologism coined by Saussure[28] to account for the logic of the origin and existence of any language: all its terms must be operative from the very start. A consequence of the rational requirement deriving from the theory that holds that all signifiers only consist of their difference regarding all others is that such a beginning cannot be dated. 'Simultaneous', on the contrary, refers to something entirely different, namely, the coincidence of a plurality of phenomena taking place at the same instant, something that can be established by means of a clock.

The battery, the treasure of signifiers and discourse are all intertwined; their structure cannot be conceived in evolutive terms. Thus, Saussure's linguistics and Lacan's psychoanalysis reject that one can posit the existence of a first element and then a series of others that follow it consecutively. Lacan solves the seemingly emerging paradox by regarding the relation between the synchronic and diachronic dimensions (at the level of spoken speech as at the level of writing each term is expressed one after the other) from two conceptual tools created by him. One is temporal: the time of the *future antérieure* (the past comes before the future and the future comes before the past); the other is spatial: the loop (a closed line) where S_1 comes before S_2 and S_2 comes before S_1. To validate ideas so subversive in relation to the prevailing configuration of Western thought, it must be kept in mind that every phrase, written or spoken, in any language requires for its interpretation to posit both that the first elements of the phrase determine (anticipate) the last ones while the last ones resignify the former. Without the period it is not possible to interpret what the first elements even mean.

6. The opposition between the two paradigms can be eloquently shown by reference to the analysis of the so-called 'adolescence crisis'. In the Western world, this is uniformly interpreted as the consequence of the evolutive growth of the biological body, which, together with the development of secondary sexual characteristics as well as sexual desire, provokes in the youth a shock that is the consequence of the rearrangement required by the hormonal and anatomic transformations of puberty, a transformation that, in turn, is reflected by their conflict with their image and their relationships. All of this appears unquestionable. However, it can be thought of in a completely different manner.

Taking up and developing N. Elias's arguments in his 'The Society of Individuals',[29] one may posit that the true conflict is social in nature and is due to the passage from the forms of life organized around tribes, family clans, and rural communities to state, urban and industrialized societies, a transformation that belongs to Western history of the last centuries.

At the end of this passage the adolescent leaves behind a habitat constituted by endogenous, protective, local (autochthonous) groups having tasks, obligations and concerns shared and distributed among all its members to arrive at a highly centralized society (nation-state), increasingly more urban and more demanding in terms of the formal studies one must undergo to achieve, after a certain age, one's independence. Thus, one is compelled to autonomously choose a course of study, a profession, a job, a dwelling place, a partner and so on, and even how one wants to dress and the music one wants to enjoy. Confronting the increasing and exponential number of possibilities on offer, the individual finds himself alone, left to his own devices, and obligated to choose.

This individuation process is imposed on each of us, especially after having achieved our alleged 'maturity'. The correlative crisis initiated by this state of affairs is not a consequence of the growth of one's breasts, hair and so on, but the result of a situation where one finds oneself having to choose, as soon as possible, among an increasing number of new alternatives available. Further, this decision is supposed to require that the individual is informed and has the proper knowledge to make up his mind without the interference of others, something that is highly praised, as autonomy is thought to prove the decision's authenticity. Its paradox is apparent when one observes the striking postmodern increase of abulia, isolation and suicide among teenagers and young adults in our consumer society, the ever-growing multiplication of possibilities offered to them, and the correlative temptation of desire to pursue them.[30] A non-contradictory expression of the same situation is the emergence of urban tribes among the youth, which constitute powerful imitations of vanished communal forms of life, groups that offer, usually at a high cost for those who enter them, a sense of belonging to a community.

Is there an adolescent crisis in those parts of the world where extended family, people, tribe or clan are still the prevailing social forms? The Eurocentrism exhibited by many of the interpretations of this problem clearly points in the direction of a negative answer to the question.

The stance being defended in this essay finds additional support through an analysis of events commonly designated as 'May '68', a series of protests led by young students against consumer society, capitalism, authoritarianism and so on, events that had repercussions in many countries. These anti-establishment protests did not aim to seize power – they were neither revolutionary nor subversive – but to change society. They were demonstrations against the system that would typically start in universities and even sometimes in high schools. During the same years, the United States witnessed the emergence of the hippie movement, an anti-establishment, anti-war and non-conformist counterculture that focused on the criticism of sexual taboos. All of these protest movements show that the basis of the conflict experienced by the youth is not biological, but social, cultural and historical in nature.

7. The primacy or original position of the drives was challenged by Lacan by making use of the idea of an echo as a particular acoustic phenomenon. He puts it as follows:

> It is only by means of its equivocal character that interpretation works. There must be something in the signifier that resonates. It is puzzling that it went completely unnoticed for the English philosophers. I call them philosophers because they are not psychoanalysts. They believe with conviction that speech [*la parole*] has no effects. They are wrong. They imagine that there are drives [*pulsions*] [. . .]. They do not imagine that the drives are the echo in the body of the fact that there is a saying [*un dire*].[31]

The idea of an echo suggests that Lacan admits that although what is at stake here is the tridimensional body (like mountains), the drives are nothing but the consequence of the impact of a saying, of speech, on the body's surface (not its interior). It is from that surface that the saying returns, which creates the tricky impression that it is from the interior of the body that one speaks. Every modern speaker is under this illusion and Lacan adds that psychoanalysts too make the mistake of believing it.

8. For psychoanalysis – as, at least, for the social sciences – there is a crucial polarization between two positions, one of which was referred to by Foucault as 'the political honor of psychoanalysis'.[32] The latter lies in the fact that its knowledge and its practice confront biopolitics, that s, politics understood as originating in and destined to uphold the management and biological control of the social, cultural and subjective realms. For him psychoanalysis is characterized – or, more rigorously, should be characterized – by its theoretical effort of reinscribing the issue of sexuality in the symbolic order's system of the law. According to his view, psychoanalysis holds that the law is to be found in sexuality as a principle.[33] This chapter advances the same thesis.

The other position argues that one is born with a balance or imbalance of the amounts of drives and/or the modalities of *jouissance.* This makes it impossible for the symbolic and the imaginary to work through them and, as a consequence, the residue of such original balance/imbalance operates as an essence for all subjects, an essence each individual is responsible for.

Conclusion

As one can attest to the existence of biopolitics, that is, the belief that the modalities of *jouissance* ground the political discourses and attitudes people embrace, it is also possible to claim that politics synchronically grounds the existing and preferred modalities of *jouissance.* If one is to admit the idea of a 'biopolitics' (the same applies to expressions such as 'sociobiology', 'ethnobiology' and 'anthropobiology'[34]), the idea of a 'politibiology' should also be admitted. Coining this neologism (1) entails the creation of a noun to designate the study of this aspect of the synchronic interactions among discourse, knowledge and *jouissance,* and (2) aims to articulate the notion that both ideas and their designations – 'biopolitics' and 'politibiology' – anticipate and condition each other. As 'biopolitics' suggests that biology is prior to and conditions politics, the neologism 'politibiology' posits that polit cs is prior to biology.

A convenient abstract model that may illuminate the discussion on this issue is the Moebius/Listing strip – a noteworthy case of simultaneous discovery, even though Listing never reached any popularity. Despite its apparent two sides, the strip is unilateral. Consider it as a two-tone (say, black and white), tridimensional paper strip existing in space. Now, join its extremes through a half-twist and make the two colours coincide along an edge.

If one starts from any of the apparent faces of the strip and one's trajectory is continuous and complete, one will arrive without crossing any edge to the other side. If one thinks of politibiology and biopolitics as the two sides of the strip, it is possible to challenge individualistic and biologistic prejudices, as well as the concept of evolutionary time. Indeed, that the basis for any argument on the subject and the social link is biopolitics or politibiology depends on what point of view is being adopted. But one would do well to keep in mind that any serious undertaking that starts from either of these perspectives will necessarily end up arriving at the other without crossing any logical or disciplinary boundary, as they are both in an interdependent relationship – interdependent, surely, but not reciprocal. Psychoanalysis should maintain its specific character as a discipline by starting off from discourse and knowledge as a way of accessing *jouissance* and its possible modalities, knowing that this way of proceeding entails the renunciation of all essence and all origin.

Notes

1 This text was translated by Dr Nicolás Garrera-Tolbert (translator).

2 Adelaida Ambrogi (ed.), *Filosofía de la ciencia: el giro naturalista* (Islas Baleares: UIB, 1999).

3 Denis de Rougemont, *Love in the Western World* (Princeton: Princeton University Press, 1983).

4 Arnold I. Davidson, *The Emergence of Sexuality. Historical Epistemology and the Formation of Concepts* (Cambridge, MA and London: Harvard University Press, 2001).

5 Georges, *Invention de l'Hystérie: Charcot et l'Iconographie Photographique de la Salpêtrière* (Paris: Macula, 1982).

6 Laqueur, *Thomas, Making Sex. Body and Gender from the Greeks to Freud* (Cambridge, MA and London: Harvard University Press, 1990).

7 David B. Morris, *The Culture of Pain* (Berkeley, Los Angeles and London: University of California Press, 1991).

8 Louis-Georges Tin, *The Invention of Heterosexual Culture* (Cambridge, MA and London: The MIT Press, 2012).

9 Marcel Mauss, *Sociologie et anthropologie* (Paris: Quadrige/P.U.F., 1997).

10 Elisabeth Badinter, *L'amour en plus. Histoire de l'amour maternel XVIIe–XX^w siècle* (Paris: Flammarion, 1980).

11 Michel Foucault, *Histoire de la sexualité. La volonté de savoir* (Paris: Gallimard, 1976).

12 Alfredo Eidelsztein, *Postmodernidad y Psicoanálisis* (forthcoming).

13 Jacques Lacan, *Seminar 17*, 5th session (11 February 1970). [I have translated all the author's quotations of Lacan's seminars from Spanish, but I have made sure that they correspond to the most accurate version of the Seminars available: www.staferla.free.fr (Translator's note).]

14 Jacques Lacan, *Écrits* (Paris: Éditions du Seuil, 1966), 437.

15 Jacques Lacan, *Television* (9 March 1974).

16 Jacques Lacan, *Seminar 3*, 15th session (18 April 1956) and *Seminar 12*, 10th session (15 April 1964).

17 Jacques Lacan, *Seminar 8*, 15th session (22 March 1961).

18 Jacques Lacan, *Seminar 17*, 12th session (10 June 1970).

19 Jacques Lacan, *Seminar 17*, 11th session (20 May 1970).

20 Jacques Lacan, *Seminar 11*, 10th session (15 April 1964).

21 Jacques Lacan, *Seminar 18*, 1st session (13 January 1971).

22 Cf. Alfredo Eidelsztein, *El origen del sujeto en psicoanálisis. Del Big Bang del discurso y el lenguaje* (Buenos Aires: Letra Viva, 2018). English translation forthcoming.

23 Jacques Lacan, *Seminar 2* (22nd session).

24 Jacques Lacan, *Rapport de Rome* (1953), *Seminar 2* (22th session), and *Seminar 7* (16th session).

25 Alfredo Eidelsztein, *El origen del sujeto en psicoanálisis. Del Big Bang del discurso y el lenguaje*.

26 Jacques Lacan, *Seminar 2*, 19th session (25 May 1955).

27 Jacques Lacan, 'Discussion of Charles Morazé's "Literary Invention"', in *The Structuralist Controversy. The Languages of Criticism and the Sciences of Man*, ed. Richard Macksey and Eugenio Donato (Baltimore and London: John Hopkins Press, 1972).

28 Ferdinand de Saussure, *Cours de linguistique générale* (Paris: Payot, 1995; Tullio de Mauro, ed.).

29 Norbert Elias, *The Society of Individuals* (New York and London: Continuum, 2001), esp. Part II-C.

30 Gilles Lipovetsky, *L'ère du vide. Essais sur l'individualisme contemporain* (Paris: Gallimard, 1989).

31 Jacques Lacan, *Seminar 23*, 1st session (18 November 1975).

32 Foucault, *Histoire de la sexualité*, 197–8.

33 Ibid., 197.

34 Sociobiology studies human society from a biological standpoint; ethnobiology examines cultural phenomena from a biological perspective; anthropobiology aims to elucidate the human diversity over time and space on the basis of biology.

Chapter 14

The jouissance of capital

Notes for a Lacanian critique of political economy

David Pavón-Cuéllar

Fantasy and its truth

Technological automation allows capital to increasingly do without human beings as subjects in order to enjoy them as objects. The jouissance of capital with regard to objects, human as well as non-human, increasingly predominates over people's ties to each other and to things. It can be said that the subjects give so much credence to capital that they become its objects.

The conversion of subjects into objects of subjectified capital is one of the expressions of alienation in the Marxian sense of the term. According to Karl Marx, the alienation of subjects is correlated to the fetishization of capital, which acts as a kind of subject by self-valorizing itself with its objective expressions, its commodities, and its human and non-human resources. Marx's *Capital* unfolds the objective fantasy of an absolutized capitalism that reminds us of Hegelian knowledge: objectively, it is as if capital, as a big Other, becomes the only subject.[1]

Of course, Marx was very well aware that capital as a subject is a fantasy of capitalism. One of the main purposes of the Marxian critique of political economy is precisely to reveal that capital is not the actual subject, that it does not even exist by itself, that its existence comes from the labour power of the proletariat. The proletariat, as represented by Marx, is the subject that underlies capital, the living core of the inert bone, the blood of the vampire, the coral life in the reef of the economy, the existence in the essence, the emptiness of the face behind the capitalist mask, the truth inherent in fiction.

The objective fantasy of capital is refuted by the Marxian demonstration of the non-existence of the big Other. Marx divides the big Other, literally crosses it out (∅), by showing that it is materially inhabited by subjects, by their lives and their class struggles, and is not merely a simple, formal, automatic, autonomous and self-sufficient signifying structure. The structure has its truth in those who support it. This truth is in the same place as the subject of the unconscious in Lacan: the place of the subject of the enunciation ($) that underlies the subject enunciated as a signifier (S1).[2]

Marx shows that the true subject of capitalism is 'us' and not capital. However, to prove it, he must first show how the capitalist system usurps our place as subjects and objectively constitutes itself, through the objective fantasy, as a self-generated totality in which there is no place for us. This must be shown because it is not obvious to the common sense of individuals who imagine themselves to be free and masters of their actions in a capitalist society.

In Lacanian terms, Marx went successively from the ego to the Other, and from the Other to the subject. First, he went through the superstructure of consciousness, the specular surface of the imaginary autonomy of the ego, to discover behind it and below it the base of the unconscious, the heteronomy of the subject in the autonomy of the symbolic system of capitalism, of capital that appears as Other, as *the subject of the subject*. Then, Marx went further to bar or cross out the Other by traversing the fantasy of the *automaton*, of capital autonomized as a subject, to come into contact with the reality of capitalism and arrive at the true subject, the proletarian as the labour force of capital.[3]

It is impossible to reach the subject without first going through the objective fantasy in which the subject is missing. In the material objectivity of this fantasy, there is no place for any subject apart from the Other – the non-subject of capital. Here, we arrive at the objectivist fetishization that Marx detects in some economists. For them, it is as if capital were sufficient to accumulate. It is also as if the economic relations of the capitalist system, relations between commodities mediated by the general equivalent of money, supplant all the social relations of the symbolic system of culture.[4]

Quantification and privatization

The fetishist supplanting of social relations by economic relations can only be possible because both are signifying relations. As explained by Jacques Lacan, the notion of the significance of both relations is essential to understanding the subsumption of culture in capitalism. This real subsumption can only be understood through the Lacanian thesis of the symbolic system of society and the economy.

Lacan is clear that both social and economic relations are established not on the basis of intersubjectivity but on the basis of an '*intersignificance*', a link between signifiers, between symbolic entities, which are only 'subjectified in their consequences'.[5] Subjects only relate to each other, derivatively, n terms of what certain signifiers represent for other signifiers. Do we not have here the universal expression of the Marxian idea of fetishism, whereby things are related through people instead of people being related through things? In the fetishist functioning of the symbolic system of culture, intersignificant relations are the basic fact.

In Lacanian terms, at the base is the 'society of signifiers' with which the human group is formed through an economy consisting of the jouissance of the 'accumulation of signifiers'.[6] Lacan observes that 'the economy, even the one attributed to nature, is always a fact of discourse', with jouissance operating 'not only as a fact, but as an effect of discourse'.[7] This Lacanian idea of the discursive economy of jouissance does not contradict Marx and several of his followers, but it is in clear contradiction with the classic Marxist economistic vision of a discursive superstructure resting on an extra-discursive economic base.[8]

The signifiers are the constitutive elements of any economic system. However, in the capitalist system, the signifiers lose their qualitative complexity and turn into simple quantitative values of exchange, values of jouissance, which represent less and less the subjects and more and more the objects of the jouissance of capital. This jouissance tends to become what is signified by all that is symbolic – by the unconscious in Freud and by the discourse of the Other in Lacan. The entire culture, the entire sphere of the Other, is subsumed into the automated capitalist system.[9]

The jouissance of capital, of the valorization and accumulation of capital, seizes the 'jouissance of the Other', of the 'passion of the signifier'.[10] The only exciting signifier is increasingly the one that comes to occupy the place of possession for possession's sake, that of the object of phallic jouissance – that is, the reiterative signifier of money. This signifier has two distinctive aspects, quantification and privatization, which explain much of what capitalism provokes in the world and in subjectivity.

In the first place, as already noted, money only admits quantitative differences. The consequence of this, noted by Marx and Engels, is that money functions as a 'common measure' and a '*tertium comparationis*' of all things and people, and allows them to be compared with each other, annulling their 'unique' and 'incomparable' character.[11] Money transmutes qualitative differences into quantitative disparities that are not even differences, since differences – as correctly indicated by Mao – meet the criterion of 'already entailing contradictions'.[12] The monetary quantitative disparities exclude contradiction and reduce the oppositions between signifiers to simple gradations of a single signifier – that of money – whose accounting allows the various dimensions of things to be dissolved into a single quantifiable dimension. Thus, money leads us to the undifferentiated one-dimensionality that increasingly reigns over life and thought, which imposes inequality without leaving room for difference, negativity, criticism, or conflict, as Herbert Marcuse masterfully demonstrated.[13]

Second, money can be privatized, become private property or belong to a single individual to the exclusion or deprivation of others. This distinguishes money from other signifiers that are usually public, always being already socialized, associating subjects and already intrinsically constituting the social.[14] Although there are insurmountable differences between the relationships that different subjects establish with signifiers, these signifiers are aspects that they have in common and that, therefore, can be at the foundation of the community and of communism, in contrast to the money that always belongs to someone and separates everyone from the rest.

Money, as Marx said, is 'the general means of separation', the 'true dividing currency', which manages to 'untie all ties'.[15] Contributing to anomie and atomization, money destroys the signifying relationships that constitute culture to replace them with exchange, trade and market relationships, which are predominant in capitalism. The mercantile exchange between private individualized spheres supplants the constitutive transindividual community of the public space of the Other.[16]

Instead of having symbols in common, we have a general equivalent with which we exchange things and people so that capital is produced and accumulated. Thus, with the subsumption of the symbolic system into the capitalist system, money becomes the only 'means of union, the galvano-chemical force of society'.[17] Only the external social link remains, mediated by the arithmetical simplicity of money, by the qualitative poverty of its quantitative wealth, where earlier there was the community that was internally constituted by the culturally qualitative diversity of the different signifiers that mediated among subjects.

It is true that the various constitutive qualities of culture have been dissolved not only through the general equivalent of money. There are other general equivalents, such as the phallus or the being that designates everything *that is*, which make possible the same dissolution of the qualitative diversity of culture. However, unlike the other analogous signifiers, money is distinguished because it dissolves community, with its public and cultural qualities, through its quantification and privatization.[18]

Jouissance as self-valorization in the general formula of capital

The young Marx marvels at how 'all human and natural qualities' can be confused and dissolved in money, in its simple and quantifiable quality, in 'the universality of its quality' which translates into 'the omnipotence of its essence', 'the property of buying everything'.[19] Similarly, Lacan describes money, the signifier that can signify everything, as the most destructive signifier – 'the most annihilating of any signification'.[20] What significance can subsist in the money that, in Marx's terms, 'transforms fidelity into infidelity, love into hate, hate into love, virtue into vice, vice into virtue, servant into lord, lord into a servant, stupidity into understanding, understanding into stupidity'?[21] Money can mean anything and so it nullifies any meaning.

Any use value or other intrinsic symbolic value of things tends to dissipate with the contact of money. The monetary substitute for the phallus, the general equivalent that does not mean anything by itself since its only use value lies in its exchange value, is thus the most perfect object for a jouissance that 'is useless' and only exists because it is ordered as an 'imperative' of the superego.[22] This superego is what impels us to enjoy – that is, to let ourselves be possessed by the enjoyment of capital, of money, as the dominant historical version of the jouissance of the signifier, of the Other, of the language of the unconscious as an 'apparatus of jouissance'.[23]

In the absence of metalanguage, of an Other of the Other, it is as if today there is only globalized capitalism that enjoys itself through and at our expense. It is this joyful *automaton* of capital that Lacan describes through his capitalist discourse. In this discourse, it is as if the subjects no longer count but in the form of simple moments of capital, either as 'personifications' of capital, as capitalists[24] or as 'variable capital', as commodified labour power.[25] Once everything appears to have been subsumed into capitalism, the capitalist system can pretend to function automatically and 'timelessly', in a 'closed circuit', with the 'eternity' of the unconscious, as already noted by Althusser.[26]

The joyous automaton of capitalism is already in an embryonic state in the self-valorization that Marx describes with his 'general formula of capital', money-commodity-money (M-C-M'), which comes to supplant the 'direct form of circulation', commodity-money-commodity (C-M-C).[27] Instead of the old peasants or artisans who went to the market to sell their products (C-M) and buy what they needed (M-C), what we now have is the capital that buys everything (M-C) to sell it at a higher price and, thus, obtain the surplus-value it enjoys (C-M'). In other words, instead of 'selling to buy', selling a commodity that is produced to obtain the money (C-M) that makes it possible to buy another commodity with a utility or qualitatively different use value (C-M), capitalism is all about 'buying to sell' – buying a commodity with a certain amount of money (M-C) and then selling it a higher price, for a greater amount of money, thereby giving it a quantitatively higher exchange value (C-M'). The purpose of this operation, obtaining more money (-M'), is precisely the jouissance of capital, its self-valorization (M-C-M'), and not simply the acquisition and subsequent use of a commodity by a subject (M-D-M).

In the general formula of capital (M-C-M'), what is important is no longer the use value of the commodity, which is not bought for its intrinsic utility but only to be sold at a higher price. As Marx says, 'the driving motive and the determining purpose' is the 'exchange value itself'.[28] It is only a matter of increasing it, obtaining more jouissance value, a surplus value that represents a *plus-de-jouir*, a surplus of jouissance or more jouissance for capital – an opportunity for capital to have more enjoyment by valuing itself through commodities.

Marx shows us how the self-valorization of capital involves various kinds of commodities that are bought and sold, produced and consumed, used and exploited. Of all these commodities, the determining factor for the generation of value is the life of the subject, a life that is exploited as labour power. This commodity is not bought simply to sell it at a higher price, as in a traditional slave market, but it is bought for a certain amount of money to exploit it and, thus, produce other goods that are sold for an amount of money greater than that which was disbursed for it.

Further, the supplementary links do not modify the process of capitalist self-valorization: the money disbursed, the capital invested, has to go through the circuit of commodities – fundamentally labour power – for it to return increased (M-C-M'). This circular automatic movement is clearly described by Lacan in his capitalist discourse, where capital (S1) must pass through the circuit of other signifiers (S2) to produce a surplus of jouissance (a) that only passes through the subject ($) to end up being incorporated into the capital (S1). This is how capital enjoys everything else – by possessing it, by subsuming it into its jouissance, by consuming it and exploiting it to return to itself with an increased supplement of jouissance, with the surplus value of capital which is the surplus of jouissance that is incessantly lost by the subject.

The vampire of capital who kisses itself

The circuit of self-valorizing capital makes us think of self-erotic, self-sufficient jouissance, which Freud compares to the mouth of one who only passes through other lips because he cannot 'kiss himself'.[29] As Lacan rightly observes when commenting on this image, the goal of the drive is a 'return in circuit'.[30] It is like what Marx reveals to us through the capital that acts 'as if its body were by love possessed',[31] the capital that only invests itself in exploited labour to return to itself increased, to enjoy itself by exploiting labour, by appropriating it as variable capital and, thus, self-valorizing with a surplus-value, with more capital.[32]

It is in order to enjoy itself, its self-valorization, that the vampire of capital must pass through the exploited worker, subsumed in the capitalist process, exactly like the kiss that passes through other lips to reach one's own lips. It must be understood that, here, the other lips are only a means, a scale, a momentary object of the drive. The final instinctual goal is the deadly fundamental fantasy of kissing oneself – that is, for capital, enjoying its own self-valorization directly, immediately and automatically, without going through the labour force. This phantasmagoria is realized not only in an imaginary manner in finance, in which money appears to multiply by itself but also in a real, impossible manner, in the always unattainable dystopian horizon of technological advances that would make it possible to completely dispense with the workforce, the workers, the subjects with their existence, with their experience and their conscience.

The paradoxical overcoming of life by technology subsumed in capital would be the most ominous outcome of a movement that blindly obeys the general law of capitalist accumulation. Such an outcome, as impossible and devastating as it appears in Marx, would absolutely consummate the process of progressive automation, which is also a process of objectivation and desubjectivization, as well as symbolization, derealization, virtualization and devitalization.[33] This process that is inherent to the capitalist discourse would finally lead to the kiss of death, to the mouth kissing itself lethally, without mediation.

An immediate self-valorization of capital would imply the absolute triumph of the death drive, which could finally surrender to a free fall in a straight line, in a short circuit, without the *clinamen* from which everything comes, without the 'deviations' and 'detours' to which the drive of life pushes.[34] These deviations and detours, in which the very circuit of the self-valorization of capital is included, are the kisses of others through which the vampire of capital must pass in order to kiss itself: thus, they are an onerous vital remnant of the past that is technologically overcome by making savings for the benefit of capital, either by reducing mediations, eliminating the links in the cycle, simplifying processes, laying off workers, looking for shortcuts, and shortening times and distances.

Renunciation and hoarding

The vampire of capital has not managed to get rid of us. It still engages in enjoyment through the mediation of subjects who only know enjoyment negatively, as something to be dispossessed, as dispossession itself, as the renunciation of enjoyment. Even the capitalist must renounce the jouissance that belongs to capital and not to the person who personifies it. This renunciation, as we know from Weber, appears as a form of 'intraworldly asceticism' that is historically associated with the spiritual rootedness of capitalism in the Protestant ethic of Calvinism and that acts 'against the carefree enjoyment of wealth' while 'it breaks the chains of the desire for profit from the moment that it not only legalizes it, but also considers it a divine precept .[35]

The *intraworldly asceticism* that Weber refers to consists of the double mandate of working to get rich and depriving oneself of enjoying the wealth that is obtained. This double mandate is summed up in the Lacanian idea of labour, which is understood as something that 'implies the renunciation of jouissance'.[36] It is not only that one ceases to enjoy working, but the fact of renouncing enjoyment can itself be labour – the labour of the renunciation of enjoyment, the labour that underlies any labour and that distinguishes it from pleasurable activities, not laborious ones.[37]

The emphasis on labour is also important to avoid confusion between, on the one hand, the purely negative experience of laborious renunciation of enjoyment by the dispassionate, cold and calculating capitalist, and, on the other hand, the negative-positive experience of joycus renunciation of enjoyment by the old greedy miser who does not stop enjoying his wealth and who appears, in Marx, as the 'hoarder'.[38] Undoubtedly, this hoarder precedes the capitalist in the art of renunciation, a precedence that did not go unnoticed by Marx, who not only discovered in hoarding a 'renunciation of wealth in its material reality' and a disdain for 'worldly, temporary, and fleeting' pleasures, but was ahead of Weber in attributing this 'asceticism' to a Protestantism that he would subsequently describe as the most appropriate form of religion for a 'society of commodity producers'.[39] Protestant asceticism is found in the same renunciation of the hoarder as in that of the capitalist, but this does not imply that it is the same renunciation in both cases.

As Marx rightly indicates, what the hoarder renounces is the *material reality of wealth* in *worldly, temporary and fleeting pleasures*. However, as Marx also recognizes, this renunciation enables the same hoarder to achieve something that must be associated with jouissance, which is understood in Lacanian terms as possession for possession's sake: the 'appropriation of wealth in its general form' as an 'eternal treasure which can be touched neither by moths nor by rust, and which is wholly celestial and wholly mundane'.[40] The hoarders enjoy themselves when they frantically surrender, in Marx's terms, to the 'Sisyphean torment of accumulation'.[41] It is for such enjoyment of the 'gold fetish' that the hoarders 'sacrifice the pleasures of the flesh'.[42] It is correlatively through their renunciation of these pleasures that they can have the jouissance – the jouissance as possession – that the capitalist renounces.

The hoarders enjoy what they have, their possession, their accumulation, while the capitalists must work tirelessly to cede their enjoyment to capital; this is because, according to what Marx observes, capitalism would be 'destroyed at its base by laying down the premise that the driving motive is enjoyment and not enrichment'.[43] In reality, the propelling motive of capital is enrichment, accumulation, the cumulative abstract enjoyment of capital and not a concrete joyful spending by the capitalist. It is not the capitalist who enjoys capital, but capital that enjoys accumulating, accumulating its own enjoyment of it and through the capitalist's work of renunciation.

As Marx masterfully says, capitalists are 'more or less unable to perform their function from the moment they represent the wealth of enjoyment, the accumulation of enjoyment, instead of the enjoyment of accumulation'.[44] The capable capitalists, the ones qualified to fulfil their function in capitalism, are the ones who work to enjoy only accumulating and nothing else. The capital that accumulates must not be wasted in enjoying something different from it: it must not serve the capitalists to accumulate a jouissance of life or the world but to deprive them of this enjoyment through a labour of renunciation, laboriously renouncing enjoyment to attempt to merely enjoy the accumulation.[45]

The important thing is that the attempt to enjoy accumulation is a vain attempt for the capitalist. The jouissance of accumulating is a jouissance not of the subject, but of the Other, of capital personified in the capitalist. For capital, to accumulate is to enjoy, to possess, to possess for the sake of possessing, while capitalists can only enjoy-without-enjoying by enjoying the renunciation of the enjoyment of the capital that inhabits them, that exploits them, that also enjoys them.

The capitalists must work to accumulate the enjoyment of capital, thereby distinguishing themselves from the hoarder who himself enjoys what he accumulates. In fact, unlike the hoarder, the capitalist only enjoys the enjoyment of the Other. Thus, it is like possessed persons who have to laboriously renounce the jouissance of which they are a part, the jouissance of the capital that is personified in them, that enjoys them and the rest through them, who possesses them just like a demon, but only to produce an increasing amount of surplus value, an increasing amount of jouissance for capital.[46]

Surplus value as jouissance of capital

At first sight, surplus value may appear as a simple supplement of purely monetary value. This is how it usually appears in the eyes of economists, but not in Marx's texts. It is true that for Marx, as we have seen, the surplus value of the capitalist is distinguished from that of the hoarder by implying renunciation, the purification of any pathological element of jouissance for the subject. However, as we have also seen, when the subject renounces the enjoyment of it, it does not imply that the capital does not enjoy surplus value.

The jouissance of capital benefits from an unpolluted, impersonal economy, without traces of enjoyment for the subjects, such as the one that the World Bank and the International Monetary Fund (IMF) attempt to impose in all countries. What happens in this context is what Lacan observed in Kant's ethics and what made him associate it with Sade's perversion: the exclusion of any experiential pathological element in the discursive formula of the moral law only serves for the Other to enjoy a 'fantasy that has no reality but of discourse'.[47] Just as the jouissance of the Other in Kant and Sade requires sacrificing utility, pleasure and everything else to the purely symbolic value of the categorical-perverse imperative, the jouissance of capital requires sacrificing use value and everything else to the capitalist imperative of production of a supplement of exchange value, of surplus-value, as a surplus-enjoyment of capital.[48]

Surplus value is a jouissance supplement to capital. It is a surplus-enjoyment produced from the renunciation of the enjoyment of the subjects, who therefore suffer from it when enjoying it, usually suffering from it as something excessive of the Other that crosses them and is left over, but that they also lack because it is not theirs ($\$$), and is also missing for the Other, the capital that cannot enjoy it, not being someone who can feel or experience something ($\emptyset$). This missing double character of jouissance partially explains its insatiable aspect, which Lacan illustrates with the mythological figure of Danaids barrel that has no bottom, that is never full, that can never be satiated, in such a manner that 'once one enters into it, one doesn't know how far one is going'.[49]

The Lacanian figure of the Danaids barrel, as a representation of jouissance, is perfectly homologous to the Marxian figure of the vampire of capital who is never satisfied by drinking the living blood that he transmutes into more and more dead money. The same insatiability and the same limitlessness appear in other enjoyments of the Other, among them the one that precedes and prepares the modern jouissance of the vampire of capital – that is, the jouissance of money for money in 'the insatiable passion for profit, the *auri sacra fames*', the thirst for gold referred to by Marx in *Capital*,[50] quoting the economist John Ramsay McCulloch, who in turn quoted Virgil: 'sacrilegious hunger for gold, to what do you not drive human hearts!'[51] As Marx recalls in the same pages, this hunger for gold was already condemned by Aristotle under the term 'chrematistics', distinguishing it from the proper economy for having its end in itself and for its resultant 'excessive' aspect, for 'having no limits', for causing the monetary wealth to be 'increased without limits'.[52]

Marx significantly evoked Aristotle's chrematistics to introduce the 'incessant' character of the movement of capital, its 'insatiable appetite', its 'absolute desire for enrichment', its 'unbridled race in pursuit of value'.[53] This insatiability in the jouissance of capital, revealing the impossible total satisfaction of the death drive, is manifested in the current devastation of the planet that continues to extinguish species and threatens to translate very soon into the extinction of humanity. The infinite phenomenon of life is the price to pay for the insatiable enjoyment of capital, for its unstoppable accumulation, for the surplus value that does not stop accumulating in the form of capital.[54]

Surplus value is the jouissance of capital. It is the fundamental manner in which the enjoyment of the Other appears in the economic sphere of the capitalist system. It must always be borne in mind that capital is not a sensitive subject and cannot have enjoyment by itself, but only value itself – that is, produce surplus value. This production of additional value is the enjoyment of capital, an enjoyment that can only be enjoyed – in the strict sense of the term – through the perverse experience of the subjects who have the sensitivity to enjoy it.

Notes

1   Beyond a simple resemblance or analogy, it is a fact that the capitalist system that Marx describes in *Capital* is a system that operates like Hegel's system of logic. Slavoj Žižek is correct in insisting on the 'properly Hegelian aspect of the capitalist economy' and to observe that 'Marx needed Hegel to formulate the logic of capital', to describe 'the objective deception; the disavowed "unconscious" fantasy (of the mysterious self-generating circular movement of capital)' (*Less than Nothing: Hegel and the Shadow of Dialectical Materialism* [London: Verso, 2012], 252–3). However, as Žižek acknowledges and as we shall now see, Marx only unfolds this fantasy of capital in order to break through it.

2   Glimpsing this truth in its materiality, Jean-Joseph Goux warns us against idealist absolutism in the structuralist interpretation of Marx and reminds us that 'the whole weight of Marx's theoretical revolution consists in refusing to autonomize the economic level as a structure without living agents or as an isolable sector of human activity' (Marx Freud, *Économie et symbolique* [Paris: Seuil, 1973], 10). Such a theoretical revolution is assumed by Goux, who also for this reason, *although not only for this reason*, defends a materialist, dialectical and historical logic of the symbolic and of symbolization, a logic based on the struggle and the 'opposition between living subjects', against a certain logic of the signifier, 'in the line of Lévi-Strauss and especially of Lacan', where there would be a risk of falling into a 'semantic philosophy' or a 'semiotic idealism' by reducing the 'economic, political, legal systems' to 'signifying systems' based on a 'formal combinatory' (29–32). We know that the risk to which Goux refers began materializing with the text '*Suture: elements of the logic of the signifier*' by Jacques-Alain Miller (*Cahiers pour l'analyse*, 1.3, 37–49). We also know that Goux's alternative position exerts a significant influence on the philosophy of Jacques Derrida and on the anti-patriarchal and anti-capitalist movement.

3   These two moments of the Marxian critical method reappear in the Lacanian analytical process, as Daniela Danelinck and Mariano Nicolás Campos show when describing the movement that goes from the imaginary superstructure understood as an empty word – as obsessive speculations or paranoid castles in the air – to the real, the subject and the drive, passing through the base of the symbolic, of the Other, and of language (Superstructure, in *The Marx through Lacan Vocabulary: A Compass for Libidinal and Political Economy* [London: Routledge, 2022], 239–45).

4   Samo Tomšič does not ignore this 'fetishist (or idealist) fantasy' (*The Labour of Enjoyment*, Berlin, August, 2019, 40), but remains trapped in it when he imagines

that 'there is no social relationship' (pp. 55, 162), that the 'central hypothesis of Marx' is that 'there is no such thing as a social relation', that there are only economic relations, including class struggles that reveal 'the non-existence of the social relation' (*The Capitalist Unconscious* [London: Verso, 2015], 9, 203). Tomšič warns that this hypothesis should not be confused with Thatcher's neoliberal formula that 'there is no such thing as a society' whose 'tacit corollary' would be 'there is social relationship' (p. 203). For Tomšič, in his reading of Marx and Lacan, the non-existence of the social relationship is correlative of an existence of society. This idea is problematic both in Marx and in Lacan: in Marx, there is something like social relations that are fundamentally among classes, while society is dissociated into social classes, having no other unity than the state-national, ideological and only apparent at the service of the ruling class; in Lacan, although there is no sexual relationship, there is also something like social relationships, which are social ties and *intersignificant* relationships; however, society is itself a dissociation correlative to the division of the subject, a disintegration that has no other unity than the imaginary, illusory, or the cultural-symbolic at the opposite pole to that of the disintegrative social (see David Pavór-Cuéllar, 'La conception lacanienne de la société', *Oxymoron* 1 (2010): 1–10). The coincidence between Lacan and Marx is evident and contradicts Tomšič's thesis: for Marx and for Lacan, there is no society in the full sense of the term, although there is something like social relationships. Of course, society can be claimed as an ideal, as a project, but then perhaps it would be better to refer to *the community* or *the common* of communism, with its intrinsic unity, which differs from the liberal or neoliberal extrinsic association between individuals in modern society (see Ferdinand Tönnies, *Comunidad y sociedad* [Buenos Aires: Losada, 1947]).

5 Jacques Lacan, *Le séminaire, Livre XVIII, D'un discours qui ne serait pas du semblant* (Paris: Seuil, 2007), 10.

6 Ibid., pp. 16–18.

7 Ibid., p. 21.

8 Jorge Alemán attacks this economistic vision, condemning it as a 'Marxist essentialism' that 'does not know that discourse and what it generates and supports, drives, affects, rituals or liturgies, do not belong to the so-called superstructure, but constitute a material force, as infrastructural as the economy itself' (*El capitalismo, crimen perfecto o emancipación*, Madrid, NED, 2018, p. 143). However, what is important in Lacan is not the infrastructural character of discourse that we are already aware of from Stalin, but rather the discursive character of an economy that does not cease to be ultimately more decisive than the discursive productions through which it operates in a subsistent and structural causality. This discovery of Marx, as current now as it was in the nineteenth century, has been lost in Ernesto Laclau and his followers, including Alemán, who return by a postmodern path to the old pre-Marxist overemphasis on political discourses arbitrarily differentiated from the economy of jouissance that produces them. It is true that Alemán rightly questions the 'Marxist theorists' who continue to distinguish 'economic truth' from 'discursive fact'; however, unfortunately, he reproduces the same distinction and limits the scope of his questioning by confining the indistinction between discourse and economics in a historical situation in which 'capital has become more significant than ever and has definitively separated itself from its referents, since the current economy of neoliberalism functions as a discourse' (p.

24). What we learn from Lacan is that any economy, not only the neoliberal one, functions as an infrastructural and determining discourse, as the very discourse of politics, whether it be that of the master, the university, the capitalist or the others in which we see articulated concrete discursive productions.

9   The Hegelian Spirit of the World, an ideological representation of the Freudian unconscious, is subsumed into Marx's capital. Such capitalist subsumption takes place in this historical order and not, as André Michels assumes, in a theoretical order in which the notion of the spirit would have been 'replaced' by the ideas of capital and the unconscious (Travail, 'aliénation, valeur. Lacan avec Marx', in *Marx, Lacan: l'acte révolutionnaire et l'acte analytique* [Paris: Érès, 2013] 173–4). What interests us here, from a materialist perspective, are not the 'founding concepts' or the 'places of registration' of history, but history itself – 'the world, the economy, the subject' (p. 174).

10   Lacan, 'Radiophonie', in *Autres écrits* (Paris: Seuil, 2001), 418.

11   Karl Marx and Friedrich Engels, *La ideología alemana* (1846) (Madrid: Akal, 2014), 390–2.

12   Mao Tse Tung, 'Sobre la contradicción' (1937), in *Textos Escogidos* (Pekín: Ediciones en Lenguas Extranjeras, 1976), 96.

13   Herbert Marcuse, *El Hombre Unidimensional* (1964) (Barcelona: Planeta, 2010).

14   As Gérard Pommier has emphasized, 'there is nothing more socialized than the signifier that will never need to be nationalized, and whose private property does not exceed that of its use' (*Freud apolitique* [Paris: Fammarion, 1998], 105). One only has to object that the signifier has no use value, that it is we, its 'employees', who have use value for it (see Lacan, *Le séminaire, Livre XVII, L'envers de la psychanalyse* [Paris: Seuil, 1991], 01.21.70, 74–5).

15   Marx, *Manuscritos: economía y filosofía* (Madrid: Alianza, 1997), 179.

16   This usurpation of the complex symbolic place of the Other by the impoverishing economic logic of the market is the fundamental historical reason for the homology between the market and the Other, a homology deepened by Christian Ingo Lenz Dunker (Market, in *The Marx through Lacan Vocabulary*, 126–33).

17   Marx, *Manuscritos: economía y filosofía*, 179.

18   It is noteworthy that Jean-Joseph Goux left aside these two distinctive processes of money, both crucial to understanding capitalism and modernity, and preferred to focus on the common denominators between currency, the 'general equivalent of products', and entities such as the concept, language, the monarch in society, the being in philosophy, the father as 'general equivalent of subjects' and the phallus as 'general equivalent of objects' (Freud, *Économie et Symbolique*, 37, 69). The different equivalents would share the 'castration' with respect to everything else (pp. 62, 68), the assignment of a 'relative value' to other beings (p. 66), the 'synthesis or subsumption' of the differences (p. 90) and a 'centralization of values' typical of the West (p. 91). These aspects are illuminating for the analysis of money and reveal its deep meaning in Western civilization as a whole, but they tell us little regarding its historical specificity in modern times and in the capitalist system, a specificity that is associated with distinctive functions such as quantification and privatization.

19   Marx, *Manuscritos: economía y filosofía*, 177–9.

20   Lacan, 'Le séminaire sur "La lettre volée", in *Écrits I* (Paris: Seuil Poche, 1999), 37.

21 Marx, *Manuscritos: economía y filosofía*, 181.

22 Lacan, *Le séminaire, Livre XX, Encore* (1973) (Paris: Seuil, 1999), 11.

23 Ibid., 72.

24 Marx, *El Capital* (1867) (Mexico City: FCE 2008), 109.

25 Ibid., 42. This is how we can explain what Marcuse has described as a 'mimesis' that is no longer a simple adaptation to the environment but 'an immediate identification of individuals with their society' (*El hombre unidimensional*, 49).

26 Althusser, 'Lettres à D . . .' (1966), in *Écrits sur la psychanalyse* (París: STOCK/IMEC, 1993), 93.

27 Marx, *El Capital I*, 103.

28 Ibid., 106.

29 Sigmund Freud, 'Tres ensayos de teoría sexual' (1905), in *Obras completas VII* (Buenos Aires: Amorrortu, 1996), 165.

30 Lacan, *Le séminaire, livre XI, Les quatre concepts fondamentaux de la psychanalyse* (Paris: Seuil Poche, 1990), 201.

31 Marx, *El Capital, libro I, capítulo VI (inédito)* (Mexico City: Siglo XXI, 2011), 40.

32 Tomšič sees here, in contrast to the self-love of the individual in Adam Smith, a 'systemic self-love or enjoyment of the system', a 'self-fetishization' and 'possession by love' that has become 'omnipresent in times of financialisation' (*The Labour of Enjoyment*, Berlin, August, 2019, 55, 92). This jouissance of capital is in Marx, as in Freud and Lacan, a drive for satisfaction. Capital satisfies a drive that Marx describes, through formulations collected by Tomšič, as *Bereicherungstrieb* (drive for enrichment), *Akkummulationstrieb* (drive for accumulation), *Selbstverwertungstrieb* (drive for self-valorization), and even 'drive for an unlimited extension of the working day' (p. 183).

33 Using Jean-Claude Maleval's idea, Pierre Bruno hits the mark by seeing here a 'fantasy' characterized by the 'foreclosure of reference' and by a 'virtualization where the human becomes integrally programmable' in a capitalist discourse that becomes the 'universe' (Lacan, *Passeur de Marx* [Paris: Érès, 2010], 204–5). Bruno is also right to associate this typically post-historical and postmodern fantasy with Baudrillard's reflection. The hyperreal and cinematographic representation in *Matrix* is a fundamental ideological fantasy of technological and financialized neoliberal capitalism, a fantasy that is being realized, *hyperrealized*, through the total desertification of reality in the current devastation of the planet (Jean Baudrillard, *Simulacres et simulation* [Paris: Galilée, 1981]).

34 Freud, 'Más allá del principio de placer' (1920), in *Obras completas XVIII* (Buenos Aires: Amorrortu, 1998), 38.

35 Max Weber, *La ética protestante y el espíritu del capitalismo* (1905) (Mexico City: FCE, 2003), 271–2.

36 Lacan, *Le séminaire, Livre XVI, D'un Autre à l'autre* (Paris: Seuil, 2006), 20.11.68, 39.

37 This notion of labour can be summed up with the Latin expression of '*neg-otium*' referred to by Jean-Louis Sous: 'the business that opposes the *otium*, the leisure of enjoyment in which one rests on his possessions', in a 'lazy hoarding' or in an 'idle squandering of profit', instead of negotiating by 'reinvesting surplus value for

the benefit of capital' (*Lacan et la politique, De la valeur* [Paris: Érès, 2017], 40). It is evident that here it is capital that enjoys instead of the capitalists who work for it, who renounce their enjoyment by negotiating, by depriving themselves of the enjoyment of leisure. This business of the new capitalist masters, conceived as 'abstinence and asceticism', is opposed by Sous as the 'joyful leisure' of the old master (pp. 94–5).

38 Marx, *El Capital I*, 88–92.

39 Ibid., 43–4.

40 Marx, *Contribución a la crítica de la economía política* (1859) (Mexico City: Siglo XXI, 2013), 118.

41 Marx, *El Capital I*, 91.

42 Ibid.

43 Marx, *El Capital II* (Mexico City: FCE, 2006), 107.

44 Marx, *Teorías sobre la plusvalía I* (1861–3) (Mexico City: FCE, 1980), 260.

45 Commenting on the last quote from Marx, Jorge Alemán shrewdly observes that 'if there were satisfaction, it would be to accumulate without limit' (*Ideología. Nosotras en la época. La época en nosotros* [Madrid: NED, 2021], 100). What we will see now is that the subject cannot be satisfied because the enjoyment, the unlimited accumulation, belongs to capital and not to the capitalists, who, as Alemán rightly points out, obey a 'law immanent in the system itself, which leads them to increase accumulation indefinitely', perhaps 'not accumulating to enjoy' (pp. 100–1), but accumulating so that capital enjoys by accumulating. This jouissance of capital is the only blind spot in Alemán's argument.

46 This distinction between hoarding and capitalism has led Tomšič to oppose the empirical and obscene form of the hoarder's jouissance to a capitalist jouissance of a treasure that 'is the more endless the more it is abstract: from gold to paper money, from paper money to fictitious capital, electronic money and so on' (*The Capitalist Unconscious*, 68–9). The truth is that the jouissance of capital is not without important empirical and obscene manifestations in phenomena such as workaholism, the entertainment industry, the frenetic consumerism of the last century, or the exhibitionist waste used as 'ostentation of wealth, and, therefore, means of credit' (Marx, *El Capital I*, 500).

47 Lacan, 'Kant avec Sade', in *Écrits II* (París: Seuil Poche, 1999), 258

48 A part of what is elaborated here is already outlined in Žižek, specifically in his association between Marx's surplus value, which 'implies a renunciation of pathological empirical use value', and Kant's ethics, in which 'all empirical pathological contents' are excluded, but concealing the fact that 'this renunciation itself produces a certain surplus enjoyment' (*The Sublime Object of Ideology* [London: Verso, 2008], 89). What is missing in Žižek is a clear distinction between the subject and the Other in relation to jouissance. This lack prevents one of the main critical potentialities of Lacan's reading of Marx from being realized – that of founding a critique of the jouissance of capital like the one outlined here.

49 Lacan, *Le séminaire, Livre XVII, L'envers de la psychanalyse*, 83.

50 Marx, *El Capital*, 109.

51 Virgilio, *Eneida* (Guanajuato: Universidad de Guanajuato, 2018), III, 57, 138.

52 Aristóteles, *Política* (Madrid: Gredos, 1988), 1257b–1258a, 70–3.

53 Marx, *El Capital I*, 108–9.

54 Capital offers us the best historical example of the 'jouissance of annihilation' that Pierre Bruno appropriately associates with the Freudian concept of the death drive and with 'the series that, from Marx to Lacan, passing through Freud, is constitutive of the category of the insatiable' (Lacan, *Passeur de Marx*, 318–19).

Chapter 15
Aggression and the future

Mia Neuhaus

Vorwärts und nicht vergessen[1]

'There's war again in Europe!' resounded excitedly through radio stations, news portals, Facebook profiles and Instagram accounts in February 2022. Europe has woken up to a different world, leading German politicians stated on the morning of the first attack. A 'turning point' (*Zeitenwende*) was proclaimed, which could refer to either the attack on Ukraine itself or the announcement that Germany would boost the military budget with a special fund of a whopping 100 billion euros, or the plan for a 'quantum leap' in the EU's security policy towards becoming a 'serious military power' (Koch, 2022). Within German discourse, this development was accompanied by fervent cries of 'Never again!' which, although related to war, frequently led back to the legitimization of hate-filled fantasies of overpowering and rearming.

Given the shock of the war, but also of the Covid-19 pandemic and the impending climate catastrophe, perhaps neither the inclination to look back into history nor the desire to describe a rupture is surprising. But since in the same channels a splitting into good and evil, a radical presentism and elements of projective identification emerged, this chapter is interested in the layers of agitation hidden below the surface and in interrogating aggression where projection emerges.

Perhaps the unspoken content of the catchphrases that emerge at the moment a rupture becomes visible, and find such a resonance that they become winged and capable of guiding action, can allow some conclusions to be drawn about the unconscious passions of our time that are negotiated in them.

'If we want to take the road to the future', Yassin al-Haj Saleh says, 'it helps us to see the "present as history"' (al-Haj Saleh, 2020, p. 32). This would require a historicization in a double sense, concerning the passage through times and the question of a *dis-covery* of the political unconscious. While a radical presentism would deny its own historicity what is in consequence the impossibility of a reference to the present itself, this chapter is concerned with 'the absence that makes memory possible in the first place' (Kläui, 2017, p. 52), with the distance, the gap, the interstice that dynamizes this reference. The question this entails is that of the connection between politics and the unconscious, which leads to that of the relationship between the subject and the Other.

This chapter argues that the dynamics of division (*Spaltung*) that accompany the multiple crises of our time render invisible the tensions crises generate, and render invisible the struggles for recognition (Honneth, 1994) or experiences of misrecognition negotiated in them. The result, it further argues, is a widespread experience of being stuck in the present, while there seems to be a lack of real visions of the future. Part of it is that the urge for change that is so desperately longed for is absorbed into the prevailing social order. Both, experiences of disregard and of a lack of a sense of meaning and 'future orientation' (Honneth, 2015, p. 15), generate frustration, helplessness and anger, which are then absorbed by the discourses of identitarianism, xenophobia and militarism that are booming everywhere, where in the same time aggression is projected onto others, where t can seemingly be defensively warded off.

As I would like to show, the closures still point to the Other that is excluded and negated. Thus the twisted 'Never again!', the quantum leap and the memorable image of a turning point are, too, related to another, hence historical. The never again always refers back to the past that it wants to banish, the quantum leap, a Janus word anyway, wants to get away from what it has to transform, and the turning point resists the dull continuity of presence and yet necessarily refers to it.

Ultimately, then, it is a matter of enduring ambivalence and at the same time being open to what comes back from the unconscious layers of history, where the unavailable, the impossible thrives for change.

'Always historicize!' Jameson (1981, p. 9) announces to us in the first sentence of *The Political Unconscious*. Rooted in the Marxist tradition, he departs from the assumption that all history is the history of class struggles and that its parts 'share a single fundamental theme', that of 'the collective struggle to wrest a realm of Freedom from a realm of Necessity' (Jameson, 1981, p. 19).

It is in detecting the traces of that uninterrupted narrative, in restoring to the surface of the text the repressed and buried reality of this fundamental history, that the doctrine of a political unconscious finds its function and its necessity. (Jameson, 1981, p. 20)

To that effect, this chapter departs from the assumption that history, as political and human history, is always a history of negations and exclusions, dislocations and the expression of a fundamental antagonism. The political shall be understood as the process of those dialectical movements of negation, as the practice within which one, alien to oneself and in an alien world, seeks to make oneself at home. It has its origin in the moment of encounter, of confrontation.

If it is practice itself that constitutes the political, this chapter pleads for a radical openness to what wants to show itself, consequently for an ethics that holds a space open for the unknown and what cannot (yet) emerge (cf Neuhaus, 2021). It is interested in the transitional space and passage (cf. Dorsch et al., 2024) – maybe into the future. For otherwise, the question of how, despite those closures, the living, disordered and unsaid can demand space and initiate *change*, is also blocked.

Turning point or end times?

We reflect on the question of the political unconscious at a time when the declaration of the 'end of an illusion' (Fromm, 2008 [1976]), that capitalism had a real promise of happiness to deliver, was followed by the end of the bipolar world order and the declaration of the end of history. While '[t]he Great Promise of Unlimited Progress – the promise of domination of nature, of material abundance, of the greatest happiness for the greatest number, and of unimpeded personal freedom – has sustained the hopes and faith of the generations since the beginning of the industrial age' (ibid., p. 1), the transition into the twenty-first century can be compared to Gramsci's interregnum, where 'the old is dying and the new cannot be born' (cf. Caccia & Mezzadra, 2015).

If we consider the image of a turning point, a *Zeitenwende*, which at the moment of the attack on Ukraine was supposed to evoke its eventful character, it has in fact been used again and again for years to describe a world in a manifold crisis, which demands radical changes in the economy, ecology and life itself – without of course being accompanied by a real awakening.

Part of the dynamic seems to be a fixation reminiscent of Benjamin's Angel of History (Benjamin, 2019, p. 697). For decades, new wars, ecological crises and the end of the fossil age have merged into a paralysing revelation of the end times that threatens to stifle all hope. This is all the more dramatic because the measures themselves, taken in the face of the world economic crisis, the coronavirus pandemic or the war in Ukraine, made it extremely clear that *another world is possible*, other choices were possible, other attempts have been made. Against forgetting must be remembered: the time we live in is the time of great social movements of feminism, of flight and migration, solidarity and anti-racism, of the *agora* and reclaiming the streets and public squares, of democratic awakenings.

So how does the impression of being stuck in the present or even of a rollback come about? Why do the counter-movements appear so strong in many places and are so brutal?

It is not a new thought that our world is full of hatred because it is full of oppression, unsatisfied longings and needs and broken promises (cf Bauman, 2016). The crisis-induced loss of structure, as well as the more fundamental loss of hope for and concrete experience of a departure into a future from which one does not simply want to flee, are accompanied by disappointment, frustration, anger and sadness, while at the same time the demands on the isolated individual increase.

However: 'consumerist post-democracy, tries to neutralize negativity by transforming politics into apolitical administration' (Žižek, 1997). If the concept of a turning point legitimizes the first great wave of militarization in Europe in this millennium, this discourse simultaneously addresses the urgent desires of our time and absorbs their progressive aspect – the longed-for quantum leap into the twenty-first century as a cypher for a different future, most urgent for those who suffer most under the existing order and its violent social relations, then becomes a leap into division and mobilization for war, the consequences of which in turn hit the same people hardest.[2]

But where the 'laudatory monologue' (Debord, 2014, p. §24) of the ruling order stifles contradiction, or where the 'creeping continuity of the machinery of annihilation' prevails (al-Haj Saleh, 2021), the penetration of the living, of the political is blocked, repressed, channelled and absorbed (cf. Jameson, 1981, p. 91).

The problem of being trapped in the present thereby also seems to lie in the projection of any possibility of liberation into the past. It rejects the possibility of a collective and conflictual processing of the consequences of our crises and the challenges of our time as a whole. At the same time, identitarian closures in thought close themselves off from the possibility of change, and all too often threaten life in a very concrete way.[3]

Defensive struggles

To pursue the question of *why this hatred?* in a historically informed way also means asking where and why it is not pursued. It means raising the question of the suppressed aggression and its projection onto the Other and understanding the will to fight it in the Other with all one's strength. It means historicizing hatred, which is in fact a very everyday hatred – and I am not talking about the hatred that is unleashed in a war of aggression but about the hatred that fuels the discourse that accompanies it 'from a tickle to an inferno' (Hewitson, 2015).

The above-mentioned elements of projective identification have been widespread for some time now. They are booming in an everyday world in which a loss of social structure and meaning favours the growth of violence, the return of identitarian closures, paranoid conspiracy theories and a sanctified hatred: 'Destructiveness is attributed to others . . . [which] is supposed to justify one's own aggressive actions by referring to their defensive nature' (Widmer, 2021, p. 18).

This defensiveness also points to an inner conviction of great dependence, to fear and the feeling of being at the mercy of others. If we consider the hatred of a withheld object to be impossible because at the same time one is radically dependent on it, then the result is the dynamic of division and projection of hatred onto the outside (cf. Klein, 1947). We can relate this dynamic to the experience of life's woes (*Lebensnot*) and radical insecurity in a world whose paradisiacal promise of total consumption (cf. Žižek, 1997) offers neither nourishment nor comfort.[4]

Part of this is a widespread inability to mourn – both in relation to the plight of others and to remember one's own finitude.[5]

According to Widmer (2021, p. 246):

> The basic instances of signifiers and finitude confront the helpless ego, dependent on others, with freedom, its freedom to reject life altogether, whether through suicide or the destruction of the lives of others, or to affirm it, which is not without conflict.

Remembering, narrating the unspoken and mourning are practices of historicizing. In contrast, the splitting into good and evil, and a completed separation from all that is ambivalent, at the same time is the negation of separateness on which historicizing is dependent on, indeed of death itself, and obstructs a working through of those basic conflicts.

Since struggles for recognition and the good life are all fundamentally connected to the Other and to social space, this dependence cannot be broken without negating the conditions of life itself. It must therefore be possible to trace the Other, and consequently the urge for transcendence, liberation and fraternization, even in everyday hatred and the urge to destroy, to sever the relationship, which also fuels the psychology of the discourse of war and crisis.

Unconsciously, the defensive struggle is for the invading Other, the New, the excessive and transgressive nature of life itself. The attempts to prevent the departure,[6] or to 'integrate' and absorb it into the existing order ultimately deny our basic experiences of radical dependence and surrender and the absolute certainty of ultimate death (cf. Kläui, 2017, p. 12). For both, the Other, the Stranger, appears as evidence that must be repelled (Bauman, 2016, p. 21 f.).

Never again

The 'Never again' proclaimed at the beginning of the war and at the same time in the prospect of the end of most of the Pandemic Measures of Social Distancing in Germany may involve multiple layers, which can be a commemoration (*Eingedenken*) as well as a refusal to look back: never wanting to hope, fight and be subjugated again, never be disappointed or betrayed again, never answering the call to the battlefields again, never seeing hundreds of thousands die again, but also never wanting to be reminded of one's own guilt or pain again, never bearing the burden of one's own anger and grief again, or enduring the tension generated by social antagonisms.

With regard to the war in Ukraine, it is the 'Never again', which in German discourse refers to the historical dimension of the 'Never again Auschwitz', with which already the first participation of the Germans in military action after the Second World War against Serbia in 1999 was justified. With regard to climate, it is a 'no further like this', and with regard to the pandemic it is a 'nothing will be the same', which is given out as a maxim for the future but at the same time lacks a future imaginary.

It is then also a 'never again the twentieth century!' – an angry rejection of that century 'that experienced "politics as destiny" but is depicted today as a slaughterhouse' (Giglioli, 2016, p. 21). Daniele Giglioli recalls the feminist struggles, the introduction of compulsory education and voting rights, how social and civil rights were fought for: 'becoming aware, speaking up, making decisions, dramatic alternatives [. . .] but above all hopes: no trace of all this. Illusions, chimeras, and blindness instead. Only the spilled blood and the senseless pain of the victims should have been true' (ibid.). Having a passion for and taking pleasure in rupture, in the 'irrational', in the subversive, in everything that goes into the open, which were also characteristic of the twentieth century, seem to have been buried.

This only apparent contradiction to the above said, namely that hope is projected onto the past, is part of the circular argument that rejects the option of liberation in the present – as violent, chaotic, 'undesirable' and unpredictable.

But as noted above, those closures still refer to the excluded. They respond to something that also emerges in the suspension of order, to a gap, to an emerging unknowing, something that is not yet comprehended, or narrativized, and yet demands space. 'The crisis of discourse [signifies] a crisis in the system of signs that [expresses itself] in a specific, narrative speechlessness and [gives rise to] a new imagery' (Perinelli, 2009, p 57).

For destructive rage and bloodlust do not only arise at the moment of the arrival of the Other (cf. Bauman, 2016), nor at the moment of war, as the masses are led onto the battlefields. Rather, subversive restlessness and transgression are channelled into the closed discourses of the national, the military and the reactionary by those movements of closure and defence, thus cementing their imprisonment in the present.

Thus it is not unrest, chaos or the fragmentary that emerges at the moment of crisis that should be demonized as 'aggression'. Rather, 'restoring to the unconscious its historical perspectives, against a backdrop of disquiet and the unknown' (Deleuze, 2015, p. 9f.), would have to be expanded to include a look at the places and subjectivities of ruptures and gaps, of heterotopias – even and especially when they are unsettling (Perinelli, 2009, p. 68).[7]

In contrast, it is precisely those everyday practices that subversively 'improvise for survival' that can come into view, as a historical perspective shows (Perinelli, 2009, p. 67). Then what is lamentable then is not the loss of structure as the 'loss' of the nuclear family, the institution of marriage and the like, as reactionaries have been lamenting for decades. Rather, it is about the precariousness and the closure or temporary loss of spaces of encounter as places of living (conflict), of social and thus subversive practice, of the movement (of negation) that accompanies struggles for recognition that cannot be stopped and attempts to be at home in the world (cf Schulte1998, p. 33).[8]

And this loss at the moment of (renewed) closure, in turn, does not mean the loss of a better past, but the loss of something that never was, which 'produces us as historical subjects' (Gast, 2006, p. 184), and the loss of a potentiality, of the moment of encounter and solidarity when the existing order is suspended, the loss of a political practice. The lack of interest in the dialectic of the loss of structure or the loss of 'security' and the passion for what is revealed in the moment of opening and disorder is also lamentable. For 'with despair also comes freedom: The freedom to do what we know must be done' (Žižek in Žižek and Barria-Asenjo, 2022).

Desiring the impossible

Barbara Marte (2017, p. 9) calls for 'an ethics separate from the good [. . .], conceived as a form of desire (and) linked to the notion of the impossible'.

Such a perspective may open onto what comes (back) from the unconscious into the struggles, the Other that is repelled, excluded, rejected. It is about the tortuous paths that the struggle for recognition takes towards an alien world and an alien self: what exclusions does it produce, and what happens to the demand for enjoyment – that is, what is the force behind the different faces or voices of the demand for recognition?

We needn't sing the praises of destruction or talk about a revival of a theory of impoverishment in order to problematize the fear of the uncertain, the new, which is inherent in the idea that only an end awaits us in the future. Instead then, these reflections amount to seeking a productive force precisely in the ruptures and interruptions, and rediscovering in the 'reprehensible', in the 'many fissures' of 'the unconscious world of politics' (Rogers and Zevnik, 2017, p. 581) the struggle for freedom and a better life. Miller (2021, p. 21) writes, 'The symptom forms the mode in which the subject expresses that enjoying is bad'. We can say it reveals and at the same time betrays[9] the existing order.[10]

If entering social space means being thrown into a world that includes in its social institutions the struggle against the Other as a struggle against the Other in ourselves (cf. Widmer, 2021), then it is dynamic negativity, 'that psychic tendency to transgress, the psychic brokenness of the human being' (Honneth, 2010, p. 259) that keeps resistance to that very thing alive. In this context, it is social space as a site of encounter, of the event and of the political itself that generates the confrontation and triggers this dynamic; it is in this space and in the abundance of the foreign and what is unavailable in it, that the actual longing to come into life, to surrender oneself to it, and to 'squander' oneself (Gast, 2006, p. 184) is present.

When living conflict is blocked, we look for the political in the unconscious, in the dream, in the symptom – also in the sense of 'social pathologies' (Honneth, 2000). A better formulation would be that it finds us – where irritation, resistance and contradictions, unrest and rebellion arise.

Thus the question of an orientation to the future is ultimately also about the question of dealing with the excessive, about the connection between enjoyment (jouissance) and aggression – and about desire. It is about discovering the violence also present in repression, and especially the kinds of aggression that are in service of liberation (Scheerer, 2013).[11] 'This leads to the paradox that hatred must not be hated, [. . .] so that work can be done on a culture that does not have to exclude [the destructive], but even recognizes it as its foundation' (Widmer, 2021, p. 246).

Notes

1 Brecht and Busch, *Solidaritätslied*, 1947.

2 And also with regard to the stresses and strains during the corona pandemic, numerous sources point out that they can be traced along the worldwide lines of social segregation and hit those worst who already suffer most from exclusion and exploitation (Barria-Asenjo et al., 2021).

3 When the present crisis occurred, the memory of the consequences of the last one, from 2009 onwards, was immediately present, when violent acts against migrants, women, queer people, children, the poor and undocumented people increased as drastically as suicide rates did.

4 This line of thought was pursued by Björn Salomonsson in his lecture 'Paradise Lost: Psychoanalytic Reflections on Climate Fears' on 19 November 2021 at the Berlin Institute for Psychotherapy and Psychoanalysis.

5 This found perhaps its most striking expression during the corona pandemic in the prohibition of end-of-life care and farewell by relatives and loved ones and in the fact that the 'public uprising of grief' (Butler, 2012) largely failed to materialize.

6 'Aufbruch', which in German means both 'beginning' and 'rupture'.

7 He opens a view onto the 'gap of domination between the disarticulated discourse of the *ventennio* and the not yet established discourse of the new republic' in postwar Italy of the 1940s and brings into focus a new autonomy of the body that emerged from this gap (Perinelli, 2009, p. 63).

8 Both Massimo Perinelli and Regina Schulte relate their remarks to the historical perspective of the postwar period before the restitution of the order of gender and the politicial system in Italy and in Germany.

9 'Verrät', which in German means both 'betray' and 'disclose'.

10 'Our society is sick', also says Nicol A. Barria-Asenjo, 'it is a society that suffers and becomes sick precisely because it is not allowed to suffer; everything invites individuals to be happy, to enjoy and to rejoice. The unrecognition or denial of the existence of panic attacks, feelings of hopelessness, melancholy, anxiety, etc., brings further problems' (Barria-Asenjo and Žižek, 2022).

11 Instead of clinging to a morality of renunciation and the affirmation of loss (of what never was, which is also supposed to not be wanted), we need to remember that regression can also be in the service of the I, can signify a letting go.

References

al-Haj Saleh, Y. (2020), *Freiheit: Heimat, Gefängnis, Exil und die Welt*, Berlin: Matthes & Seitz.

al-Haj Saleh, Y. (2021), 'Zwei Engel der Geschichte', *Medico International*, 12 April, https://www.medico.de/zwei-engel-der-geschichte-18148.

Barria-Asenjo, N. A. and S. Žižek (2022), *Un tiempo de incertidumbres* [Jacobin América Latina], 15 February, https://jacobinlat.com/2022/02/15/un-tiempo-de -incertidumbres/.

Barria-Asenjo, N. A., Žižek, S., Scholten, H., Salas, G., Constanzo, A. X. Z., Acosta, J. G., Muzzio, E. G., & Muñoz, J. U. (2021). Deglobalize Covid-19: The pandemic from an off-center perspective. *Sociedade e Estado*, 36(3), 967–87. https://doi.org/10 .1590/s0102-6992-202136030006.

Bauman, Z. (2016), *Die Angst vor den anderen: Ein Essay über Migration und Panikmache*, Berlin: Suhrkamp.

Benjamin, W. (2019), 'Über den Begriff der Geschichte', in *Gesammelte Schriften*. Bd. 1, 9. Auflage, Frankfurt: Suhrkamp, 691–706.

Butler, J. (2012), *Kann man ein gutes Leben im schlechten führen?* [Dankesrede zur Verleihung des Adorno-Preises], https://www.fr.de/kultur/kann-gutes-leben -schlechten-fuehren-11319646.html.

Caccia, B. and S. Mezzadra (2015), 'Unterm Himmel des "Interregnums"', *Blockupy Goes Athens*, http://blockupy-goes-athens.tumblr.com/post/128904606805/unterm -himmel-des-interregnums.

Debord, G. (2014), *The Society of the spectacle* (Paperbound edition), Berkeley: Bureau of Public Secrets.

Deleuze, G. (2015), 'Preface: Three Group-Related Problems', in F. Guattari (ed.), *Psychoanalysis and transversality: Texts and interviews 1955–1971*, South Pasadena: Semiotext(e), 7–21.

Dorsch, T. et al. (2024), 'A Left of the Passage', in Nicol A. Barria-Asenjo, B. Willems and S. Žižek (eds), *Global Manifestos for the Twenty-First Century. Rethinking Culture, Common Struggles, and Future Change*, London and New York: Routledge, 28–34.

Fromm, E. (2008) [1976], *To Have or to Be?* (London/New York: Continuum).

Gast, L. (2006). ,Mensch ist der, der grenzenlos verliert . . .': Zur (Psycho-)Logik des Verlusts. *Jahrbuch Psychoanalyse*, 52, 169–86.

Giglioli, D. (2016), *Die Opferfalle. Wie die Vergangenheit die Zukunft fesselt*, Berlin: Matthes & Seitz.

Hewitson, O. (2015), 'From a Tickle to an Inferno: The Theory of Jouissance in Psychoanalysis', *School of the Freudian Letter*, https://www.lacanonline.com/2015 /07/what-does-lacan-say-about-jouissance/.

Honneth, A. (2000), 'Pathologien des Sozialen. Tradition und Aktualität der Sozialphilosophie', in *Das Andere der Gerechtigkeit: Aufsätze zur praktischen Philosophie*, Frankfurt: Suhrkamp, 11–69.

Honneth, A. (1994), *Kampf um Anerkennung: Zur moralischen Grammatik sozialer Konflikte*, Frankfurt: Suhrkamp.

Honneth, A. (2015), *Die Idee des Sozialismus: Versuch einer Aktualisierung*, Berlin: Suhrkamp.

Jameson, F. (1981), *The political Unconcious*. Narrative as a socially symbolic act, Ithaca, New York: Cornell University Press

Kläui, C. (2017), *Tod – Hass – Sprache, psychoanalytisch*, Wien/Berlin: Turia + Kant.

Klein, M. (1947), 'Notes on Some Schizoid Mechanisms', *International Journal of Psychoanalysis* 27: 99–110.

Koch, M. (2022), 'EU-Eingreiftruppe: "Quantensprung" in der Sicherheitspolitik: Wie die EU zur Militärmacht werden will', *Handelsblatt Online*, 23 March, https://www. handelsblatt.com/politik/eu-eingreiftruppe-quantensprung-in-der-sicherheitspolitik -wie-die-eu-zur-militaermacht-werden-will/28185018.html.

Marte, B. (2017), *Das Begehren als ethischer Imperativ*, Wien/Berlin:Turia + Kant.

Miller, J.-A. (2021), *Die Erotik der Zeit und andere Texte über das Genießen*, Wien/Berlin: Turia + Kant.

Neuhaus, M. (2021), 'Im Raum des Anderen. Elemente einer Ethik der Solidarität', in B. Heimerl (ed.), *Unerhörte Stimmen*, 153–77, Berlin: Psychosozial-Verlag.

Perinelli, M. (2009), *Fluchtlinien des Neorealismus: Der organlose Körper der italienischen Nachkriegszeit, 1943–1949*, Bielefeld: Transcript.

Rogers, J. B. and A. Zevnik (2017), 'The Symptoms of the Political Unconscious: Introduction to the Special Issue', *Political Psychology* 38(4): 581–9.

Scheerer, A. K. (2013), 'Leidenschaftliche Aggression als Tabu?', *Psychoanalyse Aktuell*, https://www.psychoanalyse-aktuell.de/artikel-/detail?tx_news_pi1%5Baction%5D =detail&tx_news_pi1%5Bcontroller%5D=News&tx_news_pi1%5Bnews%5D=133 &cHash=4096ca3013560d35bf8b95db23d6dfa1.

Schulte, R. (1998), *Die verkehrte Welt des Krieges. Studien zu Geschlecht, Religion und Tod*, Frankfurt: Campus.

Widmer, P. (2021), *Destruktion des Ichs: Psychoanalytische Annäherungen an den Ursprung menschlicher Aggression*, Berlin: Psychosozial-Verlag.

Žižek, S. (1997, 2007), *The Liberal Utopia: Against the Politics of Jouissance*, https://www.lacan.com/zizliberal.htm.

Žižek, S. and N. A. Barria-Asenjo (2022), *Goditi la tua apatia! – L'ascesa della sinistra cilena, la pandemia, l'universalismo*, [Il Tascabile], 31 January, https://www.iltascabile.com/societa/barria-asenjo-zizek/.

Chapter 16
AOC and her boyfriend's leg

Slavoj Žižek

In late December 2021, the US nationalist Rightist Steve Cortes tweeted a photo of Alessandria Ocasio-Cortez (AOC) and her boyfriend Riley Roberts enjoying their Christmas break in Florida, commenting on it: 'Her guy is showing his gross pale male feet in public – not at a pool or beach – with hideous sandals.' AOC quipped back on 31 December: 'If Republicans are mad they can't date me, they can just say that instead of projecting their sexual frustrations onto my boyfriend's feet. Ya creepy weirdos.'[1] Her reply triggered mixed reactions – one user responded: 'Bold move . . . when people disagree with my policy positions or call me a hypocrite, I tell them they just want to f . . . me as well.' Another responded, 'Why did your mind automatically go to "dating you" and "sex"? That's very conceited.'[2]

At some level these reactions are right: it was AOC who brought sex into a situation which was not sexualized (explicitly, at least), reading Republican attacks on her policy positions as the expression of their frustration that they cannot date her. Incidentally, I don't think the reasoning implied by AOC is correct – there is another, more probable, version. Her Republican critics primarily disagree with her policies but, as most men notice her sexual attractiveness, so they bring in sexuality to devalue her argumentation in accordance with the standard male-chauvinist wisdom that beautiful women are stupid: 'Stick to sex, avoid argumentation which is beyond your league.' The implicit reference to feet fetishism (Riley's foot really protrudes a little bit excessively in the tweeted photo) is even more ambiguous: Cortes (who made this move from AOC to Riley's foot) could have made AOC mad for another unexpected reason – instead of really desiring her (as AOC's reply suggests), he seems to prefer her partner to her. The implicit surmise of her reply could thus be: 'I am the real beauty in the photo, so why do you mention my boyfriend's foot and not me, its real focus?'

Such tensions indicate that a truly radical feminism should do what Amia Srinivasan proposes in her path-breaking *The Right to Sex*[3]: she thinks 'beyond the parameters of consent' – she is not afraid to confront sex in all its complexity and ambiguity. Consent? Yes, but why is it somehow always the woman who gives consent or denies it? Why should a woman not be the active part? Plus consent relies on a logic of market exchange: 'the idea of consent presupposes a contract: someone is asking to do something to you, and they have to get permission to do it', so that consensual sex can also be exploitative. And what about my unconscious which can make me desire what I do not know, including a desire to humiliate others and myself? What if suffering brings a perverse pleasure? And what about the social dimension of desire: is my intimate desire not always affected by public and secret social norms and expectations? The image of a sexual partner who is perceived as 'desirable' obviously depends on the society in which I live. Srinivasan's general conclusion: 'We need a feminism that is truly internationalist, that centres on climate disaster, colonialism, and the voices of women in the global south.'[4]

Here is such a case from the 'global south,' the very opposite of the trifling AOC incident: a terrifying event that took place at the beginning of 26 January 2022 in a New Delhi neighbourhood in India.[5] A young woman, mother of a three-year-old child, was attacked by a mob in her paternal house, her hair chopped off and her face blackened; she was brutally slapped and kicked as others in the house clapped and cheered. The attack continued for several minutes as the woman pleaded for mercy, her body crouched and hands folded. After the beating, she was paraded in the narrow lanes of the neighbourhood and dragged by the mob to her 'victim''s house where she was gang-raped. And who was her 'victim'? The attack took place because the woman had repeatedly rejected the advances of a teenager who lived next to her parent's house. The sixteen-year-old boy's family claims he killed himself following the rejection in November last year – the teen's death caused the purported 'revenge attack'.

There are two notably shocking moments in this affair. First, a video shared on social media shows that most of the baying mob were women – when the brutalized woman was raped, the women in the same room instigated the men to be more brutal with her. Second, she was punished for refusing the boy's advances, although she was married – as her sister put it, 'she didn't do anything'. One can imagine what would have happened if she were to concede and give the boy a so-called mercy-fuck – if found out, would have been again found guilty and perhaps even more brutally punished. In short, she had a choice with both options a catastrophe for her. In the reactions to the accident, both these features are mostly accounted for in terms of 'internalized patriarchy': in patriarchal societies, women are taught they're ultimately to blame for any wrongdoing, and the scale of internalized misogyny is very large in India where women are taught to uphold patriarchal structures.[6]

However, this explanation runs all too smoothly. It is ridiculous to account for the violence women exert on other women in terms of internalized patriarchal values – where are the intense envy, hatred and violence a woman can direct at her sexual competitors? While this dimension is obviously not part of some eternal 'woman's nature' but is historically mediated by the patriarchal order, this dependence in no way implies that a woman's envy and violence directed at her competitors is somehow 'unauthentic' – as if a woman is not able to desire and actively pursue a man and thus hate her feminine competitors? In 2019 a scandal shook Slovenia: Danijela Ružič, a judge in Maribor, a northeastern town in Slovenia, an attractive lady, was brutally beaten in front of her house while returning home deep in the night – for some days even her life was in danger. The rumour was that her partner did it because the two were ending their relationship, and Angelca Likovič, an old Christian conservative politician, immediately reacted on Facebook: 'She got what she deserved!' (She deserved to be beaten for her 'immoral' behaviour because she was allegedly returning home from a meeting with a lover.)[7] Again, the shock was that it was a woman who reacted so brutally, and that even conservative politicians distanced themselves from her comment.

Furthermore, to make a woman responsible for a man's suicide just because she didn't gratify his (illicit) desire for sex, while simultaneously blaming her if she were to gratify it, attributes to women (at least those who are considered 'attractive') an extraordinary power which reduces men to helpless puppets – why is the sixteen-year-old boy not blamed for not being able to resist his desire? The true patriarchal moment of this horrible story resides also in the fact that the woman's sexual desire is never mentioned in it: to be direct, what if she also desired an adventure with the young boy but was prevented by her fidelity to her husband? Many of those solidary with her praise her for this fidelity – but did the same hold for her husband? Her sister emphasizes that she did nothing – but what if she were to do something in accordance with her desire about which we know nothing? To put it in vulgar terms, she was beaten and raped because she refused to 'act as a proper whore' and cheat on her husband – ironically, she was held responsible for NOT consenting to extramarital harassment. This perverted reversal is the hidden truth of patriarchal ethics.

Are we not here at the opposite end of the conflict around AOC's boyfriend's naked leg in Florida? Does AOC's trip to Florida not appear a trifling minor affair compared to what happened in New Delhi? Yes, but there is something that unites the two cases: upon a closer look, they both challenge the obvious account that offers itself. Cortes's critique of AOC as well as her reaction bring out not only the hidden male-chauvinist logic of the new Right but also the inconsistencies of the liberal-Leftist approach to sexuality. The scandalous affair in India is not just the outcome of 'primitive' patriarchal traditionalism: it could only have happened in today's mixture of traditionalism and modernity – only within such a mixture can a woman be perceived as endowed with extraordinary powers rendering men her helpless victim, and at the same time as deprived of their own desire.

The conclusion to be drawn is thus that, while patriarchy and other forms of oppression of women (even in the guise of false 'permissiveness') should be ruthlessly examined and punished, sexuality remains a big mess: it relies on rules *and on their codified violations*, so it is impossible to fully regulate – we have to learn to live with its crazy paradoxes. We cannot ever be sure what the consequences of our interventions, as well-meant as they are, will be. In January 2022, the Royal Opera House in London announced that it is

> consulting with Ita O'Brien – an intimacy coordinator who ensures actors feel comfortable during such scenes – for Katie Mitchell's new production of Theodora, opening on Monday. [. . .] 'There's consent each and every day. You might agree one day that you're very happy to kiss lip to lip, and then you develop a cold sore, so it's not suitable any more. So you explore what the moment is about, different ways to tell the same story,' she said.[8]

While one should support the fight against any form of harassment, there are some details in this announcement that make me 'feel uncomfortable'. First, why, again, the (implicit) reduction of women as victims of harassment here? Second, while, obviously, there are scenes in which playing a victim of rape or violence will make the actor as a person traumatized, how could one enact on screen or stage a brutal scene without feeling uncomfortable? Third, the example mentioned ('You might agree one day that you're very happy to kiss lip to lip, and then you develop a cold sore, so it's not suitable anymore.') is ridiculously obvious and has nothing to do with harassment – it throws a strange light on the entire argument by putting a cold sore in the same series with, say, touching the breast of an actress. Fourth, the very term 'intimacy coordinator' sounds (and *is*) ominous: at the end of this road lurks the idea that (why not?) even when a couple is intimate alone but not sure about how to interact, they should hire an intimacy coordinator.

Along the Lacanian and Millerian lines, Christiane Alberti[9] characterizes the MeToo censorship and regulation of language as a stance directed against phallic virility – but does phallus (in the Lacanian sense) really stand for virility? Can one really oppose gay communities held together by a phallic master-signifier and lesbian communities as communities which function as non-all, without a master-signifier uniting them? I am much more inclined to see in the MeToo strict control of language and body a phallic procedure par excellence, a desperate attempt to control and regulate our speech and bodily movements up to minor details (a gesture that I involuntarily make with my hand, how I look at a person next to me) – the target is here the inconsistent chaos of our language games invested by sexuality and power relations. In short, the MeToo control is an attempt to purify language by way of using the utmost 'masculine' procedure of totalizing control and regulation.

So let me conclude with a lighter example, a misunderstanding that happened to a philosopher-friend of mine. A young fan of his, an attractive lady, told him jokingly after a lecture: 'If you explain all this to me in private, you can have sex with me!' He took a restrained stance and explained things to her, but with no sex, claiming that doing it to get sex as a payment would amount to sexual exploitation. Later, however, he learned from her friends that, far from being impressed by his honesty, she was furious at him: she really wanted sex, and she just playfully mentioned the price he would have to pay to avoid the vulgarity of directly asking for sex. So, again, what if women are not just victims of male predators but can also subtly provoke them? And why shouldn't they do this, why should they just be passive receivers who consent or not?

In his *Interpretation of Dreams*, Freud reports on a dream dreamt by a father who falls asleep while keeping the guard of his son's coffin; in this dream, his dead son appears to him, pronouncing the terrible appeal 'Father, can't you see that I am burning?' When the father awakens, he discovers that the cloth on the son's coffin has caught fire because one of the burning candles fell down. So why did the father awaken? Was it because the smell of the smoke got so strong that it was no longer possible to prolong the sleep by way of including it in the improvised dream? Lacan proposes a much more interesting reading:

> If the function of the dream is to prolong sleep, if the dream, after all, may come so near to the reality that causes it, can we not say that it might correspond to this reality without emerging from sleep? After all, there is such a thing as somnambulistic activity. The question that arises, and which indeed all Freud's previous indications allow us here to produce, is – *What is it that wakes the sleeper?* Is it not, *in* the dream, another reality? – the reality that Freud describes thus – *Dass das Kind an seinem Bette steht*, that the child is near his bed, *ihn am Arme fasst*, takes him by the arm and whispers to him reproachfully, *und ihm vorwurfsvoll zuraunt: Vater, siehst du denn nicht*, Father, can't you see, *dass ich verbrenne*, that I am burning? Is there not more reality in this message than in the noise by which the father also identifies the strange reality of what is happening in the room next door? Is not the missed reality that caused the death of the child expressed in these words?[10]

So it was not the intrusion of the signal from the external reality that awakened the unfortunate father but the unbearably traumatic character of what he encountered in the dream – insofar as 'dreaming' means fantasizing in order to avoid confronting the Real, the father literally awakened so that he could go on dreaming. The scenario was the following one: when his sleep was disturbed by the smoke, the father quickly constructed a dream which incorporated the disturbing element (smoke-fire) in order to prolong his sleep; however, what he confronted in the dream was a trauma (of his responsibility for the son's death) much stronger than reality, so he awakened into reality in order to avoid the Real. . . . And it is exactly the same with much of the ongoing 'woke' movement: they awaken us (into the racist and sexist horrors) precisely to enable us to go on sleeping, that is, ignoring the true roots and depth and racial and sexual traumas.

Notes

1 'Ocasio-Cortez Blasts "Sexual Frustrations" of Republicans Criticizing Miami Beach Photo', *The Washington Informer*.

2 'Did AOC REALLY say Republican Men Want to have Sex with her? BF Feet Tweet Creates Uproar', *MEAWW*.

3 See Amia Srinivasan, *The Right to Sex* (New York: Farrar, Straus and Giroux, 2021).

4 Quoted from 'The Right To Sex: How Amia Srinivasan Wrote the Most Divisive Book of 2021', *AnOther* (anothermag.com).

5 www.aljazeera.com/news/2022/2/1/india-new-delhi-alleged-gang-rape-torture -woman-revenge-attack.

6 See, for example, 'Some People in a Cheering Crowd Called for her to be Raped. Many were Women', *CNN*.

7 See Likovičeva šokirala po napadu na sodnico: 'Dobila je to, kar si e zaslužila' – Slovenske novice.

8 'Royal Opera House Hires Intimacy Coordinator for Sex Scenes', Royal Opera House, *The Guardian*.

9 See www.thelacanianreviews.com/lacanian-opinion-i/?fbclid=IwAR0w4N4EubiNm tmVSp97pizHqdghbQsDYJvTW8lVYAAZ4QRxsAlsFNICMCI.

10 Jacques Lacan, *The Four Fundamental Concepts of Psycho-Analysis* (Harmondsworth: Penguin Books, 1979), 57–8.

Chapter 17

Jouissance the Levinas way

Graham Harman

Whenever the name of Emmanuel Levinas is mentioned, the first words that come to mind are likely to be 'otherness', 'alterity' or 'ethics'. This is especially true among those who emphasize his rootedness in Judaic tradition, as someone who confronts Western philosophy – not long after the *Shoah* – with its long and suddenly dubious subordination of ethics to Being. The same holds for his critics, including the somewhat admiring ones. Consider the case of Jacques Derrida's 'Violence and Metaphysics', which also bolts Levinasian thought down to the theme of otherness as a single paradox concerning the appearance of the inapparent.[1] In some ways, however, Levinas is even more interesting when approached from the surface rather than in ethico-religious depth. I refer to his remarks on *enjoyment*, which are not just intriguing phenomenologies of human pleasure, but also amount to piercing critiques of his major philosophical forerunner: Martin Heidegger.

While there are hundreds or even thousands of articles on Levinasian ethics, publications on his conception of enjoyment are comparatively few in number, overshadowed not only by his ethical writings but also by the fact that Lacanian psychoanalysis has largely cornered the market on *jouissance* in recent French thought.[2] Alphonso Lingis is generally the most reliable interpreter and heir of the sensual aspect of Levinas.[3] John Sallis wrote an article on 'Levinas and the Elemental' that makes an effort to take enjoyment seriously, and Steven Shaviro has given us a fine juxtaposition of Levinas with Alfred North Whitehead.[4] There are other scattered articles and book chapters on the topic, but it would be fair to say that enjoyment remains a somewhat marginalized topic in Levinas studies. In this article I would like to extend my previous writings on Levinas with a brief discussion of enjoyment, followed by an equally brief reflection on the political ramifications of this theme.[5] In the interest of brevity, I will limit myself to the pages of *Totality and Infinity*, where we find *jouissance* discussed in special detail from pages 109 through 142 of the Lingis translation, although Levinas's earlier *Existence and Existents* is also worth careful study.[6]

Jouissance vs infinity and equipmentality

As stated, Levinas famously develops an ethical philosophy devoted to the theme of otherness. This is true not only of *Totality and Infinity* but perhaps even more so of his other major book, *Otherwise Than Being*.[7] It almost goes without saying that the Levinasian theme of enjoyment works in the opposite register: namely, we enjoy or bathe in that which is directly accessible, not in what transcends us. This carnal or secular side of Levinas, although often neglected, is no less central to his thinking than the religious side that often annoys the self-proclaimed libertines among his critics. As the philosopher puts it: 'enjoyment is the ultimate consciousness of all the contents that fill my life – it embraces them'[8] (111). We find no chilly clericalism in the motto that '[l]ife is *love of life*, a relation with contents that are not my being but more dear than my being: thinking, eating, sleeping, reading, working, warming oneself in the sun' (112). And again: 'I eat bread, listen to music, follow the course of my ideas' (122). This is the forgotten face of Levinas, the one that more closely resembles Merleau-Ponty than the leading figures of the high ethico-religious tradition.

Of course, Levinas distinguishes *jouissance* not just from his own sphere of ethical interests. Enjoyment is something he also finds entirely lacking in his admired predecessors Husserl and Heidegger, though for different reasons in each case. His disagreement with Husserl is covered at some length by Derrida and revolves around the claim that intentionality remains within the sphere of what Levinas calls 'the same'. As Levinas puts it, in a way that is both fair and unfair at once: 'The thesis that every intentionality is either a representation or founded upon a representation dominates [Husserl's *Logical Investigations*] and returns as an obsession in all of Husserl's subsequent work' (122). Restated in a simpler formula, it is a question of '[t]he Husserlian thesis of the primacy of the objectifying act' (123). The considerable grain of truth in this way of looking at Husserl is that he does grant priority to direct intellectual intuition as the exemplary mental act: 'it is . . . a question of what in Cartesian terminology becomes the clear and distinct idea' (123). The Kantian thing-in-itself, an object of flirtation for both Levinas and Heidegger, is simply ruled out of court by Husserl as an absurdity. Yet by the same stroke, Levinas simply misses the upshot of why Husserl stresses the objectifiying act. For in fact, it is a question of Husserl's break with his teacher Franz Brentano, a figure rarely if ever mentioned by Levinas despite his strong phenomenological leanings.[9] Although on a surface level both Brentano and Husserl seem to endorse representation as the basis of all mental acts, they mean completely different things by this. Husserl is right when he rejects Brentano's thesis that intentionality is a matter of 'experienced contents', countering that it consists instead of 'object-giving acts'. The difference at stake – missed entirely by Levinas – is that Brentano is essentially signing on to a Humean doctrine of intentional objects as 'bundles of qualities'. When a horse or rabbit in our experience changes, as when for example the animal moves slightly, for Brentano we are dealing with a closely related but different intentional object. This is what Husserl opposes and also what leads to his key breakthrough. Namely, for Husserl, there is a fundamental rift between the horse and the various 'adumbrations' through which it appears from one moment to the next. The Husserlian horse is an enduring intentional object despite constant accidental surface changes, which is simply impossible under Brentano's basically empiricist model. What this emphasizes for our present purposes is that Levinas remains only half-fair to Husserl. Consider the following Levinasian indictment of phenomenology: 'The thinking thought is the locus where a total identity and a reality that ought to negate it are reconciled, without contradiction' (127). As we have seen, this is true insofar as Levinas means to criticize Husserl's belief in direct intellectual access to a reality, not haunted in the least by any infinity, any shock of unmasterable otherness. But there is another sense in which Husserl knows the world of sensibility just as well as Levinas does, since each of his intentional objects is constantly surrounded by perfumed mists of inessential qualities. This is why Merleau-Ponty was able to hit the ground running after mastering Husserl's system, much like Picasso in the wake of Cézanne; the road had been suggestively paved.

As for Heidegger, the Levinasian critique hits on the most important passage of *Being and Time*: the celebrated tool-analysis.[10] For Heidegger, not only do tools in action withdraw from visibility until something goes wrong, but they also combine in a totality of equipment subordinated to some conscious aim of human existence. Once an entity breaks loose from this invisible system, it shifts from 'ready-to-hand' to 'present-at-hand'. Essentially, Levinas holds that a more positive discourse about the present-at-hand is possible than Heidegger permits: 'Every object offers itself to enjoyment, a universal category of the empirical – even if I lay hold of an object-implement, if I handle it as [equipment]' (132–3). Far from disappearing into further ulterior purposes, 'the objects of everyday use are subordinated to enjoyment – the lighter to the cigarette one smokes, the fork to the food, the cup to the lips' (133). Far from being a holistic equipmental network, '[t]he world answers to a series of autonomous finalities which ignore one another' (133). Things do not merely vanish into networks of further things: they also pulsate as solitary termini with which one can interact directly, and with fascination.

A few more points can be made. The first is that the human does not entirely fuse with the object of its enjoyment: 'Enjoyment is made of the memory of its thirst; it is a quenching' (113). We enjoy a thing precisely because it *is not* us but almost seems to have fallen into our grasp by the luckiest of results. The object of enjoyment and I are together, jointly separate or cut off from the remaining world in a way that excludes external observers or participants; we can sit and eat bread at the same table, but your enjoyment of the bread is not my own. Peter Sloterdijk also drank from this well in the final volume of his *Spheres* trilogy, when noting that monads are actually dyads: a feature that is also characteristic of love in the great epic of Dante.[11] Moreover, we should not just think of this sincerity of enjoyment as something that partially glues subject and object together. More than this, it also selects and excludes other possible objects of interest. As Levinas insightfully notes: 'The I that thinks the sum of the angles of a triangle is . . . precisely the one that thinks of this sum, and not the one that thinks of atomic weight' (125). Rather than writing this article, I might have spent the same time learning Italian or practising the viola. Every choice of how to spend one's days excludes countless alternate options, a point that Helmuth Plessner rightly regards as more threatening than the gloomy Heideggerian meditations on mortality.[12]

Along with this separation-in-togetherness of sincerity, the enjoyment of an object is also inscribed in the simultaneous enjoyment of a surrounding medium that Levinas calls 'the elemental'. In his words: '[The things] take form within a medium in which we take hold of them. They are found in space, in the air, on the earth, in the street, along the road' (130). This medium is 'earth, sea, city, light' (131). It is 'a field cultivated by me, the sea in which I fish and moor my boats, the forest in which I cut wood' (131). He describes the experience of bathing in the element as comparable to residing 'in the bowels of being' (132). And just like the enjoyment of individual objects, '[t]he element separates us from the infinite' (132). This foray into media theory makes Levinas a rarity among philosophers: after all, our forerunners have not often thematized the relation between the things with which humans engage and their background environment with which they also engage, just as directly if often less consciously.[13] There is more that could be said about enjoyment according to Levinas, but the foregoing pages can suffice as an initial overview.

Jouissance **and politics**

We might now ask if there are any political implications of this side of Levinas, who throughout his writings is far from a militant or even a political philosopher, limiting himself mostly to powerful intermittent remarks about the Nazi genocide that decimated his family. One possible misunderstanding is invited by Levinas himself. When speaking of how human enjoyment cuts itself off from everything else, he speaks (in a seemingly positive sense) of '[t]he pathos of liberalism . . . [which] lies in the promotion of a person inasmuch as he represents nothing further, that is, is precisely a self' (120). Yet there are reasons for caution in interpreting this. The first is that it need not be solely an individual human that enjoys. Levinas himself speaks of a relation between two people which is more than the sum of its parts and has an inner life of its own, inaccessible to those left outside. Here one thinks of Sloterdijk again, with his suggestive pages on amorous couples and the mother–child relation. There is no empty alternative between individualistic liberalism and collectivized socialism: the social space consists of numerous layers of different sizes, ranging from cliquish hipster partnerships, through transient athletic and intellectual gatherings, to combative international trends in physics. We might also recall the somewhat surprising admiration of Levinas for Marx, for 'the great force' of his philosophy and its 'ability to avoid completely the hypocrisy of sermons', as it roots speculation in the needs of everyday life.[14] But more generally, it is often a bad idea to assume that a given ontology will inevitably flow into specific political consequences. Important philosophy tends to work at a layer much deeper than detailed social programmes, which is why the same philosophy often provides nourishment to vastly different portions of the political spectrum. Just think of Kant, Hegel, Nietzsche and Heidegger, all of them available in both Leftist and Rightist versions.

Nonetheless, a new ontology also tends to shed light on the strengths and weaknesses of contemporary political tropes, and this certainly holds for Levinasian *jouissance*. Some readers will immediately think of Roland Barthes's praise of the socialist Charles Fourier's attention to pleasure, a surprisingly rare preoccupation among revolutionaries.[15] If we ask how the turn to pleasure and enjoyment might jostle established political categories, at least one answer comes to mind. The first is that *jouissance* in the Levinasian sense involves an object, along with an elemental medium supporting objects within it, and it is clear that object-oriented politics has not been a thoroughly studied theme.[16] In general, modern political theory revolves not around objects but around competing tales of humans and whether they were good or evil in the state of nature, as recently re-emphasized by David Graeber and David Wengrow at the start of their much-anticipated history of the world.[17] Yet there is considerable reluctance to revise political theory in light of the object. This is due partly to the ongoing dominance of philosophies of the subject, as seen in the most popular continental thinkers of the present day: Alain Badiou and Slavoj Žižek, who double down on the modern emphasis on political subjectivity, rather than reining it in as I, for one, would prefer.[18] The same holds for the recent tendency to treat the present political stalemate primarily as the result of a failure of imagination as if the task now before us were simply to brainstorm and experiment and put an end to the sense of the inevitable that surrounds capitalism and liberal democracy.[19]

Aside from Marxist discussions of technological shifts in the modes of production, much of the attention to objects in political theory has come from the geopolitical 'realist' school, which despite its name is tied to philosophical *actualism* rather than realism. That is to say, it is typically concerned with the array of tangible forces now deployed on the earth and tends to exclude values, goods and ideals from the sphere of the real. In the words of one such realist, George Friedman, 'I try not to be drawn into matters of right and wrong, not because I don't believe there is a difference but because history is rarely decided by moral principles'.[20] Yet there is much that the political realist is skilled in *not* excluding, such as facts that cannot easily be outstripped by enhanced human imagination. One of these is geography, a long-time staple of political realism. There is good reason why, for several decades, American military equipment was designed to fight Warsaw Pact forces specifically in the Fulda Gap in Germany. Given that transport by water is by far the cheapest method of shipping goods, controlling the world's sea lanes has been the fastest ticket to empire for centuries. Since geography tends to be stable by nature, any politics tied too closely to geographical fact might seem in danger of galloping towards traditionalist authority. Yet constraint is also our friend, once we remember that it easily reverses into opportunity. Free verse is not always better than iambic pentameter, and an earth without gravity would not be more liberating in any fruitful sense of the term.[21]

Notes

1   Jacques Derrida, 'Violence and Metaphysics: An Essay on the Thought of Emmanuel Levinas', in *Writing and Difference*, trans. A. Bass (Chicago: University of Chicago Press, 1982), 29–67.

2   Jacques Lacan, *The Seminar of Jacques Lacan, Book VII: The Ethics of Psychoanalysis, 1959-1960*, trans. D. Potter (New York: Norton, 1992), 167–240; Jacques Lacan, *Encore: The Seminar of Jacques Lacan, Book XX: On Feminine Sexuality, the Limits of Love and Knowledge*, trans. B. Fink (New York: Norton, 1999), 1–13.

3   See Alphonso Lingis, *The Imperative* (Bloomington, IN: Indiana University Press, 1998).

4   John Sallis, 'Levinas and the Elemental', *Research in Phenomenology* 28 (1998): 152–9; Steven Shaviro, 'Self-Enjoyment and Concern: Whitehead and Levinas', in *Beyond Metaphysics? Explorations in Alfred North Whitehead's Late Thought*, ed. R. Faber, B. Henning, and C. Combs (Leiden, The Netherlands: Brill, 2010), 249–57.

5   In chronological order, they are as follows: Graham Harman, *Tool-Being: Heidegger and the Metaphysics of Objects* (Chicago: Open Court, 2002), 235–43; Graham

Harman, *Guerrilla Metaphysics: Phenomenology and the Carpentry of Things* (Chicago: Open Court, 2005), 9–20; Graham Harman, 'Aesthetics as First Philosophy: Levinas and the Non-Human', *Naked Punch* 9 (Summer/Fall 2007): 21–30; Graham Harman, 'Levinas and the Triple Critique of Heidegger', *Philosophy Today*, Winter 2009, 407–13; Graham Harman, *Skirmishes: With Friends, Enemies, and Neutrals* (Brooklyn, NY: Punctum, 2020), 141–66.

6 Emmanuel Levinas, *Totality and Infinity: An Essay on Exteriority*, trans. A. Lingis (The Hague: Martinus Nijhoff, 1979); Emmanuel Levinas, *Existence and Existents*, trans. A. Lingis (Pittsburgh: Duquesne University Press, 2001).

7 Emmanuel Levinas, *Otherwise Than Being or Beyond Essence*, trans. A. Lingis (The Hague: Martinus Nijhoff, 1998).

8 Throughout this article, all page references in parentheses refer to Levinas, *Totality and Infinity: An Essay on Exteriority*, trans. A. Lingis (The Hague: Martinus Nijhoff, 1979).

9 Franz Brentano, *Psychology from an Empirical Standpoint*, ed. L. McAlister, trans. A. Rancurello, D. B. Terrell, and L. McAlister (London: Routledge, 1995); Edmund Husserl, *Logical Investigations*, 2 vols., trans. J. N. Findlay (London: Routledge & Kegan Paul, 1970).

10 Martin Heidegger, *Being and Time*, trans. J. Macquarrie and E. Robinson (New York: Harper & Row, 1962).

11 Peter Sloterdijk, *Spheres, Volume 3: Foams. Plural Spherology*, trans. W. Hoban (South Pasadena, CA: Semiotext(e), 2016), 58; Graham Harman, *Dante's Broken Hammer: The Ethics, Aesthetics, and Metaphysics of Love* (London: Repeater, 2016).

12 Helmuth Plessner, *Levels of Organic Life and the Human: An Introduction to Philosophical Anthropology*, trans. M. Hyatt (New York: Fordham University Press, 2019), 200, 318.

13 See Graham Harman, 'The Two Faces of Mediation', in *Phänomenologie und spekulativer Realismus/ Phenomenology and Speculative Realism/Phénoménologie et réalisme spéculatif*, ed. Nicolás Garrera-Tolbert Jesús Guillermo Ferrer Ortega, and Alexander Schnell (Blaufelen: Königshausen & Neumann, 2021), 12–15.

14 Emmanuel Levinas, *Existence and Existents*, trans. A. Lingis (Pittsburgh: Duquesne University Press, 2001), 37.

15 Roland Barthes, *Sade/Fourier/Loyola*, trans. R. Miller (New York: Hill & Wang, 1976).

16 Latour borrowed my term 'object-oriented politics' in Bruno Latour, *An Inquiry into Modes of Existence: An Anthropology of the Moderns* (Cambridge, MA: Harvard University Press, 2013), 337. See also Graham Harman, *Bruno Latour: Reassembling the Political* (London: Pluto, 2014).

17 David Graeber and David Wengrow, *The Dawn of Everything: A New History of Humanity* (New York: Farar, Straus, & Giroux, 2021).

18 Alain Badiou, *Theory of the Subject*, trans. B. Bosteels (London: Bloomsbury, 2013); Slavoj Žižek, *The Ticklish Subject: The Absent Centre of Political Ontology* (London: Verso, 1999).

19 Graeber and Wengrow, *The Dawn of Everything*; Mark Fisher, *Capitalist Realism: Is There No Alternative?* (Winchester: Zero Books, 2012); Peter Hallward, 'The

Will of the People: Notes Towards a Dialectical Voluntarism', *Radical Philosophy*
155 (May/June 2009), https://www.radicalphilosophy.com/article/the-will-of-the
-people; Catherine Malabou, 'Le vide politique du réalisme contemporain', in
L'écho du réel, ed. C. Crignon, W. Laforge, and P. Nadrigny (Sesto San Giovanni:
Mimesis, 2021), 485–98. For a response to the latter article see Graham Harman,
'Malabou's Political Critique of Speculative Realism', *Open Philosophy* 4 (2021):
94–105.

20 George Friedman, 'Viewing Russia from the Inside', *Stratfor Global Intelligence*, 14
December 2015, https://www.stratfor.com/weekly/viewing-russia-inside.

21 On this point see Ian Bogost, *Play Anything: The Pleasure of Limits, the Uses of
Boredom, and the Secret of Games* (New York: Basic Books, 2016).

References

Badiou, Alain (2013), *Theory of the Subject*, trans. B. Bosteels, London: Bloomsbury.

Barthes, Roland (1976), *Sade/Fourier/Loyola*, trans. R. Miller, New York: Hill & Wang.

Bogost, Ian (2016), *Play Anything: The Pleasure of Limits, the Uses of Boredom, and the
Secret of Games*, New York: Basic Books.

Brentano, Franz (1995), *Psychology From an Empirical Standpoint*, ed. _. McAlister,
trans. A. Rancurello, D. B. Terrell, and L. McAlister, London: Routledge.

Derrida, Jacques (1982), 'Violence and Metaphysics: An Essay on the Thought of
Emmanuel Levinas', in A. Bass (trans.), *Writing and Difference*, 29–67, Chicago:
University of Chicago Press.

Fisher, Mark (2012), *Capitalist Realism: Is There No Alternative?* Winchester: Zero Books.

Friedman, George (2015), 'Viewing Russia from the Inside', *Stratfor Global Intelligence*,
14 December. https://www.stratfor.com/weekly/viewing-russia-inside.

Graeber, David and David Wengrow (2021), *The Dawn of Everything: A New History of
Humanity*, New York: Farar, Straus, & Giroux.

Hallward, Peter (2009), 'The Will of the People: Notes Towards a Dialectical Voluntarism',
Radical Philosophy 155. https://www.radicalphilosophy.com/article/the-will-of-the
-people.

Harman, Graham (2002), *Tool-Being: Heidegger and the Metaphysics of Objects*,
Chicago: Open Court.

Harman, Graham (2005), *Guerrilla Metaphysics: Phenomenology and the Carpentry of
Things*, Chicago: Open Court.

Harman, Graham (2007), 'Aesthetics as First Philosophy: Levinas and the Non-Human',
Naked Punch 9: 21–30.

Harman, Graham (2009), 'Levinas and the Triple Critique of Heidegger', *Philosophy
Today*, 407–13.

Harman, Graham (2014), *Bruno Latour: Reassembling the Political*, London: Pluto.

Harman, Graham (2016), *Dante's Broken Hammer: The Ethics, Aesthetics, and
Metaphysics of Love*, London: Repeater.

Harman, Graham (2020), *Skirmishes: With Friends, Enemies, and Neutrals*, Brooklyn, NY:
Punctum.

Harman, Graham (2021), 'Malabou's Political Critique of Speculative Realism', *Open
Philosophy* 4: 94–105.

Harman, Graham (2021), 'The Two Faces of Mediation', in Nicolás Garrera-Tolbert, Jesús Guillermo Ferrer Ortega, and Alexander Schnell (eds), *Phänomenologie und spekulativer Realismus/ Phenomenology and Speculative Realism/Phénoménologie et réalisme spéculatif*, 12–15, Blaufelen: Königshausen & Neumann.

Heidegger, Martin (1962), *Being and Time*, trans. J. Macquarrie and E. Robinson, New York: Harper & Row.

Husserl, Edmund (1970), *Logical Investigations*, 2 vols, trans. J. N. Findlay, London: Routledge & Kegan Paul.

Lacan, Jacques (1992), *The Seminar of Jacques Lacan, Book VII: The Ethics of Psychoanalysis, 1959–1960*, trans. D. Potter, New York: Norton.

Lacan, Jaques (1999), *Encore: The Seminar of Jacques Lacan, Book XX: On Feminine Sexuality, the Limits of Love and Knowledge*, trans. B. Fink, New York: Norton.

Latour, Bruno (2013), *An Inquiry Into Modes of Existence: An Anthropology of the Moderns*, Cambridge, MA: Harvard University Press.

Levinas, Emmanuel (1979), *Totality and Infinity: An Essay on Exteriority*, trans. A. Lingis, The Hague: Martinus Nijhoff.

Levinas, Emmanuel (1998), *Otherwise Than Being or Beyond Essence*, trans. A. Lingis, The Hague: Martinus Nijhoff.

Levinas, Emmanuel (2001), *Existence and Existents*, trans. A. Lingis, Pittsburgh: Duquesne University Press.

Lingis, Alphonso (1998), *The Imperative*, Blocmington, IN: Indiana University Press.

Malabou, Catherine (2021), 'Le vide politique du réalisme contemporain', in C. Crignon, W. Laforge, and P. Nadrigny (eds), *L'écho du réel*, 485–98, Sesto San Giovanni: Mimesis.

Plessner, Helmuth (2019), *Levels of Organic Life and the Human: An Introduction to Philosophical Anthropology*, trans. M. Hyatt, New York: Fordham University Press.

Sallis, John (1998), 'Levinas and the Elemental', *Research in Phenomenology* 28: 152–9.

Shaviro, Steven (2010), 'Self-Enjoyment and Concern: Whitehead and Levinas', in R. Faber, B. Henning, and C. Combs (eds), *Beyond Metaphysics? Explorations in Alfred North Whitehead's Late Thought*, 249–57. Leiden: Brill.

Sloterdijk, Peter (2016), *Spheres, Volume 3: Foams. Plural Spherology*, trans. W. Hoban, South Pasadena, CA: Semiotext(e).

Žižek, Slavoj (1999), *The Ticklish Subject: The Absent Centre of Political Ontology*, London: Verso.

Index